Marketing the Wilder...

MARKETING THE WILDERNESS

Outdoor Recreation, Indigenous Activism, and the Battle over Public Lands

JOSEPH WHITSON

University of Minnesota Press

Minneapolis

London

Published by the University of Minnesota Press
111 Third Avenue South, Suite 290
Minneapolis, MN 55401-2520
http://www.upress.umn.edu

ISBN 978-1-5179-1510-0 (hc)
ISBN 978-1-5179-1511-7 (pb)

A Cataloging-in-Publication record for this book is available from the Library of Congress.

Printed in the United States of America on acid-free paper

The University of Minnesota is an equal-opportunity educator and employer.

34 33 32 31 30 29 28 27 26 25   10 9 8 7 6 5 4 3 2 1

It is hereby declared to be the policy of the Congress
to secure for the American people of the present
and future generations the benefits of an enduring
resource of wilderness . . . administered for the use
and enjoyment of the American people.
[. . .]
A wilderness, in contrast with those areas where
man and his works dominate the landscape, is
hereby recognized as an area where the earth and its
community of life are untrammeled by man, where
man himself is a visitor who does not remain . . .
retaining its primeval character and influence, without
permanent improvements or human habitation.

—Excerpts from The Wilderness Act of 1964

Contents

Introduction

Wildernessing

I n the early 2010s, as a recent college graduate putting to use my newly minted history degree, I found myself working at a state-level park district in the cultural heritage department. Among the historic homes, ruined mills, and restored train depots we cared for throughout the Twin Cities region were thousands of Indigenous cultural sites, including burial sites. Despite a comprehensive education in the field of history, this was my first practical exposure to the laws, practices, and institutional ethics surrounding Indigenous history and presence on American public lands—the management of physical sites, the creation and interpretation of complex narratives, and the balancing of outdoor recreation with best practices in historic preservation.[1]

The district was required by laws like Section 106 of the National Historic Preservation Act, the Native American Graves and Repatriation Act (NAGPRA), and Executive Order 13175 to consult on a government-to-government basis with federally recognized tribes connected to these sites and work closely with State and Tribal Historic Preservation Officers (SHPO/THPO). For the people in the cultural heritage department, this was more than due diligence. They were committed to narratives and historical interpretations that took Indigenous history seriously and respected the wishes of Indigenous collaborators on how sites should or should *not* be interpreted or accessible to the public. While the systems were far from perfect, often deeply unequal, and largely still designed to serve the settler state, it was clear that the stories of public lands, colonial settlement, and Indigenous history and presence were deeply intertwined. Outdoor recreation management was often the result of a negotiation between state land priorities and contemporary Indigenous governance.

While I was learning to navigate public land politics, I was simultaneously working as a social media "brand ambassador," writer, and photographer for a handful of local outdoor recreation companies. Similar to my work with the park district, I was responsible for crafting a narrative about the relationship between humans and the outdoors, public lands and recreational spaces, and what it means to engage in outdoor recreation in general. However, unlike the park district, these companies were unbound by federal law and internally governed along a very different set of ethical commitments. These marketing narratives sought to present a deeply uncomplicated representation of outdoor recreation and the land on which it depends. The companies, aligning themselves with liberal-leaning and progressive environmental politics, presented the land in what they viewed as an idealized state, pristine and untouched, a wilderness waiting to be explored.

Read back-to-back, the industry's total absence of any engagement with Indigenous people and their investment in actively *suppressing* these counterclaims to land seems unmissable. However, even as someone who was actively engaged in a far more complicated process of recreation and land management with the park district, I blithely reproduced the companies' narratives for them, becoming an unaware accomplice in a century-old system of wildernessing that I was only beginning to understand.

Marketing the Wilderness emerges from these two experiences. It follows the intertwined and deeply fraught relationship between the outdoor recreation industry and Indigenous people, showing how this tension has shaped America's public lands both politically and in the settler imaginary. Our contemporary understanding of wilderness— the idea that land and ecosystems exist, unpeopled and untouched, outside of the rest of society—was sold to the American public by the outdoor recreation industry, an ideological advertisement that spanned decades and reshaped the very landscapes we see as natural today. This idea molded the public land policy that has created, and continues to create, outdoor recreational spaces that have been scoured of contemporary Indigeneity and designed to support the settler fantasy of terra nullius—land that is at once no one's and everyone's.

I call this process *wildernessing.*

The concept of wildernessing is designed to provide a lens for understanding one of the many ways the interconnecting system of laws, narratives, and individual actions that perpetuate the ongoing replacement of Indigenous people and culture with settlers and settler culture, known as settler colonialism, is structured in nations like the United States. Wildernessing describes the process by which the entire outdoor recreation-industrial complex—from outdoor corporations to public land policy to everyday recreators—contributes to the physical removal of Indigenous people from their homelands. It contributes to the narrative erasure of Indigenous lives from the histories of recreational spaces and the production of the "pristine, empty lands" that ideologically and economically undergird the outdoor industry and, more broadly, maintain the legitimacy of the U.S. occupation of these areas. The creation of wilderness as an idea and its implementation on public land is not simply a frantic reaction to escalating environmental loss or the brainchild of a small group of inspired men, as it is often described; it was and continues to be the outdoor industry's most successful marketing campaign.

Wildernessing positions the outdoor recreation industry as itself a force of extraction and dispossession on public land, addressing the myth that the outdoor industry is a natural ally for Indigenous people, set in opposition to traditional extractive policies. Outdoor companies like Patagonia and The North Face are akin to mining, drilling, and other resources extraction industries. While the physical and ecological impacts of these industries are obviously different, the companies approach land management and relationships to environments from an equally colonial perspective, treating the land as a resource on which to capitalize. This remakes the land from a space compatible with Indigenous ways of life and relationships into a space that meets the economic needs of the company. Our National Parks, our wilderness areas, our state nature reserves, our boondock sites, our lakes and forests and mountains and coasts are not untouched oases. They exist not as remnants of a preindustrial world, but as modern products designed for consumption, part and parcel of the same capitalist landscape that enables unchecked extraction, industrial agriculture, and sprawling urban development.

In many ways, this book is an indictment of outdoor recreation in the United States. I speak from personal experience when I say that hiking, camping, climbing, paddling, surfing, or engaging in any activity in the wilderness can be a deeply meaningful, even transformative, experience, a chance for people deeply disconnected from land to forge a relationship with the natural world. But for many of us, it remains a human-centered, one-way relationship. Wilderness recreation facilitates the dualistic understanding of humans as separate from nature. We explore, we experience, we categorize *this* as wilderness, untouched, worth preserving, worth connecting to and *that* as wasteland, exploitable and fallen.[2] Then we return home, and we remain just as alienated from the nonhuman world around us as we ever were. Outdoor recreation companies capitalize on this disconnect, reinforcing the idea that specific kinds of recreation in specific kinds of landscapes are the only ways to truly, authentically connect with nature. And then they sell us access.

At the same time, this book serves as an invitation to profoundly rethink the kinds of relationships we build with the nonhuman world—urban, rural, and "wilderness" alike. What would it mean to think of humans as fundamental and necessary parts of a healthy ecosystem? What does a truly two-way, reciprocal relationship with nature look like? Is a more relational form of recreation, a form that is more integrative, more giving, and more respectful, possible? Many of our fellow beings on this planet are at or past crisis points and only a radical realignment of our ecological relationships can alter this course. For much of the last hundred fifty years, outdoor recreation has been a significant way Americans have come to know the natural world—a trend that is only increasing. If it can break from its colonial origins and corporate gatekeepers, I believe outdoor recreation can be part of the reciprocal path forward as well.

In this introduction, I delve deeper into the concept of wildernessing, laying out a process I will return to throughout the book as I examine specific strategies and examples of the outdoor industry's colonial complicities. I then position this work within the field of environmental justice and, in particular, Indigenous environmental justice. As a project that turns a critical theory lens to land, this book is inherently invested in understanding the power structures that produce environmental and political inequities in the United States. Finally, I turn to my digital methodologies. I discuss my own positionality as a non-Indigenous person within the research that forms the groundwork for this book and include what I hope will be a useful blueprint for future digital ethnographers attempting to navigate new, rapidly changing, and increasingly ubiquitous digital sources, archives, and communities.

Wildernessing

For the outdoor industry, creating and realizing a wilderness replacement narrative happens through the process of wildernessing. Wildernesses have had to be narratively and physically created since European settlement brought the concept to the continent. Through their marketing, targeted activism, and political involvement, the outdoor industry is a part of the system establishing the representational and ideological conditions necessary for the physical creation of wilderness—in whatever way "wilderness" is defined in any given period. The outdoor industry is invested in this idea, relying on wilderness areas as the government-funded arenas in which their products are used. It actively promotes the wildernessing of public lands and other outdoor spaces through their representations of these lands as well as through political lobbying and environmental activism. The industry then populates these imagined worlds with the consumers of their products under the guise of explorers, allowing each consumer to narratively lay claim to the lands they explore.

With the term *wildernessing*, 1 draw from historian Traci Voyle's theorization of "wastelanding." Voyles looks at lands, in particular the uranium mining region in Diné Bikéyah, that have been represented as wastelands, as places uninhabited and uninhabitable, worthless places. She argues that the representation of these lands is inextricably connected to the physical transformation of these spaces into wastelands. For example, in the eyes of extraction companies and policymakers, the representation of Navajo land as valueless and uninhabitable made it a landscape that could be polluted, sacrificed for a national need. Then the actual process of uranium mining in this space made a landscape that had healthily supported an entire Indigenous nation, toxic, making "real, material, lived—what would otherwise be only discursive."[3]

Although resulting in the construction of a different environmental space, wildernessing functions in a way similar to wastelanding—as the environmental realization of a narrative. As a result of the historical and continuing representation of certain environmental spaces as inherently unpeopled and unmanaged, wilderness areas as we know them today were constructed through the active removal of Indigenous people and the erasure of their impacts on the environment.

At the same time, the story of wildernessing is more complex. In some ways, this is a process that has already happened. American Indian nations across the country have already experienced removal due to conservation and the creation of parks and wilderness areas. This is a long and difficult history that I dive into more in the following chapters. But suffice it to say that not only are all public lands carved out of the homelands of various Indigenous nations, but many Indigenous people also experienced removal, land loss, or resource dispossession explicitly to create "natural" areas for recreation. But it is not *only* a process that has already happened. Settler colonialism is an ongoing process and must constantly be maintained, especially when it comes to control over resources and sovereignty over land. Even while vocally and sometimes financially supporting certain kinds of Indigenous activism efforts, the outdoor industry is still invested in public, state control of land and wilderness as the land ethic that most profits their businesses.

As I discuss in Chapters 2 and 3, the idea of what exactly wilderness is has not been static and has evolved alongside shifting U.S. policy around conservation, U.S.–Indian relations, and American recreational practices. While most of this book engages with wilderness through our contemporary definition of a pristine, Edenic landscape outside of time and society, this has not always been the representational strategy the outdoor industry has used and likely will not always be in the future. Like many strategies of settler colonialism, wildernessing is adaptive and is more concerned with the creation of consumable spaces that can be easily marketed rather than maintaining any one specific representation. However, because this relationship to land requires the commodification of space and unquestioned recreational access, wildernessing will always be invested in the settler colonial agenda.

As I have developed this model, there have been two conceptual frameworks I have found helpful in contextualizing the idea of wildernessing. The first is *colonial terraforming,* a form of settler colonialism that involves the intentional cultivation of settler cultural ecosystems at the expense of Indigenous ones. The second is the recently articulated concept of the *outdoor recreation-industrial complex.* These two concepts help untangle the deeply emmeshed relationships among outdoor companies, government institutions, consumers, markets, and ecosystems that drive this process, and its role within a larger settler colonial structure. In the following chapters, as I examine the history, strategies, and political motivations involved in wildernessing, readers might also find these frameworks, which I expand on in the following sections, useful tools in unpacking the logic behind the industry's often contradictory actions and representations.

Colonial Terraforming

In his foundational discussion of settler colonialism, historian Patrick Wolfe uses the term *territory* instead of *land* in his descriptions of the colonial process, denoting a political structure, a bounded space.[4] This has historically been a common framing within settler colonial studies, especially among the Australian and American settler scholars like Wolfe, Lorenzo Veracini, and Walter Hixson who worked to define it as an academic field.[5] The goal of these scholars was in many ways to understand the settler state through the lens of territory, which naturally led to the important focus on political replacement and the state-sponsored genocide of Indigenous people as central aspects of settler colonialism. As scholars in the field of Native American and Indigenous Studies (NAIS) increasingly adopted the term to describe the Indigenous experience under colonial occupation, territoriality—especially in the context of political sovereignty, cultural sovereignty, and sovereignty over land— has remained a central thread. Historians like Lenape scholar Joanne Barker, for example, emphasized the diversity and locally specific nature of Indigenous sovereignty often overlooked in settler-state-focused histories of setter colonialism, and Kevin Bruyneel pushed back against a one-sided focus, revealing the constant negotiation between state and Indigenous sovereignties in a settler colonial context.[6]

When I refer to land, political territoriality is, of course, one aspect of it. I draw on Indigenous theorists like Glen Coulthard and Leanne Simpson, who move away from settler colonialism as a political abstraction and recenter occupation and control over land and physical space as the fundamental goal of the colonial state. Sovereignty over territory, unrestricted access to resources, and the power of decision-making over land use are all part of what settlers desire. However, as Kyle Whyte, Zoe Todd, and others have shown, territoriality is only part of the equation. Land also includes its community of life and ecological systems. Settler colonialism is a dual assault on both Indigenous political existence as well as on Indigenous life and the nonhumans and environments that make this life possible. The replacement of Indigenous people with settlers is predicated on the replacement of Indigenous ecosystems with settler ecosystems.[7]

In science fiction, the ecological transformation of a newly settled planet to support the lives and economies of those from Earth is known as terraforming. Settler colonialism is a form of colonial terraforming. Terraforming has been aptly invoked as a metaphor for a range of settler colonialism impacts on the ecosystem, including oil infrastructure, agriculture, and, of course, recreation.[8] European settlers arriving in North America found an environment that, while sustainably supporting millions of Indigenous people, was incompatible with European lifestyles, worldviews, and economies. The subsequent environmental transformation of the continent has had the dual effect of allowing settler society to thrive while undercutting Indigenous society. Conflicts over land use, land management, and ecological decision-making, and about the distribution of environmental risk and equity of access, are conflicts about colonialism, about who will be valued and supported at the most fundamental level. Political territory and ecological life are not so easily separated.

Like settler colonialism, colonial terraforming is designed to seem a natural, even inevitable, transformation of land and ecosystems, and no aspect of it is as naturalized as wildernessing. Wilderness spaces are often seen as exceptions to the much more obvious ecological changes throughout the rest of country. But of course, these lands have explicitly been shaped for outdoor recreation, for the reenactment of a colonial fantasy of exploration only possible in carefully managed environments, emptied of Indigenous people.

The Outdoor Recreation-Industrial Complex

Another way to look at the outdoor industry's commodification of public land, its complicity in settler colonialism, and the physical and ecological impacts that go along with this is to understand it as part of a larger outdoor recreation-industrial complex, whereby the industry (outdoor retail in particular, but also outfitting, guiding, hospitality, and other outdoor tourism businesses) has become deeply entwined and codependent with political institutions (the National Park Service and other recreation-mandated land management agencies). The United States, through its militarily backed colonial occupation, provides the outdoor industry with openly accessible public lands, the lands upon which the industry is built. The outdoor industry, through its marketing rhetoric and public-pleasing narratives, provides the United States with legitimacy and justification for its continued occupation and, eventually, its extraction of natural resources. This alliance serves the underlying capitalist interests of both parties at the expense of the raison d'être of these institutions. As Nick Estes, Melanie Yazzie, and others have shown in related circumstance, the colonial and capitalist interests of the state and of industry become inseparable as access to existing "wilded" land and acquisition or cultivation of new such land (wildernessing) becomes a primary source of wealth creation, forming a classic feedback loop that exists to serve only itself—not ecological sustainability, not Indigenous people, not even settlers or consumers.[9] This physical transformation occurs alongside increased consumer alienation to non-wilded lands through both environmental degradation and ideological marketing, increasing the value of and demand for wilderness areas.

Environmental historians have paid close attention to the way the American state has used public lands and wilderness areas as tools of settler colonialism. Mark David Spence, Karl Jacoby, and Dorceta E. Taylor, for example, show how environmental and public land policy in the United States has been explicitly designed to dispossess and criminalize Indigenous people, freeing land for a variety of settler uses, including recreation.[10] However, by engaging primarily at a policy, state-centered level, these histories have little to say about corporate complicity, especially of traditionally nonextractive industries like outdoor retail. Wildernessing, by engaging with the entire outdoor recreation-industrial complex, allows for a more multifaceted analysis of public lands and colonialism.

That is not to say that the industry has gone completely unquestioned. There has recently been an emergent understanding of the outdoor recreation industry as an inherently paradoxical system, where fiscal growth becomes incompatible with the industry's supposed purpose—that is to facilitate recreation in outdoor, natural, or wilderness spaces. This reinterpretation of what had long been framed by outdoor consumers as a "good" or even anticapitalist industry and its articulation in terms of the "outdoor recreation-industrial complex" gained increased public attention and credence during the summer of 2020, when Covid-19 shutdowns and quarantines drew unprecedented crowds to wilderness spaces at the same time as it dramatically reduced the ability of management agencies to maintain them.[11] Overcrowding, lack of visitor education, and a scarcity of resources led to trashed parks, damaged ecosystems, and a diminished recreational experience. The industry, however, boomed. Outfitters and resorts saw record visitation and even outdoor retail, hampered by labor shortages and supply chain challenges, outperformed expectations. The stress of the Covid-era outdoor recreation boom may have exposed some contradictions in the system—revealing to many visitors the intense management needed to create pristine nature as well as the unsustainability of the industry's growth—but it has largely been framed by the outdoor industry as the result of exceptional circumstances, rather than an under-the-hood look at the industry's standard mechanics. The industry failed to reckon with its own colonial history or its entanglement with settler colonial policy. Indeed, as demonstrated by Patagonia's move to "make the earth its shareholder," a novel corporate strategy I examine in more detail in the conclusion, companies have doubled down on their vision for American land use and management, a vision necessary to maintaining tight control over wilderness access and environmental relationships. In its attempt to address certain forms of environmental injustices, the industry has cemented others.

Indigenous Environmental Justice

Holistically examining why the outdoor industry has failed to, or refuses to, address these colonial underpinnings, is an important goal of this book, which, through its analysis, speaks to community members, scholars, and readers from a wide range of fields and interests. For environmental historians and political ecologists, it reveals the role of outdoor corporations in the shaping and reshaping of environmental spaces. Drawing from Indigenous and American studies, it moves beyond wildernessing as a settler colonial analytic that helps us map systems of oppression and examines the failures of this process, looking at the ways Indigenous people have engaged, pushed back, and taken control of environmental narratives. For outdoor recreators and all lovers of a Patagonia puffy jacket, it provides a lens for critically engaging with the marketing material they encounter every day and a toolkit for examining their own behavior and relationships to the natural world. Most importantly, however, as a project that deals with land in a settler nation, *Marketing the Wilderness* is fundamentally an environmental justice project. I see environmental justice as an intersection where fields and audiences come together, using various methodologies and theories to ask questions about society's often complex, often unequal, often harmful relationships to the environment and to each other, while looking for ways to make them better.

Broadly, environmental justice engages with the spaces in which we live, work, play, and pray.[12] It seeks to understand and suggest solutions to social and political violence as well as inequity related to environmental issues. It is concerned with issues of equitable representation, access to, and investment in outdoor spaces and is sensitive to the ways both environmental conservation and environmental degradation have been used as weapons against marginalized communities. Scholarship around critical environmental justice—or environmental justice that emphasizes how intersecting structures of power and difference shape these issues on multiple scales—has refined what this means.[13] Environmental justice has been used as a lens to look at issues as diverse and multiscale as global migration due to climate change, decisions about waste disposal, and privatization of DNA.[14] While this broadening of the field has brought holistic environmental critiques to an array of issues, their tether to the importance of land and colonialism as one of the foundational pillars of environmental justice in a settler society has become increasingly tenuous.

The original Principles of Environmental Justice drafted at the 1991 National People of Color Environmental Leadership Summit cites colonialism as one of the core underlying causes of environmental injustice. Number eleven on their list of seventeen principles reads, "environmental justice must recognize a special legal and natural relationship of Native Peoples to the U.S. government through treaties, agreements, compacts, and covenants affirming sovereignty and self-determination."[15] Environmental justice in the United States must always address the structure of settler colonialism because settler colonialism always comes back to land. It is about access to land, acquisition of land, and ownership of land. As historian Patrick Wolfe argues, land is settler colonialism's "specific, irreducible element."[16] Settler colonialism is a structure of intersecting systems of power designed to bring land and its resources under the control of the colonial state and into the capitalist market. Political theorist Glen Coulthard argues that the "constellation of power relations" that encompass settler colonialism is the basic political and social structure that makes possible other forms of power and oppression—patriarchy, white supremacy, state hegemony—and, in turn, is maintained by them.[17] Methods of settler colonialism are varied and far-reaching—war, genocide, forced removal, detribalization, assimilation—but the fundamental goal, the voracious appetite for land, has remained consistent.

This is true for more traditional cases of environmental injustice like toxic water supplies in low-income communities and carcinogenic dumps in communities of color. The land they are on, the resources involved, and the ways they are inequitably distributed are inseparable from their colonial past and ongoing market forces. However, when it comes to American public lands, the lands I focus on in this book, the settler colonial aspects come into sharp focus. In an urban landfill, for example, you might have to dig through many layers of representation, policy, development, and power dynamics—physically, archivally, and in communities—to uncover the site's Indigenous history and its impact today. On public land, you barely have to scratch the surface. While all land has Indigenous history, on public land in outdoor spaces, the wounds of colonialism are kept open and raw through contemporary conflicts over resource management, treaty rights, access to sacred sites, required consultation with tribes, cultural appropriation, and representation.

Just as we cannot talk about environmental justice without engaging settler colonialism, we must place both into conversation with capitalism or, more specifically, the drive of unregulated capitalism to transform everything—land and landscape, life and lifestyle—into commodities that can be atomized, marketed, and owned. Historian Nick Estes's work describes the codependent relationship between capitalism and colonialism, forcefully arguing that one cannot be challenged without challenging the other.[18] In a settler colonial society, land is wealth, but only once it is owned within the capitalist system of wealth production. Indigenous people are represented as occupiers, not owners, and as an obstacle to be removed. These connections are well understood by environmental justice scholars and activists who engage with colonial histories. They are often deeply concerned with how market forces intersect with the politics of race, gender, and class to produce an unequal distribution of environmental risk. Traci Voyles, David Naguib Pellow, Winona LaDuke, and others have shown that equity and fair distribution of environmental risk and access without a fundamental change in the system can never achieve the "justice" of a colonial/capitalist system designed to create these inequalities and oppressive power structures.[19] As Voyles succinctly puts it, "a state that has structurally excluded populations of color, the queer, immigrants, and others is not compatible with meting out justice for those communities, precisely because it is constituted on and through their exclusion."[20] She argues that seeing environment justice through this lens requires us to rethink what we mean by justice and injustice and demand a new system altogether.

While the colonial forces may become clearer when dealing with public land, the capitalistic forces seem to become obscured. These are *public* lands, not private lands; therefore, it is implied that there is something unique and anticapitalist about them. This is just semantics. Facilitated by the state, these lands are still very much active commodities. The narrative of public land as being outside the market is itself a part of its market value. Through outdoor recreation, public lands are the site of a literal reenactment of the violent, historical process of colonization that brought these spaces into the market to begin with through the removal of Indigenous people and commodification of land through narrative and representation. Although this process is sanitized and performative, its effects are still very real.

Wildernessing, the outdoor recreation-industrial complex, and their inherent environmental injustices are the result of a system working on many levels—policy, enforcement, individuals acting on the ground— with narrative and representation undergirding all of them. Representation creates the conditions necessary for the physical realization of ideas and is, in turn, reinforced by its own manifestations.[21] Increasingly, these representations exist and spread through social media.

Why Instagram?

This book interrogates the relationships between outdoor recreation and land representation and policy; corporations and activists; and, broadly, people and the outdoors. The dynamics of these relationships are always shaped by and play out over the dominant media and technology of their time. When I look at the history of the outdoor industry, I analyze physical space, catalogs, print advertising, and television commercials. Part of my argument is that the investment of the outdoor industry in the settler colonial project is resilient, reimagining itself as culture and technology change around it. The large processes and values remain the same while the micro-level functions change. At the moment in time when this research was conducted, the industry was reimagining itself around social media and around Instagram in particular as the most influential platform among the communities with which I engage.

Founded in 2010, the image-sharing social media platform grew rapidly, particularly from 2017 on. As of March 2018, Instagram had reached one billion monthly users who collectively posted just under a hundred million photographs a day.[22] Thirty-four percent of Americans used Instagram, including 73 percent of teenagers, making it the second most used platform after Facebook for all users (second after Snapchat for teenagers), which owns Instagram.[23] Instagram also had by far the highest engagement rate (percentage of followers engaging with a post) of any social media site, ten times that of Facebook, and a high conversion rate (the percentage of consumers who see an advertisement and buy the product). Eighty percent of users followed a business account and 20 percent engaged with businesses on Instagram daily.[24] It is no surprise then that businesses and advertisers flocked to the platform. Seventy-three percent of all U.S. businesses had an Instagram account, including 96 percent of clothing brands.[25] In 2019, Instagram made $14 billion in ad revenue, up from just $3.6 billion in 2017, numbers that did not include the nearly $6 billion paid directly to influencers through sponsorships.[26] While all these statistics represent Instagram during the period of my research between 2017 and 2019, as of 2023, Instagram had two billion users and nearly $40 billion in ad revenue, only cementing its place at the center of the marketing world and largely resisting the disruption created by the rise of TikTok.

These numbers mean that Instagram was among the most prolific sites of media production, distribution, and consumption across all retail, a trend that is magnified for the outdoor industry. Every major outdoor company was on Instagram, many with several million followers. A 2018 panel on outdoor advocacy on social media at Outdoor Retailer, the industry's largest conference, barely mentioned other platforms, referring to their work on "Instagram and other social media." Forbes cited the outdoor industry as the most able to take advantage of lifestyle marketing on Instagram.[27] In January 2023 for example, Patagonia had 5.1 million followers (twice what they had just two years earlier), REI had 2.3 million, and The North Face had 5.4 million. Instagram gave these companies a greater reach and higher engagement rates on the platform, which meant consumers were not just seeing the pictures posted by the companies, but commenting, liking, and reposting—building the kind of one-way, parasocial relationships marketers love. While many different industries were seeing high engagement and conversion rates on the platform, the outdoor industry's higher reliance on the kind of images already popular on the platform—see Chapter 4—made Instagram a better choice than other social media platforms for this industry in particular. On top of this, the way land is represented on other platforms was influenced by the intentionally nostalgic aesthetic of Instagram. People were responding to these campaigns not only by buying outdoor products but by increasingly using public lands in new ways based on what they saw happening in the posts of companies and influencers. Through Instagram, these companies were not just selling products; they were selling lifestyles and shaping land use. While correlation does not equal causation, National Park visitation went up 20 percent in the first decade after Instagram was founded, and people were making this connection with a slurry of doomsday articles around the lines of "Instagram is ruining public lands."[28]

When I started this work, I originally meant to answer the question of the outdoor retail industry's complicity in settler colonialism. I had expected to draw out general themes about outdoor marketing and the industry's relationship to land, environmental policy, and Indigenous people. How was land being portrayed and discussed? What histories were being told and to whom? Who was being represented, who was not, and in what ways? I also expected to develop a better understanding of the power dynamics within the industry. Which accounts followed who? Who was driving the conversations and who was reacting? Who were the network hubs? What did these relationships look like? I found answers to many of these questions, and they are embedded in the arguments I make throughout my work.

However, what I did not expect was for 2017–18 to be a year of rapid and intense politicization of the outdoor industry around several issues, most significantly around the issue of public lands, which arose in response to specific threats to Bears Ears National Monument. This played out most radically in a lawsuit filed by Patagonia against President Trump in December 2017, but also included things like The North Face's not so subtle "Walls Are Meant for Climbing" campaign, the Outdoor Industry Association's boycott of the state of Utah, and REI's "We [heart] Public Lands" campaign. While the questions above remained important in understanding the colonial politics of the outdoor industry generally, the reason behind this politicization became the central question. What exactly about this threat to public lands drove the industry to enter the political sphere suddenly and in such a dramatic manner? My social media analysis, particularly an analysis of Patagonia's marketing campaign around the Bears Ears conflict, answered this question from the corporate side—the economies and narratives these companies are invested in and the strategies they are using to maintain them. But there was another side to these issues as well.

More important than Instagram being the most significant site of media production around public land and outdoor recreation in the 2010s, is that this was the digital space in which outdoor advocacy groups had coalesced. Instagram's design made it an especially effective space for organizing. While Facebook groups continued to be the go-to platform for social media organizing, they tended to be slow growing, insular, and populated by outside links rather than original content. Instagram had no formal "groups" setting, but it was more deeply networked than Facebook and the line between personal and organizational profiles blurred, which lowered the barrier to connection both among peers and between normal individuals and powerful influencers and corporations. While this point was sometimes overstated, the platform was still much more egalitarian than nondigital organizing often is. The platform also only allowed external links in very limited ways, driving the creation of more original content including long captions. I examine these reasons in greater detail in Chapters 4 and 6. This fertile digital environment with flexible communities and an overwhelming amount of information provided both opportunities and challenges for research. Challenges I approached using adapted forms of digital ethnography.

Digital Ethnography

Digital ethnography is not a new methodology—researchers have been embedding themselves in online communities since the internet became widely available in the 1990s—but it is a dynamic one that must constantly be reimagined to keep up with rapidly changing technologies and user interfaces.[29] While the nuts and bolts of the research might shift, larger ideas about their use and impact on society can be sieved out.

Instagram works well for this kind of qualitative, ethnographic research. New artificial intelligence technology is being used to analyze posts by Instagram itself. However, for outside researchers, the complexity of networked social media analysis, the difficulty of accessing Instagram's API through Meta, and the relatively small sample size of the industries and communities I engage with make quantitative, big data research on the platform difficult and expensive.[30] Digital ethnography can be done at a small scale and provide more nuanced insight into the relationships and activities on the platform.

Digital ethnography can refer to a wide range of research methods. Scholars have drawn from various aspects of traditional ethnography and applied them piecemeal to digital scenarios. For this project, I used two of the methods most commonly used by consumer insights researchers in the marketing industry—social media analysis and embedded ethnography—which I describe in detail below. These methods made sense for me for several reasons. First, they are methods that can be applied to or easily adapted to a broad range of different digital platforms and environments. By necessity, marketers must be able to rapidly shift with technology. Flexible methods that are not tied to specific interfaces but that can quickly take full advantage of them are important. Second, this is a project that focuses heavily on marketing, within a specific industry, and using these methods has helped reverse engineer some of the marketing choices these companies made. Finally, there is more written about digital research methods in the context of consumer insights and market research than there is for humanities scholarship. The lag time in peer-reviewed academic publishing means that even the most recent publications are drawing from research conducted at minimum several years earlier (this book notwithstanding).

The industry's digital ethnographic methods can be broken up into three categories: digital focus groups, social media analysis, and embedded ethnography. These are my terms used for the sake of clarity in this project as all these methods are interchangeably referred to as digital ethnography, "Netnography," digital anthropology, or other terms depending on the author and the context in which they are used.[31] I only use the latter two in this project but want to briefly address the first as well. Digital focus groups use technology to hybridize traditional focus groups—where marketers will bring in a small, diverse group of people to discuss, analyze, or test new products—with traditional consumer insight ethnography—where marketers spend hours or days physically observing people using products in their homes or work. In this model, researchers will recruit a target group of people and have them record themselves using products in their personal spaces with, for example, wearable cameras provided by the company or preexisting social media platforms and accounts. While this method gives marketers immediate environmental context for product use without the awkwardness of in-person observation or formality of in-person focus groups, it does not do as good of a job building the larger cultural or relational context in which the products are used. This makes it less than ideal for humanities research in which understanding the larger narratives of both the company and their consumers is the more important goal.

My focus instead has been on social media analysis and embedded ethnography, which I used in both independent and overlapping ways to look at the two distinct but interconnected communities of outdoor recreation and Indigenous-focused outdoor activism. Social media analysis, the closest comparable method to what is sometimes known as "Netnography," involves gathering user-generated data created organically on social media (Facebook, Instagram, Twitter/X, TikTok), other web-based community platforms where conversations occur like review sites (Yelp, Google), or multi-use forums and news aggregators (Reddit, Quora). This includes collecting videos, images, comments, captions, and other text from targeted communities and analyzing them using various established methods like visual analysis, semiotic analysis, and network analysis.[32] Social media analysis has an advantage over digital focus groups in that it can draw from a much larger, more diverse sample size and, most importantly, see the relationships that connect users to each other, to companies, and to other cultural hubs. While less complete than a constant video feed from a focus group, users are not creating media with companies in mind, giving researchers much more natural, less self-conscious information about the account owner's habits and practices. This can give a much clearer outline of cultural norms and trends within a group.

I used social media analysis not to look at outdoor retail consumers like a marketing team would, but to understand the culture and context of the outdoor industry itself. Over the course of a year, from May 2017 to May 2018, I gathered data from fifty-five accounts on Instagram associated with the industry including companies, publications, and influencers with over a million followers. Data from posts include the media posted by the original poster—the main image (or images, GIFs, and video), the caption, hashtags, and geotags—as well as comments by followers. Together, these accounts encompassed a network of over fifty million people and connected many of the main nodes of the outdoor industry.

Social media itself, as both a text and community, requires a multi-method approach to analysis. Social media functions as a microcosm of larger society, and a truly comprehensive view of the platforms and posts would require a level of interdisciplinarity that is outside the scope of this project. Social media scholar José van Dijck, for example, argues that social media analyses need to consider not just content but also users, technology, ownership, governance, and business models, all of which can and should be approached from the fields of information technology, social science, humanities, economics, law, and political communication.[33] Looking broadly at digital sources, cultural studies scholar Mark Andrejevic brings forward the problem of information overload. Simply the amount of information flowing through these platforms—nearly a hundred million posts a day on Instagram alone—causes a breakdown of normal, human information processing and requires new methods to sift through it. Since these often highly technical methods, Andrejevic argues, are outside the means of the general public, too much information is as damaging to understanding a subject as too little information.[34]

I have chosen to primarily use content analysis, looking at what the images themselves are representing and the ways images, captions, comments, and geotags interact in a post to shape a certain argument. However, I also interrogate the other elements of the platform, especially users and technology. Who is posting and who is following? What is their positionality? Are they producers or consumers or both? Are they professionals or amateurs? What are their connections and relationships to each other? Technology seems simpler since I am only looking at a single platform and Instagram is a mobile-only application. But how does the relationship between photographer and camera change when the camera is also a computer, telephone, shopping mall, and map? How is Instagram integrated with other applications and software? I look at ownership, governance, and business models only to the extent that they directly impact the actions of the users.[35] What does it mean to do activism work on a private platform? How does Instagram's need to make money shape how they interact with businesses and consumers using the platform—what they see and to what functions they have access? I approach posts with these questions in mind.

Following van Dijck's model, my social media analysis relies on methods that combine Actor-Network Theory (ANT) with political economy (or in my case also political ecology).[36] ANT requires the analysis of how all the atomized pieces of a single post, including but not exclusive to human users, function together to create meaning.[37] A post is fundamentally relational and to the extent that it can be considered a single artifact of analysis, it is an artifact that is both human and technology indivisible. Political economy/ecology, on the other hand, is concerned with power relationships, both how preexisting systems of power shape the creation of posts and are reinforced by them as well as how new systems of power develop in this new digital environment. The individual users and corporations on the platform are political actors and the platform itself is a political actor. Drawing any meaning from a post requires an understanding of them as such. Both of these approaches are necessary to analyze socially networked media.

While social media analysis provides broad insight, it is less effective at depth and complexity than embedded ethnography. Embedded digital ethnography is the digital method most similar to traditional ethnography. A researcher is embedded in a specific online community for an extended period of time either as an active participant or as a nonparticipant observer. This is a method that is used in the marketing world, but less often than other methods because it is too time consuming for quick campaign turnarounds and involves a small sample size. Like traditional ethnography, there is the idea that this method is objective, that the observer is within but not of the community they are researching. The myth of objectivity is reinforced by the use of technology, the physical distance between community members supposedly allowing for emotional distance. This is not the case, and the inability to objectively disconnect from communities you are working with has deeply informed this work.

Unlike in-person ethnography where the presence of the researcher inevitably has an impact on the community they are observing, it is possible to truly be a nonparticipant observer in online communities, colloquially known as lurking. As long as it is a public group, a lurker can observe conversations and interactions, get a feel for cultural norms, and explore larger group dynamics without actually influencing the community. That does not mean, however, that they are not part of the community or that the community is not impacting them or their perceptions or objectivity. Every group has lurkers—not necessarily researchers—people who are silent members, closely following the more active members while not participating themselves. These people often feel that they are connected to the community, however, and have a relationship with frequent posters despite the posters having no idea they exist. This is an important aspect of group dynamics and is known as a parasocial relationship—a one-way relationship between a follower and an influential member of the community.[38] Parasocial relationships are often intentionally cultivated by marketers for whom they have become an important way to build trust with consumers. Consumers see company accounts as individuals with whom they can have a relationship, mistaking familiarity for intimacy.[39] These relationships exist within noncommercial communities as well and are an important part of developing political awareness as a group, something I explore in Chapter 4. Lurkers are influenced by what they see and read, and they mimic the views of the more influential members. This is as true for researchers as it is for normal silent community members.

If nonparticipant observation is not objective, it goes without saying that neither is participant observation. The history of participant observation as a method, and its claims to objectivity in particular, are deeply steeped in racist rhetoric and extractive practices with white researchers portrayed as objective, neutral observers of non-western communities. Activist Rachel Cargle captures this issue well, writing: "White people over history considered themselves the default for humanity. One way this shows up is in the colonization of intellect. In academia white people are the knowers and everything is to be known. White people are the explorers and everything else is to be discovered. White people are the academics and every other culture is to be studied, critically approached and picked apart through the white lens. #decolonizeintellect."[40] While contemporary researchers are (or should be) more aware of their own subjectivity and the impact of their presence on the community, the idea of participant observation still suggests the possibility of an insider/outsider status that carries objective observation. It is possible for digital ethnographers to fall even deeper into this narrative because digital space always involves some level of anonymity and performance.

My work and involvement with the outdoors activist community on Instagram through Indigenous Geotags (@indigenousgeotags) falls broadly under the category of embedded ethnography, but while I learned much about and from this community throughout this process, my work is as autoethnographic as it is ethnographic. I can draw only from my perspectives and experiences as a white academic and activist. My analyses of social media activist work and the engagement of Indigenous activists and non-Indigenous allies committed to decolonial work with the outdoor industry is shaped by and in many ways speaks to this positionality. The primary example of this is the fact that many of the processes and structures I write about throughout this book—that outdoor recreation and American public lands are fundamentally colonial systems for instance—are already well-known by Indigenous people and are part of the everyday, lived experience for Indigenous outdoor recreators. Other people approaching this same issue would see or choose to emphasize different aspects, find different things remarkable, or catch nuances I miss. Work on the outdoor recreation industry from Indigenous perspectives is critical to addressing these issues and is already being done by activists in public spaces on social media.

That being said, the perspective I bring is important to the work of articulating these structures within a certain genre, as I do in this book, and to a certain audience, as I do in my public work on Instagram. This story was not obvious to me before I began this research; as a photographer and writer for outdoor companies, I was in fact an active participant in the creation of the media I critique. It continues to be surprising and sometimes extremely challenging for other non-Indigenous outdoor recreators to accept, often undercutting deeply help beliefs and identities (not to mention income streams). My work on Instagram through Indigenous Geotags was designed to do two things. I wanted to challenge non-Indigenous outdoor recreators to rethink their relationship to land and the industry within the context of settler colonialism, and I wanted to use my connections and skills as a researcher to serve as a resource for the community. This book and its "ethnography" are part of this same project.

Chapter Summaries

Marketing the Wilderness's six-chapter arc begins by laying out the political, social, and environmental stakes of the project and contextualizing the relevant systems. It then jumps back in time to trace the history of the outdoor industry and its connection to Indigenous people before returning to contemporary outdoor conflicts and digital interventions. It concludes with a look toward Indigenous, decolonial futures and questions about what a post-wilderness land system might look like.

Chapter 1 analyzes the political and social framework undergirding the rhetoric of collective ownership of public land. Outdoor recreation corporations, despite their obvious capitalist positioning, espouse an anticapitalistic rhetoric in the context of public land, emphasizing its collective ownership and strongly condemning the privatization or, ironically, the commercialization of outdoor recreational space. The outdoor industry's deep investment in this idea stems from its reliance on public land as a massively subsidized arena for outdoor sporting goods. While the claims are transparently disingenuous since the outdoor industry actively commercializes public land as a way to sell outdoor products, the idea that collectively owned public land, of land that "belongs to you and me," is inherently good and progressive is a deeply treasured belief within the outdoor recreation community, including individuals within the industry itself. The existence of this ideology is only possible as the result of a combination of policy and representation driven and abetted by the outdoor industry to narratively and physically empty public lands of contemporary Indigenous people and their counterclaims to American collective ownership. This chapter grounds this argument in a handful of concrete spaces that highlight the contradictions inherent in the "our land" construction of public lands including the Boundary Waters Canoe Area Wilderness, the Arctic National Wildlife Refuge, and the National Marine Sanctuary and Marine National Monuments.

Chapter 2 serves as a prequel to a larger contextualization of the contemporary politics and strategies of the outdoor industry. I use the term "frontier wilderness" to describe the outdoor industry's general representational and marketing strategies and understanding of wilderness as a space inextricably connected to the presence of Indigenous people. Using historical advertisements from early outdoor companies like Abercrombie & Fitch and railroad tourism boards, I show how until as late as the mid-twentieth century, Indigenous people were seen as part of and even authenticators of wilderness and natural places outside of "civilization." This was especially prevalent beginning in the 1890s when, after the massacre at Wounded Knee, the end of the Indian Wars, and the increasing confinement of Indigenous people to reservations, Indigenous people took on a mythological status, representing a lost and longed-for American past and the boundless nature it had contained.

Chapter 3 explores the shift in representation within the outdoor industry from centering or acknowledging Indigenous presence to eliminating it. This turn toward an "untrammeled wilderness," a term drawn from the language of the Wilderness Act, began in the first half of the twentieth century, but coalesced in the 1950s, '60s, and '70s with the explosive growth in popularity of outdoor recreation and the founding of some of today's most influential outdoor companies including Patagonia, The North Face, and Black Diamond. This shift in representation is deeply connected to the passing of a series of conservation laws designed around the idea of an unpeopled wilderness as the most pure and sustainable form of nature. The construction of these spaces and the land management practices that maintain them have gone largely unchallenged by environmentalists and outdoor recreators in the fifty years since they were enacted, naturalizing the myth of wilderness within mainstream American thought. By examining the origins of these ideas, in particular the early outdoor recreation advocacy group The Wilderness Society, and the 1960s Yosemite climbing community, I show the profound impact midcentury outdoor recreation has had on contemporary environmental thought within the outdoor recreation industry, and the outdoor recreation community in the United States more generally.

Chapter 4 looks at the shift in corporate marketing strategies made possible by social media and digital technologies. I argue that this digital turn in marketing and social interaction in general is redefining the relationship between the outdoor industry and Indigenous people as power over representation and control of media is increasingly fragmented and, potentially, democratized. While this opens the possibility of a third paradigm shift away from the untrammeled wilderness model toward a potentially decolonial future, the outdoor industry has thus far successfully adapted their strategies to maintain the status quo. The outdoor industry's embrace of technologies like augmented reality and digital photography as well as adapting psychological theories like enclothed cognition, digital place attachment, and archetype identification to digital platforms has allowed the industry to individually target consumers and engage them in virtual worlds. Furthermore, the increasingly instantaneous and socially networked nature of digital technology has enhanced the scale and flexibility with which these ideas circulate. I use a range of examples from across the outdoor recreation industry to demonstrate how these strategies function, focusing on the industry's use of the explorer archetype to allow consumers to embody and reenact this colonial figure. Drawing on cultural nostalgia and American explorer mythologies, marketers use a range of strategies in their digital advertisements that allow consumers to inhabit the explorer identity first digitally and then, through the consumption of the company's products, physically. This construction makes Indigenous people and history illegible in recreational spaces, at best invisible and at worst an active and unwelcome obstruction to the enactment of the explorer fantasy.

Chapter 5 uses the conflict around the reduction of Bears Ears National Monument in 2017 and the yearlong marketing campaign Patagonia built around it as a concrete case study for how wildernessing functions in the contemporary outdoor recreation landscape. I argue that Patagonia's campaign to save Bears Ears, and adjacent campaigns by other corporations, set the social and political agenda for the progressive and environmental side of the conflict. The original Indigenous-centered purpose for the park was eclipsed by recreational interests, cementing Bears Ears as primarily a recreational site and weakening Indigenous claims to the land. The Trump-era monument boundaries, which included the original monument's best climbing routes but eliminate some of the most important Indigenous sacred sites, revealed the impact of this type of campaign. This chapter draws from social media marketing, commercials, digitally interactive media, and court cases to show how Patagonia has controlled the conversation.

Chapter 6 examines the ways Indigenous activists on Instagram have appropriated and redeployed digital strategies used by the outdoor industry to disrupt the wilderness narrative and illegibility of Indigenous people in recreation spaces. In the wake of the Bears Ears conflict, a community of Indigenous and decolonial activists began using their platforms to challenge the duality of the extraction versus recreation narrative employed by Patagonia, the Sierra Club, and similar organizations.

I look at their position within the larger history of Indigenous digital activism and position their innovative strategies as models for future digital activism. Like with Bears Ears, this activist community has put the outdoor industry in a new position of having to defend its ideologies. While using social media has its drawbacks, including working within a privately owned communication sphere, this movement still marks an important realignment of power between the outdoor industry and Indigenous people, one that is already driving a shift in representation if not yet in the physical management of land.

I use my conclusion to emphasize that the arguments I am making are relevant beyond the political moment of Bears Ears and the Trump administration. I look at Patagonia's move to "make the earth its only shareholder," and the limits of even the most liberal attempts to adapt the corporate system. These representations and policies are systemic and connected to the treatment of land as a commodity under capitalism and the structure of the United States as a settler state. I also suggest we might be at a point of change in outdoor representation and relationships. I look at how a post-wilderness world might function, either as a continuance of colonial systems in a new guise or by embracing a radically different Indigenized approach.

1

This Land Is Our Land

If you ask people what is the United States, they say
"freedom," and what is that? It's public lands.

—Luke Nelson, Trail Runner for Patagonia,
Bears Ears: Sport

▌n early 2019, I attended a screening of a short film by Native Outdoors
founder and Diné scholar Dr. Len Necefer about the Gwitch'in people's
fight to preserve the Arctic National Wildlife Refuge (ANWR). The film,
produced by Patagonia and shown at a Patagonia store in St. Paul, Minnesota, attracted an almost all-white audience who sat surrounded by
racks of puffy jackets and branded fleece vests hastily pushed to the
edges of the converted auto garage space. Images of people wearing
those jackets covered the walls, advertisements featuring mostly thin,
mostly white people paddling across pristine lakes and hiking through
untrammeled forests. The film dealt with many of the issues I discuss
later in this chapter around ANWR and the complications of tribal sovereignty and activism. The post-film conversation largely focused on
how ANWR benefited the Gwitch'in and the seemingly natural allyship
between environmental conservationists and Indigenous people in the
shared goal of protecting the nonhuman world. Comments and questions from the audience took this stance for granted, clustering Indigenous people, conservationists, and corporate supporters like Patagonia
together on one side of a political and ethical spectrum with extractive

industries, colonial governments, and other obviously environmentally destructive forces on the other.

In response, Necefer diplomatically agreed collaboration was an important aspect of pushing more sustainable and eco-friendly legislation forward, but also mentioned the role conservation activism, public lands, and outdoor recreation have played in the history of Indigenous removal and genocide, citing as an example the exceptionally violent removal of the Ahwahneechee people from what would become Yosemite National Park.[1] This screening had brought together a group of people who cared deeply about environmental issues and were invested in outdoor recreation, and yet, at Necefer's words, the audience let out a collective gasp. Was this true? How could they not know this history? Didn't white environmentalists and Indigenous people both care about the environment? Hadn't they always been on the same team?

The audience's shock stemmed from an assumption that conservationists and Indigenous environmental activists had shared goals when it came to public land and had equivalent, if slightly different, experiences when these lands were threatened. This assumption is both widespread and demonstrably false, betraying a deep misunderstanding of the ideological foundations of conservation, the structure of American settler colonialism, and the ways they support each other. For the audience members asking these questions, the potential for drilling in ANWR was a question of environmentalism, a threat to a pristine land and the caribou it supported. But for the Diné filmmaker and the Gwitch'in people featured in the film, the drilling was a question of political sovereignty and environmental justice—another example of how environmental risks are unequally distributed across society, disproportionately impacting historically disempowered people and people of color. While their intersection on this particular political action gave the impression of long-term alignment, the two groups not only had fundamentally different objectives for this space; they also had a deeply divisive history of which the white conservationists, at least, were unaware.

Conservation in the United States has been and continues to be complicit in environmental injustices against Indigenous people. By contributing to the political dispossession and violent removal of Indigenous people from their land, and erasure from their lands' histories and representations, American conservation is part of a power structure that perpetuates the continued colonization of Indigenous people and normalizes the occupation of land by settlers.[2] The government's acquisition and nationalization of land to be held in the public trust for the public good—the lands that would become public land as we know it—was the mechanism used to turn Indigenous homelands into an exploitable resource. While advocates tend to make a sharp distinction between environmentally destructive extraction industries and management for recreation, the distinctions fade when looked at through a lens of settler colonialism. Recreation, rather than an uncomplicated positive use of land standing in opposition to polluting industry, becomes another method to generate wealth from stolen land and a widely supported justification for continued state occupation.

This chapter unpacks the rhetoric of "our land," breaking down the ways in which public land is an investment in colonial state building and showing the outdoor industry's role in this system. As is true in all settler colonial nations, control over land in the United States, whether public or private, is essential to maintaining a myriad of intersecting systems of power including capitalism, patriarchy, white supremacy, and state hegemony. Through the outdoor industry's public land advocacy and its campaigns for wilderness, the rhetoric of collective good is weaponized as a tool of capitalism, commodification, and, ultimately, colonialism, ensuring these lands remain accessible for wealth extraction and state building. Public lands are the most foundational aspect of the industry's wildernessing campaigns. The land itself provides the physical space for the realization of wilderness, while its political construction as public and unowned provides the mythology necessary to support the recreator's exploration fantasy.

I break down the outdoor industry's profit-driven investment in the idea of collectively owned land as a public good, the industry's deep, if ambivalent, relationship to federal politics (i.e., the outdoor recreation complex), and the consequences of this system for Indigenous people. The binary framings of land use in the United States—public versus private, conservation versus exploitation, recreation versus extraction—are artificial. They are all, intentionally or not, colonial constructions, designed to legitimize American presence and erase Indigenous claims. Recent wins by Indigenous activists notwithstanding, public land as a legal framework for protecting Indigenous resources and sovereignty is extremely precarious, leaving the land vulnerable to the whims of the state and undermining Indigenous long-term relationships to it.

"This Land": Public Lands and the Outdoor Industry

When Jennifer Lopez sang "This Land Is Your Land" at the inauguration of President Biden, it was meant to signal a change in direction for the country, a message of unity and openness after an era of divisiveness. The song, written in 1940 by Woody Guthrie as a pro-immigrant response to growing nationalist sentiments, deftly ties together environmental imagery with the deeply held, if amorphous, American ideals of freedom and mobility.[3] It describes an open nation, open not only externally to immigrants who come from abroad and who share a collective and God-given right to the land, but also internally to those who wish to travel across and throughout it. This accessible, collectivist sentiment is made unambiguous in several verses Lopez did not sing—verses explicitly rejecting private property and positioning trespassing laws as illegitimate. The land, it is implied, exists apart from these artificial constructions as a common resource for all. Despite her omission, Lopez's version still gets at the heart of the song. As a people, as a nation, this is our land.

For many people on the political left in the United States, Guthrie included, this collective positioning of America and American land has been a deeply compelling idea. Decidedly welcoming, it builds on the narrative of the New World as a home for the homeless, the tired, the poor, the tempest-tossed, but it is also implicitly anticapitalist. The American dream of individual material wealth is replaced by a sense of collective ownership. The land, in its beauty and its expanse, is a source of wealth for the people. Of all American institutions, it is public land that comes closest to the reality of this vision, so it is no surprise that in recent years the song has increasingly been associated with public land, conservation, recreation, and, not coincidently, the industries that depend on them.

For Indigenous people, however, the song and what it has come to represent evokes an altogether different response. Expressions of distress and discomfort quickly filtered through social media networks in the wake of Lopez's performance. For example, both Lakota activist Jordan Marie Daniel of @_NativeInLA on Twitter and Jolie Varela of @indigenouswomenhike on Instagram posted their visceral responses upon hearing the song, describing the possession of land as illegitimate.

"Y'all are on stolen land," Daniel states.[4] Others like Potowami author Kaitlin Curtice and TikToker @kat_jefferson proposed alternate lyrics to the song, in Jefferson's case, completely rewriting it.[5] The song and its increasingly land-based associations within Indigenous communities was a potent reminder that even this new, liberal administration was still fundamentally a colonial one. For Indigenous people, "your" land is first and foremost stolen land.

In the song, the land of "This Land" refers to both the land itself as well as the nation it makes up, a complete conflation of the two. For the outdoor industry, however, the message of a nondiscriminatory civic conception of the United States as a nation is less important than the message of a communal investment in the physical land. It plays

FIGURE 1. Screenshot of tweet from @_NativeInLA (Jordan Marie Daniel).

FIGURE 2. Screenshot of tweet from @KaitlinCurtice (Kaitlin Curtice).

on, and reinforces, the deep emotional bond many outdoor recreators have to public land built on the narrative of collective public ownership, land that exists outside the market and represents the quintessential American ideals of freedom and democracy. This type of land is critical to the creation of wilderness. Wilderness is ahistorical and untouched, always waiting to be explored and claimed. Private ownership, while ultimately the goal of exploration, is fundamentally incompatible with this idea. Private land has already been surveyed, mapped, enclosed, and exploited. Only on public land can the fantasy of wilderness be realized.

The connection and sense of ownership Americans have over public lands arises out of many different kinds of relationships to these spaces. Ranchers and others who make their living off subsidized resources on public lands, for example, have a very different investment than ecologists who rely on the relatively undeveloped ecosystems that certain designations preserve. For 164.2 million individual Americans, however, the relationship to public land is born from recreation.[6] Few people own or have access to private land for outdoor recreation of the size and variety available to them through the public trust. These are the landscapes people see in each other's photographs and in advertisements, the landscapes they use and have a relationship with. There is not much data on private land recreation. However, preliminary data from the 2018 National Woodland Owner Survey conducted by the U.S. Forest Service, which included questions about land use, suggests that nonhunting recreation is a much lower priority for landowners than uses like timber products or land investment.[7] Furthermore, the National Public Landowners Survey conducted by the Department of Agriculture showed that while as many as 70 percent of private landowners recreate on their own land—mostly for hunting—fewer than half allow nonfamily members to and only 12 percent would consider allowing people they do not personally know to recreate on their land.[8] Most access to private land for recreation are trail easements connecting noncontiguous sections of public lands and negotiated by government agencies. The Bureau of Land Management (BLM), on the other hand, estimated over 67 million recreational visits in 2017 alone.[9] The narrative among white environmentalists and outdoorspeople of wilderness and national parks as a universal public good—the Ken Burns narrative of "America's best idea"—has remained largely unchallenged by the outdoor industry and is one of the few issues that has historically had widespread bipartisan political support.[10]

Today public land is naturalized within our political system, a vast complex of departments and designations used to manage federal, state, and local land on behalf of the American people, but "our" land has a complex, difficult history, and it remains deeply unequal in whom it serves. Hidden behind the industry's beautiful images of mountain wildernesses is the reality that American public land is built on the dispossession of Indigenous people. This is not a new argument and the details have been covered by scholars in environmental history, Indigenous studies, new western history, and other fields.[11] Public land exists as the result of the massive transfer of land from Indigenous nations to the U.S. government through often coercive treaties, U.S. legislation, executive order, war, and illegal infrastructure projects, among other methods. The history of these transfers is, in many ways, the history of the United States and is largely beyond the scope of this book, but understanding the fate of these lands *after* incorporation in the nation is critical to understanding the public land system of today.

Most of the 2.3 billion acres of land taken from Indigenous nations was redistributed to white Americans or private corporations through legislation like the Homestead Act, various railroad acts, and land grants like the Morrill Acts of 1862 and 1890, eventually becoming the basis for nearly all private property in the United States. However, over 800 million acres are still under direct government control and considered "public" land—roughly a third of the country. Currently, the U.S. federal government holds in trust for American citizens 640 million acres of land with another 198 million acres owned by individual states.[12] Ninety-five percent of this land is administered under just four departments: the Bureau of Land Management (BLM), the National Park Service (NPS), the Fish and Wildlife Service (USFWS), and the Forest Service (USFS). Even after the era of treaty-making ended in 1871 and after American Indians experienced the largest single loss of their land as the result of allotment and the Dawes Act of 1887, these departments continued to chip away at the remaining 55 million acres of American Indian trust land in the name of the American public, environmental conservation, and economic development.[13]

The role that national parks specifically have played in Indigenous dispossession is among the most egregious if only because of the inclusive and almost universally positive rhetoric surrounding the system. Historian Mark David Spence delves into the Indigenous history of three of the most well-known parks—Yosemite, Yellowstone, and Glacier National Parks—revealing how western ideas of wilderness, preservation, and land use drove the creation of spaces incompatible with Indigenous use. The origin of the park movement was about allowing urban white Americans to truly encounter nature, experience the sublime, and regain some form of lost masculinity. It is no accident that they arose roughly concurrently with what historian Frederick Jackson Turner called the closing of the frontier. Turner argued that the "American" was a product of his encounter with the untamed frontier; its closing was a threat to the very identity of the country. Parks, then, were managed and contained reproductions of Turner's lost frontier where the pioneer spirit of the country could continue to thrive.[14] Since the unpeopled wilderness deemed necessary for this type of interaction simply did not exist in the United States, it had to be created through the forced removal of entire Indigenous communities from these newly created parks.[15]

The parks Spence writes about are just the tip of the iceberg. Conservation-driven dispossession was a model used repeatedly throughout the nineteenth and twentieth centuries. For example, the tribes that make up the Colville Nation in Washington never signed a treaty giving up the land that is now North Cascades National Park, leaving them without even the usufructuary rights over the resources tribes with treaties can claim. Likewise, President Herbert Hoover simply ignored the presence of the Timbisha Shoshone when he created Death Valley National Monument, now a national park, effectively stripping them of their homeland through executive order. Every park has its own story of dispossession.[16]

Today, federally managed public land in the United States is, in a legal understanding, held in trust by the government for all American citizens.[17] This is a definition that is interpreted in many ways, but in the context of outdoor recreation and when used by the outdoor industry, it is commonly described as a form of collective ownership by the American people. While this applies to all public land regardless of designation, in the context of outdoor recreation it usually refers to conservation-based public land with recreation management use in mind. These include, but are not limited to, national parks, national monuments, national recreation areas, national conservation land, and wilderness areas.[18] The NPS exclusively manages national parks while the rest are managed by various agencies depending on which agency managed the land before its designation, including the USFS, the USFWS, and the BLM. Public lands outside of conservation- and recreation-focused designations are also managed for recreation to a lesser extent but rarely at the expense of the extraction economy. For example, Patagonia pronounced the reversion of Bears Ears land from national monument status back to general BLM management a theft of "your" land and an attack on the idea of public land in general, even though it would technically remain public land under federal management.[19]

From its beginnings as an industry, outdoor companies have closely tied their brands and marketing narratives to the idea of wilderness, a process I examine in detail in the following two chapters. Building on the narratives of early outdoors advocates like John Muir and Theodore Roosevelt, outdoor recreation was promoted as a way to discover America anew, fresh and untrammeled. In these sellable stories, Indigenous people were first romanticized and then excluded altogether, despite their obviously central role in the mythology from which the industry was drawing. The new adversary for the American explorer was nature itself.

The outdoor industry's current wilderness narrative, that there needs to be natural spaces, separate from the rest of human activity, formed the ideological foundation for the American recreation landscape based on public lands. Wilderness was land for visiting, not staying, not making a living off of, and certainly not exerting sovereignty over. It is a fundamentally colonial construction of space that precludes Indigeneity. The creation of the National Park Service, a whole department dedicated to managing public land for recreation rather than extraction, has become the centerpiece of this land use strategy, but it spread through other public land departments as well. By the mid-twentieth century, the United States Forest Service and the Bureau of Land Management were increasingly managing land for recreation in addition to extraction—a change driven by the need to keep up with increasing use by outdoor tourists rather than the result of top-down policy decisions. These narratives, wilderness as natural and wilderness as a necessity, were finally written into law in the Wilderness Act of 1964, defining wilderness as "an area where the earth and its community of life are untrammeled by man, where man himself is a visitor who does not remain" and the eventual creation of over 109 million acres of wilderness-designated land, 4.5 percent of the entire United States.[20]

While couched in the language of conservation, this narrative was fundamentally about recreation. This was made clear when the first area designated as an official "wilderness" under the Wilderness Act of 1964 was named the Boundary Waters Canoe Area Wilderness (BWCA). Since it banned commercial activity by local Ojibwe nations, including the word *canoe* in the official name designates the land for exclusively recreational paddling. The area was also composed of second-growth forest dotted with tourist resorts, an industry that was, unlike Indigenous livelihoods, completely compatible with wilderness. Furthermore, unpeopled wilderness is not a natural state of land in North America. The ecology of the land had coevolved under the management of local cultures—most notably maintaining certain ecosystems with fire, but including all kinds of human-nonhuman relationships. The legislation never intended to conserve actual natural environments. It instead sacrificed the opportunity to create ecologically stable areas in favor of creating the kind of spaces most desired by advocates of outdoor recreation, like the members of the Wilderness Society.[21] Despite including groundbreaking ecologists like Sigurd Olson and Aldo Leopold who were working on breaking down long-held assumptions of how these ecosystems functioned, members of the Wilderness Society still perpetuated the wilderness myth throughout their writings and photography, often coupled with descriptions of the joys of primitive recreational activities like canoeing and camping.

While extractive industry and water management have typically been centered as the main drivers of dispossession on public land—and with good reason—outdoor recreation has been an equal player in this process, working in tandem with extraction industries to cement American control over land. This is most obvious in the creation of the national parks and other conservation areas where Indigenous people were physically removed. However, the outdoor recreation industry is also essential to maintaining widespread support for the continued colonization of these spaces through two narratives about public land it has perpetuated and reinforced—the naturalization of wilderness (wildernessing) and the collective ownership of public land.

"Your Land": Collective Ownership Is State Ownership

In his discussion of the representational power of maps in the Philippines, geographer David Garcia describes this process of conservation to colonization succinctly in three steps: "delineate a national park, remove Indigenous people, extract resource."[22] The role of publicly funded conservation efforts in opening up land for both public and private resource extraction is most often brought up in the context of exploitative development projects in the global south, particularly in African and Pacific nations. It is a process, however, that was pioneered in the United States. Today known as the "Yosemite Model" of conservation, this process continues to create millions of conservation refugees, displacing Indigenous people worldwide to serve the needs of first-world tourism.[23]

Recreation, as I have argued, functions as an extractive industry on public land, impacting ecosystems and physical landscapes as well as treating the land as a consumable product. More importantly, recreation is often a precursor to traditional, and much more ecologically destructive, mineral extraction. It is a politically salient justification for obliterating competing claims to land but becomes a flimsy shield in the face of ever-occurring energy and resource crises. Recent repeals of the conservation statuses on public lands, particularly the reduction of Bears Ears National Monument that I detail later in the book, lay bare the political realities of supposedly protected spaces. Assumed to be conserved in perpetuity, state abrogation of these protections is neither unprecedented nor illegal but is part of a power system that keeps these lands open and available for future state access and appropriation.

I do not want to suggest that public land advocacy on the part of the outdoor industry is ingenuine or part of a secret state-centered cabal. For example, Patagonia's founder Yvon Chouinard and former CEO Rose Marcario used their company as a real advocacy tool. The kind of awareness and political clout they generated is critically important to a particular, if colonial, kind of environmental conservation in the United States. While it is true that outdoor retail sales have directly benefited from their participation in advocacy and that public land is of financial interest to them, profit margins do not seem to have been the only driver of their conservation work.

Nevertheless, the outdoor recreation-industrial complex is inherently self-defeating. The system of environmental conservation and land ownership for which the industry advocates serves its own interests and, whether intentionally or not, ultimately that of the colonial state. The public land conservation system is still grounded in the same Euro-American land ethic that put the land at risk to begin with. At best, it produces a temporary reprieve from intensive exploitation, and at worst, it further entrenches the very systems the industry claims to oppose.

No level of land acknowledgment, inclusion of Indigenous voices, or recognition of cultural resources changes the fact that Indigenous sovereignty over off-reservation land and resources (and to a lesser extent on-reservation land and resources) is perpetually vulnerable under America's public land system for which these companies advocate and from which they profit. No amount of anticapitalist posturing around the concepts of "public" and "wilderness" changes the fact that these companies are commodifying these lands for the creation of wealth. Profitability, not conservation, remains the fundamental value system associated with public lands.

As I discuss in later chapters, Indigenous people have sought to use conservation designations of public land to preserve connections to land and cultural resources. In particular, activists have looked to the national monuments, which can be created unilaterally under executive order, as a viable option. The creation of Bears Ears National Monument by President Obama was seen as proof of concept for the success of this strategy. However, even under the most sympathetic administrations, Indigenous people are still working within a fundamental set of laws and regulations primarily designed for and operationalized by corporations for generating revenue. A colonial state will not, cannot, give up sovereignty over its land, even in the limited scope desired by Indigenous activists. Dene political theorist Glen Coulthard argues that colonialism—and in this case, I see colonialism as fundamentally about maintaining control over land—is the point of convergence for a "constellation of power relations." It is the basic political and social structure that makes possible other forms of power and oppression, and that in turn is maintained by them.[24] Coulthard demonstrates this by showing how the discourse of reconciliation in Canada, while seeming to signal a realignment of relations among the Canadian government, settlers, and First Nations, in reality served to further entrench the colonial state. While certainly cathartic for individual victims, on a political level, recognition only calcified historical land occupations and made invisible contemporary colonial conflicts.

America's public land system is analogous to reconciliation in Canada both in its liberal, progressive discourse as well as its role in naturalizing dispossession. Setting aside land for conservation, even the granting of comanagement privileges for Indigenous communities, is not a relinquishment of power by the state or by interested corporations. It is merely a reconfiguring of power that leaves both the environment and Indigenous sovereignty over it as vulnerable as ever.

The true configuration of power over public lands is revealed during times when the state decides that, due to exceptional circumstances of one kind or another, a "state of exception," resources that would otherwise be protected are needed. Giorgio Agamben describes states of exception as times when a state of emergency demands a suspension of normal laws and rights and an undemocratic concentration of power into the hands of a few.[25] In this theorization, ultimate sovereignty lies in the ability to proclaim and enforce these exceptions. Typically, the idea of states of exception is used to describe how governments justify human rights abuses or the breakdown of normally functioning democracies, but in settler states like the United States, emergencies and exceptions have been an important political tool in undercutting Indigenous sovereignty for the purpose of acquiring land and resources. Agamben also argues that "exception" is a misnomer in that for many governments the exception becomes the rule, and a state of normalcy is never restored.

The government's use of states of exception to continue to maintain control of and acquire more Indigenous land throughout the twentieth century is seen most clearly in spaces where Indigenous people retain the greatest sovereignty—Indian reservations.[26] The emergency demanding these exceptions is almost always defense and security. Repeatedly, defense and security have been used as justification for the seizure, destruction, and inundation of reservation land. Sometimes this is for direct military action as in the bombardment of Cheyenne River

Reservation in South Dakota for military air drills and weapons testing or in the use of Gila River Reservation in Arizona for Japanese internment camps during World War II.

More often, however, *defense* and *security* are used as euphemisms for energy production. Historically, this has been highly visible in hydroelectric projects where dams would literally flood Indigenous communities, transforming important sovereign land bases into state power production or water management. Again, Cheyenne River was a victim of this when a 1948 Missouri River dam flooded 8 percent of the reservation. Similarly, the 1938 creation of Lake Havasu on the California/Arizona border eliminated eight thousand acres of the Chemehuevi Reservation.[27]

More recently, this was seen in the routing of the Dakota Access Pipeline through the watershed of the Standing Rock Sioux Reservation instead of the "high consequence area" of Bismarck, North Dakota.[28] This is not to say, of course, that Bismarck or any other community should have had to accept the risk of an oil spill and water contamination in place of the Standing Rock Sioux, but instead that the decision to build an oil pipeline at all constitutes both corporate and federal willingness to prioritize fossil fuel consumption over human and environmental well-being. That Standing Rock was the community that would experience some of the greatest adverse effects in the case of a spill is the result of settler colonial policies that have allowed Indian Country to be valued less than other equally rural and environmentally sensitive spaces.[29]

Because of the investment many white outdoor recreators and sportsmen have in them, public lands under conservation designations are in some ways more difficult for the government and industries to appropriate for other uses than reservations are. In other ways, however, they lack the legal protections of treaty-guaranteed trust land, so when they are appropriated, changes can be both more permanent and more pervasive. Both differences—white investment and legal construction—make public lands an especially precarious choice for American Indians seeking protection of and control over cultural and environmental resources. They become subject to the needs and whims of the state across the political spectrum around environmental issues.

In later chapters, I dig into Bears Ears National Monument, the most obvious example of the outdoor industry maintaining colonial land systems. Here, however, I want to examine two recent examples of the precarity of using federally managed land to protect both ecosystems and Indigenous sovereignty.

The first of these is the opening of the Arctic National Wildlife Refuge (ANWR) for oil and gas exploration. ANWR is a roughly 19-million-acre refuge on the coast in northeastern Alaska created to preserve fragile arctic ecosystems and species, especially polar bears and caribou, as well as to preserve the "wilderness" nature of the region. Upon signing the bill creating the refuge, along with nearly 100 million additional acres of protected land in Alaska, President Carter said, "We cannot let our eagerness for progress in energy and technology outstrip our care for our land, water and air and for the plants and animals that share them with us."[30] Eight million acres were designated as a Wilderness Area protected under the regulations put forth in the Wilderness Act. An additional 10 million acres are minimally managed and, while eligible for increased protection as a Wilderness Area, remain vulnerable to reduced protection. However, the bill also included a compromise that allowed 1.6 million acres, known as the 1002 Area, to be opened for oil and gas exploration and drilling with congressional approval.

While the possibility of oil and gas exploration in ANWR has been hotly debated since the refuge was created in 1980, neither side of the debate had been able to get a firm victory. A 1996 bill, for example, allowing exploration was defeated by presidential veto and a 2014 proposal to designate the entire section as a Wilderness Area failed to gain traction. In December 2017, the Senate slipped a clause into the year-end tax bill that seemed to officially end the debate and allowed for drilling exploration. Despite the introduction of the Arctic Cultural and Coastal Plain Protection Act, which was designed to reverse the tax law provision and was passed by the U.S. House of Representatives on September 12, 2019, the Bureau of Land Management completed an expedited Coastal Plain Environmental Impact Statement and approved the entire 1002 Area for oil and gas leasing. Leases were auctioned off in December 2020, generating less than 1 percent of projected revenue, and were subsequently canceled in 2023. A second lease sale occurred in December 2024 and received no bids. As of the winter of 2025, the reserve remains in limbo.

For local Indigenous communities, this is a complicated issue on many levels. The 1002 Area is traditional Inupiat land and falls within the

Arctic Slope Regional Corporation (ASRC), one of the thirteen Alaska Native Regional Corporations held by Alaska's Indigenous people in exchange for their aboriginal claims to the land as a settlement under the Alaska Natives Claims Settlement Act of 1971. As shareholders of ASRC, the Inupiat rely on gas and oil leasing for their livelihood and many, although not all, support oil and gas extraction in ANWR for this reason. The Gwich'in people live to the south and are shareholders in Doyon Ltd., a Native corporation that will see little of the profits coming out of ANWR. However, many Gwich'in communities rely on the Porcupine caribou herd that migrates through the 1002 Area of ANWR and fear that the herd and their livelihoods may be impacted by extraction. Many, but not all, Gwich'in people oppose gas and oil exploration in ANWR for this reason. Many people in both communities oppose it due to a host of environmental reasons and the fear that the interests of the Indigenous corporations are not accounting for the concerns of local communities.[31]

However, one way it is not complicated is how this whole situation shows the meaninglessness of the Wildlife Refuge status. It is unusual that protections around the 1002 Area were explicitly designed to be temporary—the writers of the 1980 bill must have known that a loophole allowing for eventual oil and gas extraction would inevitably be used at some point—but the reality is that this precarity extends beyond the 1002 Area to the ten million acres designated as "minimal management." This includes direct easements allowing for roads and pipelines as well as impacts like noise pollution or pollution footprints. However, it also sets a precedent of extraction in the area that could push for reduced protections in the non–Wilderness Area sections of the refuge should (when) the need for resources in this space arises. Conservation-based land designations are only valid until state or corporate interests decide they are needed for any other reason.

The second example is the 2018 reassessment of the National Marine Sanctuaries and Marine National Monuments. Relevant here are two executive orders that challenge and reverse Obama-era expansions to protected marine areas, especially in the Pacific Ocean. In the wake of the 2010 Deepwater Horizon oil spill, which leaked 4.9 million barrels (210 million gallons) of oil into the Gulf of Mexico, the Obama administration dramatically expanded marine protections originally enacted under the Antiquities Act of 1906, the National Environmental Policy

Act of 1969, and the Ocean Act of 2000. This included an expansion of the Pacific Remote Islands Marine National Monument to encompass a total of 490,343 square miles, six times its original size.

While in Bears Ears, the Trump administration consistently tried to hide the fact that the reduction of the monument was about oil and gas leasing, claiming it was about the legal limits of the Antiquities Act, President Trump's executive orders regarding marine protections are explicitly about resource extraction. They were part of a series of larger deregulation policies focused on "energy independence" and "energy security" that have collectively gutted nearly fifty years of environmental protection policy. The first, Executive Order 13795, "Implementing an America-First Offshore Energy Strategy," came on April 28, 2017, just months after Trump was inaugurated.[32] This order, among other things, required an assessment of energy and mineral resources within protected marine spaces as well as a review of all National Marine Sanctuaries and Marine National Monuments created or expanded under the Obama administration. This review was to be conducted by the Secretary of Commerce in consultation with the Secretaries of Defense, Homeland Security, and the Interior. This is similar to the review President Trump ordered for national parks and monuments more broadly and resulted in Secretary of the Interior Ryan Zinke recommending a reduction of size and protection of the Pacific Remote Islands, Rose Atoll, and Northeast Canyons and Seamounts Marine National Monuments.[33]

The second executive order came over a year later on June 19, 2018, and further prioritized extraction as a use for public land. Executive Order 13840, "Ocean Policy to Advance the Economic, Security, and Environmental Interests of the United States," reverses President Obama's Ocean Policy—Executive Order 13547, "Stewardship of the Ocean, Our Coasts, and the Great Lakes." In addition to showing the fragility of public lands and environmental protections created through executive order, which include national monuments, Executive Order 13840 brings into focus the connection between these attacks on environmental protections and challenges to Indigenous sovereignty. While including language that requires consultation with "state, tribal, and local governments," as required by law but often ignored, the order eliminates commissions that included Indigenous representation.[34] The previous policy had actively brought Indigenous voices into the decision-making

process on an equal basis around the protection of these waters, something rare in marine conservation. Like the protections themselves, Indigenous equity was a fragile thing, quietly and easily removed.

Bears Ears, ANWR, and the Ocean Policy are just a few more publi-
cized examples of the recent reduction of protections over public lands.
According to a 2019 study published in *Science,* since 2000, over a million square miles of protected land had been eliminated or experienced
a reduction in protections globally, with 62 percent of all elimination
or reduction events being due to the expansion of extractive industry. In
the United States, this is even more extreme with around 276,000 square
miles of land impacted by reduced or eliminated protections since 2000,
of which 99 percent was due to industrial development.[35] Although these
reductions have accelerated in the last twenty years, they have occurred
historically as well, as long as environmentally protected public lands
have existed. This has become standard operating procedure for the
United States with respect to public land.

I want to conclude with one final example to bring this story back to
how state appropriation and preservation of public land serves settler
colonial goals. The National Bison Range was 18,800 acres of federal
public land in Montana, an enclave surrounded by the Flathead Reservation. The Confederated Salish and Kootenai Tribes (CSKT) of the Flathead Reservation ceded the land in 1908 but were compensated at less
than a seventh of the actual value of the land—the difference of which
they would not get for another sixty years. In 2016, after years of con-
tention, CSKT thought they might finally get their land back when the
Fish and Wildlife Service recommended transferring the land to CSKT to
be put back into trust for the tribe. This was in part a financial decision
since the tribe would then take on the operating costs of the refuge, but
would have been a victory for the community who had been fighting for
over a hundred years for the return of this land. According to Secretary
Zinke, however, the federal government was not in the business of giving
away public land, especially to Indians. The former Montana representative reversed the Obama-era management plan, choosing to keep the
National Bison Range under the control of the Fish and Wildlife Service.
He did not want to reduce public land, stating that he had committed to
not sell or transfer any public land.[36]

Zinke had no problem removing federal protection of land, as he
had demonstrated earlier that year at Bears Ears and Grand Staircase-

Escalante National Monuments. However, transferring the National Bison Range to BIA trust land—since this is still a colonial country and tribal land is still considered government trust land—was represented as selling off public land, despite CSKT's proven record of quality resource management and stated commitment to keep the land accessible. The common thread between Zinke's seemingly opposite policies at Bears Ears and the National Bison Range is an investment in settler control of land and resources and a blow to Indigenous sovereignty.

The Bison Range was eventually returned to the CSKT under the Biden administration. This could be a step in the right direction, or it could merely be another swing of the pendulum for Indigenous land activists, one that could swing back at any time.

"Made for You and Me": Turning "Our Land" into a Brand

The precarity of wilderness in the face of potential energy extraction needs means that recreation-focused designations must constantly be defended. The outdoor industry, for which these designations and the appearance of wilderness is a financial imperative, has sought to forge a close association between the American sense of collective ownership over public lands and recreation-specific designations that conform to the wilderness ideal (e.g., Wilderness Areas, national parks). The idea is to convince their consumers that the use of public land for anything other than western-style environment preservation and outdoor recreation is an attack on the institution of public land itself. Mining, logging, ranching, and gas and oil extraction, while all valid uses of public land according to U.S. land management agencies' multi-use mandates, are represented as theft, even desecration, when allowed on any public land. The opening of land previously designated exclusively for recreation, no matter how recently, becomes anathema. It is this connection that allows a company like Patagonia to unironically declare that "the president stole your land" in response to what is a simple, if deeply consequential, redesignation of federal land.

To dig deeper into this carefully crafted association, I want to return to the outdoor industry's use of "This Land Is Your Land" in its marketing and brand management. I find the industry's co-option of the song provides a powerful metaphor for its larger co-option of public land systems. It is illustrative of how the rhetoric of "our land" was beginning to be used within the outdoor industry, as the crystallization of several decades of reimagining the colonial relationship between Americans and public land. It shows that this language and the ideas behind it were more than a reaction to Trump-era public land policies that threatened the industry but were already a proactive campaign positioning the industry as a champion of the collective ownership of these lands. Finally, it reveals an ambivalent yet indispensable relationship between the industry and the federal government around the issue of public lands.

The outdoor industry is far from the first to appropriate "This Land" for its own purposes. Written in 1940 by Woody Guthrie as a response to what he saw as excessive jingoism in Irving Berlin's "God Bless America," "This Land" was meant to shine a critical, but also hopeful, light on the plight of the working class in America.[37] In the original version, the ending refrain of each verse "This land was made for you and me" begins seemingly sincere, but grows increasingly ironic in the final verses as Guthrie switches from describing the natural beauty of the country to its exclusionary practices and hungry masses. In the final verse, it appears as a question: "Is this land made for you and me?"

In the following decades, "This Land," almost always omitting the verses critical of the United States, has become something of a second national anthem, part of the "bloodstream of our nation's cultural body."[38] "This land was made for you and me" turned out to be a highly portable concept. It was used in presidential campaigns of candidates as diverse as Ronald Reagan and Bernie Sanders. It has been used to protest war but was also nearly used by the U.S. Army to recruit soldiers. And, of course, it has been used repeatedly in marketing.

While "This Land" has been used uncritically to connect products to the wonders of traveling through the United States, its more recent uses have surprisingly cleaved much closer to the original spirit of Guthrie's lyrics, including some of the most politicized commercials of the 2010s. Jeep, for example, used it in a 2015 Super Bowl commercial. Hardly the first car company to seize on the potential that lines like "this ribbon of highway" present, Jeep sparked controversy by juxtaposing the lyrics of this American anthem against footage of international travel, giving "your land and my land" a global connotation that made many Americans uncomfortable. Likewise, Johnny Walker used a mixed English/Spanish spoken-word version by Chicano Batman in a 2017 commercial. Beginning with the usually elided "no trespassing" verse, the commercial is, like many uses of the song throughout the Trump administration, a clear critique of U.S. immigration policy.

Most relevant, however, is the 2014 The North Face commercial released as part of the company's #SeeForYourself campaign.[39] The campaign, the company's largest up to that time, featured, among other things, user-generated content on social media to show how everyday people experience outdoor spaces, as well as a taxicab in New York City that would allow people to opt for a surprise adventure rather than continuing their planned trip. It utilized an "anti-social media" rhetoric that encouraged potential consumers to move beyond the beautiful images they see on-screen and take ownership over their experiences, to see for themselves and, despite the narrative, to share their experiences on social media. The central tenet was to help people reimagine "exploration" as not just a pastime for extreme athletes like those sponsored by the company, but as something they could participate in themselves.

The commercial was a joint effort among The North Face, the band My Morning Jacket, who recorded the version used in the commercial, and the U.S. Department of the Interior, which was in the process of launching a new Conservation Corps program.

Directed by outdoor photographer and athlete Chris Burkard, the commercial is emotionally resonant, the swelling of the music a powerful partner to the cinematic scenes of unspoiled landscapes and feats of extreme athleticism. The advertisement begins by panning out from the iconic Yosemite Valley Half Dome peak mirroring its own simulacra in The North Face logo. Opening with Yosemite, the spiritual heart of the National Park system and the birthplace of The North Face as a company, hits the perfect balance of grandeur and familiarity to draw the viewer into the narrative. It then alternates between showing The North Face's sponsored athletes performing incredible acts in remote places—camping suspended from a cliff, slacklining over waterfalls, summitting glacier-encrusted mountains—with shots of ordinary people engaging in everyday activities—running across the Brooklyn Bridge, jamming together in a drive-in campsite, carrying a surfboard onto the subway. In between, Burkard included frames of unpeopled wildernesses and landscapes synonymous with remoteness, areas like dense, moss-covered forests, snowcapped mountain peaks rising into the distance, and a herd of bison (the only animals featured) stampeding across a snowy prairie. It ends with flashes of diverse, weatherworn faces, and The North Face's

then team captain, backcountry skier Hilaree Nelson, before transitioning to the company's logo and tagline, "Never Stop Exploring."
The takeaway is that outdoor recreation, the unparalleled beauty of
America's public lands, and, by extension, The North Face products are
accessible to everyone. This is hardly a controversial stance, although it
is a consequential one. It speaks to a recreational focus for land use and
emphasizes the thrill of exploring remote places and pristine landscapes.
Like the Johnny Walker commercial, the company's unusual decision to
include the "no trespassing" verse gave the advertisement's message a
more subversive and politicized tone than it otherwise would have had.

As I went walking I saw a sign there
And on the sign it said "No Trespassing."
But on the other side it didn't say nothing
That side was made for you and me[40]

The commercial shows a rancher opening a gate with a "Private Property.
No Trespassing" sign for a group of backpackers. While not quite the so-
cialist manifesto a labor advocate like Guthrie might have envisioned—
The North Face is after all a for-profit subsidiary of a giant multinational
corporation—it does reveal the land ethic the company wants to project
to its consumers, one that is broadly accessible, inclusive, and, if not
exclusively recreational, at the very least multi-use. It is an implicit rejection of private (i.e., not recreational) interests on public lands and an
embrace of a kind of collectivism almost unthinkable in any other corporate campaign. It is this land ethic that makes "This Land" such a salient
choice for The North Face's marketing campaign, a union of political
and commercial goals that for once seems to actually serve the people.
The commercial concludes with the oft-omitted "Freedom Highway"
verse, further projecting a sense of the right of American outdoor recreators to these spaces and explicitly connecting it to the idea of freedom.
Interestingly, the full version of the song released by My Morning Jacket
included Guthrie's original verse about hungry, unemployed workers
standing at a church relief line asking, "Is this land made for you and me?"
The fact that The North Face decided not to include that verse in the final
version of the commercial is unsurprising as the nod to the class consequences of capitalism does not as easily fit the message of abundance and

openness evident in the rest of the song. Overall, the meaning is clear. As consumers, as recreators, as Americans, this is *our* land.

This commercial is also a powerful example of the kind of state-corporate partnership that is central to the outdoor recreation-industrial complex. It was made in collaboration with the Department of the Interior (DOI) as part of their launch of the 21st Century Conservation Service Corps (21CSC), essentially serving as a well-funded and widely distributed PSA for the public land system. This partnership was likely instigated by then Secretary of the Interior Sally Jewell. Jewell was trained as an oil industry engineer and served as the CEO of REI from 2005 to 2013. With a background and connections in extractive industry, outdoor recreation, and federal public land management at the highest level, Jewell exemplified the connections, politically and ideologically, among these stakeholders and fully understood the power of outdoor industry marketing in cultivating American bonds to public land. Since this was connected to the 21CSC program, the DOI leaning into The North Face's wilderness vision for public lands makes sense for the purposes of this campaign. However, the DOI is also the department in charge of oil leasing and has a much more multi-use vision for public lands than the company. While investing in the "your land" rhetoric may dampen American enthusiasm for nonrecreational uses, the goodwill generated for federal oversight and ownership of these lands and the total erasure of competing claims is far more important to the department's long-term strategic goals.

When Guthrie wrote about "our land," his focus was on countering anti-immigrant sentiment and addressing the vast wealth inequality of his time. As his advocacy for projects like the Grand Coulee Dam showed, he was not deeply concerned about either environmental issues (which as I discuss in the following chapters were still largely recreation focused in the 1930s rather than the justice-focused activism that Guthrie might have more seriously engaged in) or Indigenous issues. While the Indigenous critiques of his song became evident to non-Indigenous activists long before the song became an environmentalist anthem in the twenty-first century or the 2020 inauguration and its backlash, they were critiques that for the most part were conveniently ignored. Folk singer Pete Seeger tells the story of being confronted, half-jokingly, by Lakota activist Henry Crow Dog at the 1968 Poor People's Campaign in

Washington, DC, regarding the song. After the song ended, Crow Dog quipped to Seeger and fellow singer Jimmy Collier, "Hey, you're both wrong. It belongs to me."[41] This brief, lighthearted interaction deeply troubled Seeger for the rest of his career. Although in later recordings he ended up adding an additional verse addressing Indigenous claims and the difficult history of public lands, the contradiction of "This Land" being deeply inclusive while at the same time serving as a reminder of American genocide was one that he never managed to fully reconcile.[42]

For much of the American public, however, the contradictions inherent in "This Land" remained and continue to remain unproblematic. The idea of public land as "our land," rather than a reason to address a difficult history, is a welcome reprieve from increased privatization in other sectors of society. It is the one unquestionably supported land management choice, "American's Best Idea."

The idea that public lands—at least land designated under national park or national monument status—are a universal public good is far from a new idea, but its use in the marketing rhetoric of the outdoor industry and its circulation in online communities reached a fever pitch in response to the Trump administration's energy-first policies toward public land. While the commercial by The North Face was in development at least a year before Trump's campaign really took off, the outdoor industry took the opportunity presented by his rhetoric to press home their arguments about the collective good of these spaces. The industry contended that the administration's attack on them was exceptional and un-American.

Outdoor recreation and the outdoor industry that supports it has been central to the modern American conservation movement since it began in the late nineteenth century by creating, reproducing, and disseminating some of the most widespread—and most colonial—narratives that ideologically undergird the movement. Outdoor recreation is in fact at the center of an environmental justice issue of which many environmentalists are ignorant and in which they are themselves complicit. The industry contributes to these injustices while at the same time fostering the perceived alignment. While eye-opening to Necefer's white audience, Indigenous people have long experienced the negative impacts of conservation and are increasingly confronting the outdoor recreation industry's role in it. Necefer himself is part of a growing community of Indigenous activists working to intervene in the industry both physically on the ground as well as, importantly, representationally over social media. In the following chapters, I lay out the history of the ideologies upon which American colonial public land systems are built, the strategies the outdoor industry has used to promote them, and the ways Indigenous people have resisted them.

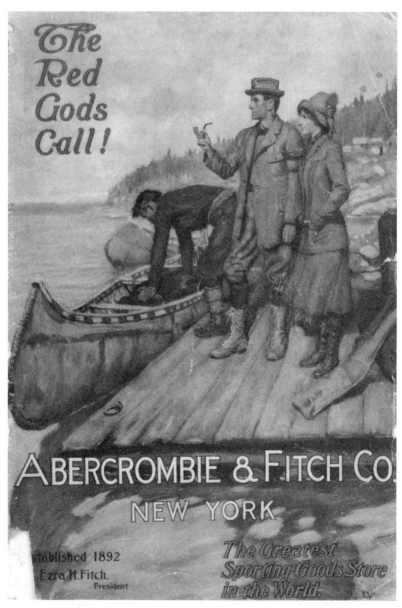

FIGURE 3. Abercrombie & Fitch, 1913 catalog cover.

2

The Frontier Wilderness

The frontier is the outer edge . . . the boundary
between civilization and savagery.

—Frederick Jackson Turner, *The Significance
of the Frontier in American History*

A 1960 headline in the *Cook Country News Herald* out of Grand Marais,
Minnesota, read, "Labor Day Fire Destroys Historic Indian Princess
Grave." The "royal remains," as the article puts it, of an eight-year-old
Kawnipi Ojibwe girl had been a popular canoe destination for paddlers
on Lake Saganaga in what would become the Boundary Waters Canoe
Area Wilderness on the Minnesota-Ontario border. According to the
legend, sometime around 1902, the princess and her chiefly father had
been caught in rough waters on their way to a neighboring village when
their canoe capsized, and the girl drowned. The chief and his band re-
covered the body and laid her to rest on an island with an array of grave
goods to honor her before continuing their journey in mourning. The
grave goods would be almost immediately looted, but the body and the
possibly apocryphal story that went with it remained an important landmark and tourist spot for the following sixty years until it was destroyed
by a fire started with a careless cigarette.

While a deeply macabre attraction, the article leans into the romance
of this "Indian" story, repeatedly calling the girl a princess, recounting
the later tragic death of her father, and even suggesting her body had
magical properties. "Mysteriously," it claims, "the many bears, wolves,

and foxes in the area never disturbed the remains."[1] Tourists did not see this as the grave of a child as they might a white child in a Christian cemetery, but as a tangible connection to an almost mythical being. The bones of the princess proved to the paddlers that they were truly outside of civilization and in the "wild" Gunflint country at last. They did not visit to pay their respects to the victim of a tragic accident or even simply to sate some dark curiosity; they visited to authenticate their wilderness experience. The presence of an "Indian Grave Island" in the nearby Basswood Lake suggests that the Indian princess's grave was not the only Indigenous grave used as an authenticating tourist destination for early recreational canoers in the region, but part of a pattern of exoticizing the Indigenous history and culture of a recreational area slowly taking on the mantel of a twentieth-century wilderness.

This chapter examines how and why early twentieth-century wilderness ideology became so closely tied to the idea of Indianness, or a set of romanticized Indian stereotypes that exist independently of and often opposed to actual Indigenous people, and the role of recreational marketing in this process.[2] For many recreators of the era, the modern understanding of wilderness as an untouched space outside of *all* human influence would have seemed foreign. Instead, wilderness, including the new national parks, were very much "Indian" spaces, imbued with, and indeed inseparable from, the wild romance of Indian princesses and tragically lost chiefs, most of whom barely resembled the actual Indigenous people and communities who still lived in these spaces or who had only recently been removed to create them. Like the untrammeled wilderness of today, this early wilderness was a narrative construction, an early form of wildernessing, reflective of the physical spaces described only to the extent that these spaces, and the people in them, were shaped to fit the preexisting narrative.

I call this wildernessing narrative the *frontier wilderness*. This was an idea created out of scarcity mentality around the disappearing frontier that prompted the creation of the American public land system—a system that balances conservation, extraction, and recreation—that still exists today. It was a wilderness explicitly designed to serve as an ideological replacement for the American frontier. The frontier wilderness was an idealized American West held in constant temporal suspension, in a tension between being always undiscovered and constantly explored. Like all wilderness, the frontier wilderness was a place outside of civilization, outside of the normal workings of society. Moving beyond early representations of wilderness as threatening and unproductive, it drew on ideas from the Romantic movement to become a retreat, a place where Americans could go to restore themselves and rediscover what it was to *be* American. Unlike the Romantics, who discovered truth through art and poetry, Americans explored through recreation. They went to reenact the country's mythic origins, to play the explorer, the pioneer, and the cowboy. All archetypical identities constructed, not coincidently, with and against the figure of the Indian.[3]

Like all wilderness, frontier wilderness was deeply invested in the settler colonial project. Reflecting a shift in federal Indian policy at the time, it was about the maintenance and production of a racial hierarchy that gave white settlers the freedom of movement and leisure while assimilating Indigenous people through intense surveillance and containment. The wilderness belonged to the settler state—national parks as a possessive as much as a descriptor—and, while Indianness was valued, Indigenous people themselves increasingly became an obstacle to the outdoor experience. Marketing materials and other representations of parks and wilderness areas played into these stereotypes, presenting Indigenous people as passive, subservient, and welcoming, emphasizing easily consumed Indian iconography more than complex Indigenous people themselves.

Media production in the era was centralized and top-down with corporate marketers and governments having an outsized influence on all kinds of representation. At the same time, parks and wilderness areas were less accessible and democratic than they are today, meaning more people relied on a smaller sample of representations to understand what these spaces and their people were like. Despite this, Indigenous people used their physical presence in these spaces and their integration in the local tourist economies to push back against harmful stereotypes and colonial policies and take agency over their own self-representation. They developed strategies that would be adapted in later decades as wilderness ideology and modes of media production began to change.

Before the Frontier Wilderness

The definition of wilderness is hard to pin down, largely because the connotations associated with the word have been in flux for the past several hundred years. It is a term continually used under the assumption that the meaning is self-evident, static, and natural. Like the concept it describes, however, nothing could be further from the truth. The term *wilderness* is codified in the 1964 Wilderness Act as "an area where the earth and its community of life are untrammeled by man, where man himself is a visitor who does not remain"—a definition used in the protection of 106 million acres of federal land.[4] The WILD Foundation, responsible for international wilderness guidelines, describes wilderness as legally protected and biologically intact areas.[5] However, a short look at the history of wilderness in America reveals that the most accurate definition is the one given on Urban Dictionary, an online, crowdsourced lexicon—"Wilderness is what you make it to be."[6]

The word itself comes from the Old English term *Wildeornes,* literally meaning "land inhabited only by wild animals," and early writings from the seventeenth and eighteenth centuries describe such places as terrifying, even heathen. Drawing on classical and biblical texts, early settlers regarded the wilderness as any place outside the moralizing influence and structure of civilization, but unlike their ancestors in medieval Europe who avoided the wilderness, these new settlers approached it with the lens of missionaries and capitalists. The wilderness was a place to be conquered, tamed, and brought into the enlightened influence of western society.[7] Alexis de Tocqueville famously observed during his 1831 journey that Americans "do not perceive the mighty forests around them till they fall beneath the hatchet. Their eyes are fixed upon . . . draining swamps, turning the course of rivers, peopling solitudes, and subduing nature."[8]

Despite rhetorically describing it as a place of only wild animals, early settlers never actually considered the wilderness to be an unpeopled place, merely uncultivated and uncivilized. From the very beginning of American settlement, Europeans were interacting with Indigenous people. The two groups traded, married, and warred and, at least in the eyes of the Europeans, the difference between them was as much about the environment as it was about race or skin color. The settlers had subdued the land they occupied, cultivated it, and brought it into what they saw as productive use. Indigenous people were considered the people of the wilderness, seen by settlers as making no productive use of the land—occupiers as the animals were occupiers, but not possessors.

Indigenous people were in fact integral to the settlers' understanding of wilderness. Environmental historian Mark David Spence argues that, at least through the mid-nineteenth century, Euro-Americans "did not conceive of wilderness and Indians as separate."[9] Through the work of Romantic-era artists like Thomas Cole and travelers like George Catlin, Spence shows that the presence of Indigenous people was an authenticating feature of the wilderness. Without Indians, the territory was just land, possibly wasteland, but more likely land already occupied by non-Indigenous settlers. The association was also just as strong the other way around. If wilderness was authenticated by the presence of Indians, Indians were authenticated through their presence in wilderness.[10]

Euro-American views toward wilderness began changing in the antebellum era from something to be destroyed or cultivated to something that just might have intrinsic value. This was, among other influences, the result of the European Romantic movement, a movement in part inspired by the seemingly untouched landscapes of the New World, finally taking root in America. In his study of wilderness in America, Roderick Nash describes how core concepts of Romanticism like the idea of the sublime and the value of primitivism gave Americans the language to begin seeing the rugged, undeveloped lands around them as beautiful.[11] A journey into the wilderness no longer needed to fill one with otherworldly panic and "restless dread" as it did Roman poet Titus Lucretius Carus.[12] Instead, it became transformative, a way to shed the excesses of society and find that, as Henry David Thoreau wrote, "in Wildness is the preservation of the world."[13]

While European Romantics looked longingly at what they saw as the primeval state of American landscapes, land as it was on the first morning of creation, American Romantics, despite their best efforts, could not escape the reality that these places were not empty gardens, but the homelands of hundreds of Indigenous nations and communities. Philosophically, this proved not to be a problem. Had not Indigenous people already been deeply associated with, even integral to, wilderness for hundreds of years? Artists and writers merely incorporated Indigenous people into their idea of what wilderness should look like—or at least a version of Indigenous people—leaning into the idea of the Noble Savage as an innocent, almost childlike figure. Like wilderness itself, the Noble Savage was a being closer to the point of creation, a purer, if more primitive, form of human. Indigenous people featured heavily in the wilderness art of Thomas Cole and George Catlin, whose controversial 1853 London exhibition led to the popularization of the Noble Savage trope.[14] The figures of Uncas and Chingachgook in *The Last of the Mohicans* owe their representations to this folding of wilderness and Indianness.

This romanticized version of Indianness, however, failed to hold up to the American Romantic's actual encounters with Indigenous people. It quicky became clear that while narratively, these people of the woods enhanced settlers' growing understanding of wilderness as sublime, actual Indigenous people hindered it. They created a more complex version of the land that suggested multiple relationalities, challenging settler legitimacy and, more critically, settler comfort. After his rather traumatic experience in the Maine woods, Thoreau described the Indigenous people there as "sinister and slouching fellows," as "degraded savages," and as "making coarse and imperfect use . . . of nature." "No wonder," Thoreau wrote, "that their race is soon to be exterminated."[15] Early canoe recreator and Romantic Charles Lanman described the beauty of northern Minnesota as unparalleled, while regretting that his encounters with Ojibwe people at Leech Lake caused him to "utterly despise the character of the whole Indian race."[16] And of course John Muir, the patron saint of wilderness, described the Miwok in the Sierras as "dark eyed, dark haired, half happy savages" who were a stain on the othewise "clean wilderness."[17] It was these views, this growing divergence between the idealized Noble Savage and actual Indigenous people struggling against the increasingly heavy hand of U.S. colonialism, expansion, and military action, that set the narrative stage for the emergence of frontier wilderness alongside the rise of the outdoor recreation industry.

Frontier Wilderness

This national embrace of wilderness was well underway when, in the 1890s, it ran headlong into another recent American idea—outdoor recreation. Before the late nineteenth century, except for a handful of wealthy eccentrics, spending time out of doors was a necessity rather than a pleasure. Historian Phoebe S. K. Young describes how it was nostalgia for the military encampments of the Civil War that first drove the average man to pursue camping for recreation, a way to reexperience the comradery of the campfire and a simple, ordered life.[18] These encampments, true to their origin, were open-field affairs, more likely to happen on the outskirts of a town than deep in a forest.

In the century's final decade, however, a number of factors came together to jumpstart a form of recreation that would shape Americans' understanding of wilderness for the next sixty years. The decade was an era of transition. The 1890 census declared the American frontier closed, prompting Frederick Jackson Turner's frontier thesis—placing confrontations with the frontier at the center of American identity creation—and Theodore Roosevelt's crisis of masculinity.[19] In a nation with new overseas imperial ambitions, the genteel Victorian gentleman had given way to a more aggressive form of American masculinity, one Roosevelt saw as formed out of the crucible of man's encounter with a rapidly vanishing wilderness. In particular, he lamented the possible end of wilderness hunting. This coincided with growing interest in the conservation movement. John Muir published his first book and founded the Sierra Club in 1892. The Audubon Society was formed and quickly spread across the country. Out of this same energy, Yosemite and Sequoia became the second and third national parks in 1890 and the first national forest was designated under the leadership of conservationist Gifford Pinchot in 1905.

Most importantly, the 1890s marked a radical shift in U.S.–Indian relations, one that allowed the nascent philosophies connecting a deeply romanticized version of Indianness (though, again, not actual Indigenous people) with the experience of wilderness to fully mature. Throughout the nineteenth century, the United States had focused on Indigenous *removal* though treaties and war. However, 1890 saw the massacre at Wounded Knee, the last "battle" of the wars with the Lakota and the end of any serious Indigenous military resistance to the United States.[20] With nowhere left to push Indigenous nations, the Bureau of Indian Affairs pivoted from removal to focusing on *containment.* Reservations had been used extensively throughout the nineteenth century and were important parts of treaty negotiations. Many treaties included a number of reserved rights to ceded, off-reservation land, and the reservations themselves were spaces of reserved absolute sovereignty that allowed tribal citizens freedom of movement to travel, hunt, or work on or off reservation.

Containment policy, however, turned these reduced homelands into the most heavily surveilled spaces in the United States, drastically reducing the freedom of movement that Indigenous people who had signed treaties had previously enjoyed. While the Indian Appropriations Act had officially ended treaty making and rejected the sovereignty of Indigenous nations in 1871, the 1890s demilitarization and increased bureaucratization of Indian policy aggressively pushed assimilation policies designed to break traditional ways of life. The most extreme example of this was the Indian Boarding School system, which sometimes encouraged and sometimes forced Indigenous children to leave home and enroll in U.S.-run schools where they were stripped of their language and culture in an attempt to make them "productive" citizens.[21] The implementation of the Dawes Act or General Allotment Act, initially passed in 1887, was intensified, which resulted in the loss of ninety million acres of land, the largest single dispossession of Indigenous land in U.S. history. Even as the U.S. government was leaning into the idea of land held collectively for the public good regarding environmental conservation, it was privatizing and atomizing Indigenous land. These genocidal policies contributed to Indigenous people in the United States hitting their lowest total population in 1900.

This process was exacerbated by a concerted effort by conservationists and the National Park Service to make the new national parks feel safe for white, middle-class tourists—through violence if necessary. Fort Yellowstone was established in the park in 1891 to prevent poaching by the Shoshone and other tribes and keep them from causing alarm among tourists.[22] In 1906, the Ahwahnechee were burned out of their villages in Yosemite Valley for the second time.[23] The end result of these efforts was that, for most outdoor recreators, Indigenous people were out of sight and out of mind. The "Indian Problem," which had been a driving force in American politics and society since the nation's inception, seemed solved and Indigenous people could safely be considered a thing of the past.

Because actual Indigenous people and nations were being removed from these newly constructed wildernesses, outdoor recreators were able to fully embrace what historian Philip J. Deloria calls "Indianness," or the appropriation of a romanticized version of American Indian identity by non-Indigenous people, without the threat of actual Indigenous people challenging these perceptions like they did for Thoreau.[24] Would-be explorers and adventurers at the time of this shift in wilderness mythology still associated the increasingly contained American wilderness with Indians—George Catlin even went so far as to suggest that the government create a national park to protect Indigenous culture and society, an action he saw as crucial to and inseparable from wilderness preservation. Frontier wilderness, then, was defined not by its connection to real Indigenous people, but to Indianness as an idea. Both the space and the people were romanticized and sanitized simulacra of the spaces and people they replaced and represented.[25] It is this fundamental association with Indianness that sets frontier wilderness apart from the untrammeled wilderness that emerged half a century later and continues into the twenty-first century.[26]

Deloria presents Indianness as an archetypical identity that non-Indigenous people don in an attempt to perform their own Americanness. It "provided impetus and precondition for the creative assembling of an ultimately unassemblable American identity."[27] To dress up as an Indian and throw tea into Boston Harbor is to stake a claim to an Americanness fundamentally separate from Europe. Because American Indians had been so narratively tied to the American continent, inhabiting this mythical version of them authenticates one's Americanness. Deloria cites the Boy Scouts of America as a quintessential example of this, where, as the organization moved from Britain to the United States, "playing Indian" was written into the organization's early models.[28] The organization was even originally called "Woodcraft Indians" when it was founded in 1902. This has been somewhat scaled back today, but Indian Lore is still a merit badge and the Order of the Arrow—the Honor Society of Scouting—still has the practice of dressing in costume regalia and performing pseudo-Indian ceremonies, despite these rites being officially changed in 2019. Far from an isolated example, the Boy Scouts were representational of the larger outdoor recreation culture.

Because American Indians had been mythologized alongside the idea of wilderness for so long, in the frontier wilderness model, Indianness continued to authenticate the wilderness experience. Generally, outdoor recreators are not playing Indian to authenticate their experience as Deloria describes. It is instead their encounter with Indianness, with the idea of a wilderness deeply imbued with Indian mythology, that proved to the would-be explorer that they had finally left civilization behind.

The frontier wilderness and its obsession with Indianness as a stand-in for authenticity was created by the collision of a romanticized wilderness, a growing interest in recreational camping, and a profound shift in U.S. Indian policy, but it was sold, as later wilderness constructions would be, through marketing by the outdoor industry. The nascent outdoor industry, rapidly growing up around the still-developing frontier wilderness idea, leaned heavily into this representation, both mirroring and reinforcing larger social constructs.

The 1913 Abercrombie & Fitch (A&F) catalog is a good example of the frontier wilderness era, one where Indianness still played an integral part of the wilderness experience, but the threat posed by actual Indigenous people to white travelers—both physically and ideologically—was largely gone. Founded in 1892, the same year Turner was penning his famous frontier thesis, A&F was among the earliest companies to capitalize on the growing interest in outdoor recreation, branding itself as the "Greatest Sporting Goods Store in the World." A&F was one of the most influential and certainly the most prestigious outdoor retail company at the turn of the twentieth century. The company ran a twelve-story flagship store on Madison Avenue in New York—complete with a shooting range, art gallery, putting range, and fly fishing pool—and was the main outfitter for the expeditions of men like Theodore Roosevelt, Ernest Hemingway, and Robert Peary.[29] It outfitted the era's most significant and groundbreaking explorations, including the first expedition to the North Pole and the "discovery" of Machu Picchu in Peru. It had positioned itself as *the* go-to outfitter for high-society exploration, a fashionable symbol of American imperial reach. Wearing A&F and paddling the Adirondacks with an "authentic Indian" guide was a way to be a member of the global colonial elite in a settler context. Like Patagonia or The North Face in a later era, A&F's marketing, especially its famous catalogs that ran up to four hundred pages long, helped shape public perception of the natural world and how potential explorers were meant to interact with it.

The 1913 catalog features a white man and woman dressed in A&F wear standing on a dock, their gaze fixed on some unseen vista across the lake (Figure 3).[30] Behind them an Indigenous man, presumably their guide, is bent over a birchbark canoe, loading their baggage and in the top left corner is written, in bold red letters, "The Red Gods Call!" The wilderness depicted in this image is one that reflects the new ideas of natural spaces. It is easy to see echoes of the imagery of British colonialism in Africa and India in the A&F advertisement, except rather than extracting ivory, gold, and cotton, the resource American travelers were after was leisure. This aesthetic mimicry is deeply connected to white American imperial aspirations of the time. Far from the hostile unknown of the early settlers, this land is welcoming and accessible, though not *too* accessible. The white travelers are there for sport and leisure, performing the part of the explorer and pioneer but importantly without the dangers, real or perceived, experienced by actual pioneers. Like the soldiers at Fort Yellowstone, A&F is highly concerned with the comfort of its consumers.

At the same time, this is not yet the "untrammeled" wilderness of the latter half of the twentieth century. As I examine in greater detail in the following chapter, contemporary outdoor retailers go to great lengths to present wilderness as ahistorical and pristine. A&F, however, conspicuously features an Indigenous guide. He is not wearing A&F products, so we can assume he is not a target for the advertisement. Instead, he is there as part of the world constructed by the company into which its consumers desire to enter—subservient and nonthreatening. The guide plays the same role as the birchbark canoes (another important signifier of Indianness), the sparkling water, and dark forested ridge. He serves to authenticate the wilderness, to realize the myth, to show that the white travelers are now truly outside the confines of their civilization in a space and time fundamentally different from their own.

More than any other aspect of the image, it is the advertisement's tagline that sets A&F's wilderness apart. The tagline, "The Red Gods Call!," is purely narrative. The image of the Indigenous guide is an important signifier, but the work could be done by this one line alone. Reminiscent of the now-ubiquitous quotation from John Muir, "The mountains are calling and I must go," A&F's version again explicitly connects the wilderness to Indianness, a place untouched not by people, as later companies claim, but by civilization, modernity, and Christianity. And it is welcoming you! In many ways this is a replacement narrative, encouraging a kind of settler indigenization.[31] Indigenous people are gone, but the Indian spirit still remains in the forest and it needs the white recreator to be its physical manifestation.

The 1909 A&F catalog presents a similar theme. This was the company's first catalog and signaled to its fifty-thousand-person readership the kind of world A&F would give them access to. This was a massive marketing investment for the company and, with the same image reproduced for the 2010 catalog, would have had an outsized influence on how outdoor consumers viewed their sport. A white hunter aims his rifle at some out-of-sight game while the Indian guide skillfully maneuvers the birchbark canoe into the natural blind of the overhanging pine. While in the 1913 image the guide is primarily distinguished from the white recreators by his clothes and labor, here the two men's clothing is less distinct and the role of guiding the stern of a canoe is one that could have fallen to a companion of the hunter instead of an Indigenous guide. Instead, the guide is distinguished primarily by skin tone, racialized facial features, and the headband, a common signifier of Indianness in the era. This clear racialization of the guide is important because it signals to the consumer that the guide is facilitating the hunter's wilderness experience not only in a practical sense—though his knowledge of the waterways and his skills at paddling and finding game—but also through his Indianness.

The recreational tableaux A&F created are fantasies. They are aspirational, mythic experiences using the romance of the frontier wilderness ideology to sell their products. The reality was that most people who would see these images would not be able to afford the products inside, let alone a long hunting vacation into the wilds of the lake country. Instead, they experienced these spaces primarily though imagery like this that presented recreation as mediated through Indianness while presenting Indigenous people as tractable background figures. In order for A&F to sell the attraction of wilderness, the company chose to also center Indianness.

Like all marketing representations, for consumers with the privilege to actually embark on expeditions like those in the advertisement, the on-the-ground reality was more complicated. Instead of an abstract vestige of Indianness used for authentication, tourists found themselves entering Indigenous spaces where Indigenous communities were working to survive in and navigate a changing world. And yet, primed as they were to only see Indigenous people as guides and to understand Indianness as an abstraction rather than a lived reality, they were often blind to these complexities and blithely reenacted the tourist experience A&F had set before them.

While it is unclear exactly what geographies the A&F images are meant to portray—I would argue this is intentionally vague since the consumer can then fill the void with spaces with which they are familiar—one

FIGURE 4. Abercrombie & Fitch, 1909 catalog cover.

of the most popular destinations for canoe and backcountry fishing trips at the turn of the century was the north woods of Wisconsin and Minnesota.[32] Like Indigenous communities around the country, the Ojibwe who called this region home were feeling the impact of changing federal policy around both assimilation and conservation. Despite treaty agreements that had been designed to reserve the right of hunting, fishing, and economic activity on all ceded territory, Ojibwe communities quickly found that they would have to abide by the recreational limits and seasons set by state conservation guidelines.[33] The abrogation of these rights, which were not restored until the 1990s, was part and parcel of larger assimilation strategies pushing these communities into a cash economy closely tied to local and state settler economies.

Guiding provided an important alternative source of income for Ojibwe men in particular, who became indispensable to the experience of canoe tourists.[34] A guide would be paid around three dollars a day and would provide services like pathfinding, managing the canoe, and cooking. Guides also found that they often took the role of an instructor, teaching their wealthy urban clients everything from how to find good fishing spots to how to hold and shoot a gun.[35] The relative helplessness of the tourists is not portrayed in the advertisements, which present their consumers as highly competent. Despite sometimes performing every step of a hunting expedition apart from pulling the trigger, drawing on generations of knowledge about hunting and this specific geography, guides were rarely credited. For tourists, the guide was simply another essential part of the outfitting package like the boat or tent. They were usually hired by the outfitter or through the Indian agency in charge of supervising the reservation instead of directly by the tourist and were certainly not part of the hunting or fishing party.[36] When the guide played the part well, they were often praised by their clients in language that evoked the ever present Noble Savage stereotypes.[37] The patient instructor and the wild nobleman were always, however, acts, masks that could be dropped by accident or intentionally in ways that revealed the colonial and racialized nature of these stereotypes.

For Ojibwe men, guiding was what Hal Rothman describes as a Devil's Bargain.[38] On one hand, participating in the tourist industry provided much-needed income while also allowing the men to engage in, at least to some extent, the traditional hunting and fishing practices that had been increasingly curtailed more generally.[39] It was a skilled job that allowed for a greater degree of autonomy than something like agricultural day labor. Local tribes also used guides as a way to reinforce to tourists that these wilderness spaces were still very much Indigenous spaces, often requiring the use of an Ojibwe guide for on-reservation travel.[40] Guides were also expected to provide their own boat and, bucking the A&F expectations, were more likely to provide a motorboat than a canoe—and charge more for it as well.[41] In her study on Ojibwe labor practices, Chantal Norrgard describes how guides sometimes intentionally upended that marketer's carefully crafted expectations. For example, one guide, claiming to know authentic Indian woodcraft to start a fire in the rain, proceeded to pour kerosene on the tinder and light it with a match.[42]

On the other hand, guides were constrained by the expectations that representations like the A&F catalog created in their consumers. Tourists often expected a level of subservience from their guides. Guides also had to manage the delicate balance of using their skills in order to be a good guide with avoiding being seen as a challenge to the tourist's masculinity. Sometimes this balance tipped too far and tourists were confronted by the fact that their guide was not merely an inanimate stereotype facilitating their wilderness experience, but an actual Indigenous person with agency beyond their role as a guide. This could happen if the guide spoke their own language and the tourist felt they were being made fun of or if the guide's instructions made the tourist feel inadequate in their own wilderness abilities.[43] This is, of course, another aspect of wilderness travel not emphasized by A&F in their campaign.

When this happened, tourists would switch to white guides or attempt to not use a guide at all, instead embracing "Indianness" through highly mediated performances put on by local communities or safely engaging with Indigenous culture without actual people involved at all. Sites with interesting "Indian" stories attached to them were among the most popular canoe destinations in the north woods including the grave of the Indian princess described in the introduction and the Hegman Lake petroglyphs. Like the Indian aura attached to the, ultimately rarely used, birchbark canoe in the A&F ads, the body of an Indian princess and the imprints of ancient artists proved more effective at authenticating wilderness than living Ojibwe guides who inevitably challenged the perceived sanctity and purity of these outdoor spaces.

FIGURE 5. *Sunset* magazine, May 1904 cover.

Yosemite As a Frontier Wilderness

In May 1904, the Southern Pacific Railroad featured a painting by Yosemite-based artist Chris Jorgensen on the cover of its marketing publication, *Sunset* magazine.[44] The painting prominently features an Ahwahneechee basket weaver working in front of her hut with the snow-capped peak of Yosemite's famous Half Dome rising starkly in the background. The scene is intimate, domestic, and, while it obscures much about the on-the-ground reality for Indigenous people in Yosemite at the time, it is clear the editors at *Sunset* saw some version of Indigenous people, even if a highly exoticized version, as an important selling point for potential tourists. The presence of an Indigenous woman is, literally, foregrounded.

While it is now common for outdoor companies to draw from well-known features of American public lands and national parks in their marketing materials, in the early twentieth century, outdoor companies like A&F, L.L.Bean, and H. Channon more commonly presented a general outdoor scene that could take place in any wilderness area.[45] Many of the features were less familiar to the consumers and all were less accessible. Additionally, Indian motifs or people could be used in a general way, allowing for unchallenged stereotypes that might be contested when talking about specific nations or cultures.

Railroad companies, however, leaned into the specific. L.L.Bean boots could be used anywhere, but it was not enough to encourage a general tourist railroad vacation. Railroads therefore became some of the strongest and earliest corporate supporters of national parks and recreational public lands. To draw people to ride western lines through lands populated by settlers, the railroad made comparisons between visiting American national parks and touring Europe's cathedrals and ancient cities—including America's own unique Indigenous cultures. The most famous of these efforts was the Great Northern Railroad's "See America First" campaign that chided tourists for prioritizing international travel over the wonders of their own country. These kinds of marketing campaigns peddled many of the same ideas as the campaigns of more traditional outdoor retail companies, shaping and being shaped by changing ideas of wilderness. Their strategies paralleled those of Abercrombie & Fitch and were an important precursor to how the contemporary industry continues to use public lands—as important federally subsidized products critical to selling their services. Selling these spaces *was* selling their services since for most people, riding the railroads was an essential part of visiting the parks. Each railroad had its park. The Great Northern invested in Glacier National Park, while the Northern Pacific built lines through Yellowstone. For the Southern Pacific Railroad, the destination was Yosemite National Park, and for much of the early twentieth century, experiencing Yosemite also meant engaging with the Ahwahneechee.

Yosemite is among the most mythologized locations in the United States, heavy with layers of meaning and identity. It was the site of John Muir's ramblings and early environmental awareness and was one of the first outdoor spaces in the country to be conserved specifically for recreational and scenic value, pioneering the "Yosemite Model" of conservation that has since become the global standard for park formation. Essayist Rebecca Solnit called Yosemite "the very crucible and touchstone for American landscape," a lens into "the peculiarities, blindnesses, raptures, and problems that constitute the Euro-American experience of landscape."[46]

Unlike the generalized wilderness of A&F, Yosemite was also a specific space with a rich, and violent, history of Indigenous communities and American colonialism. Like the terror of Ojibwe guides speaking in their own language, the physical presence of the Ahwahneechee did not always match the romanticized version of the Indian that wilderness explorers expected. Despite this, Yosemite was no exception to the frontier version of wilderness consumption. The park and the marketers that relied on it were unable or unwilling to change potential tourist conceptions of Indianness, so they instead went to work on changing the Ahwahneechee community itself.

In the first few decades following the official protection of Yosemite Valley in 1864, when Yosemite was first becoming established as a tourist destination, the park tolerated, even occasionally celebrated, the presence of the Ahwahneechee villages in the park.[47] They served to authenticate the valley as a true wilderness destination and were a draw for tourists. The Ahwahneechee themselves incorporated the growing tourist presence into their seasonal economies, charging to pose for pictures, hosting tourists for meals, and selling baskets. This was still an era when the Romantic narrative of the Noble Savage and the physical presence of Indigenous people had not yet fully separated. However, this era of relatively mutual tolerance began to change as Yosemite officially became a national park in 1890 and park managers began to increasingly manage the landscape for their *perceived* ideas of wilderness. The Ahwahneechee themselves and their traditional lifeways and economies were no longer necessary to authenticate the valley and, in fact, seemed to obstruct the park's vision.[48] While the Ahwahneechee had no treaty with the United States and therefore no reservation land, the park itself stepped into the surveillance role played by Indian Agents and the Bureau of Indian Affairs (called the Office of Indian Affairs at the time) in other communities. Park management focused on bringing the community into a cash economy and assimilating them under park management.

The extent of the park's curtailment of Ahwahneechee activity is most visible in the environmental changes in the park. Paintings of Yosemite Valley in the mid-nineteenth century show open park-like land with scattered trees—as seen in representations like Albert Bierstadt's dramatic 1867 painting of the valley—a landscape that was the result of controlled burns and other environmental management practices of the Ahwahneechee.[49] Ironically, it was this humanmade landscape, carefully constructed to meet the needs of the Indigenous community, that park advocate John Muir would call a "pure wilderness" where "no mark of man is visible upon it." However, even by the end of the nineteenth century, the valley floor had become mostly forested as the result of the park's suppression of Ahwahneechee burning in deference to American tourists' expectations of a forested wilderness, as seen in postcards and photographs from the era.[50]

Following national trends, the Ahwahneechee were being increasingly confined and their activity increasingly restricted. Indianness was still a highly valued attraction for the park, so while other Indigenous people were removed or confined to reservations, the Ahwahneechee were initially allowed to stay in the park under specific circumstances that served to further authenticate the space as wilderness.

However, it quickly became clear that the park was not interested in Ahwahneechee-ness specifically, but in a more general, easily commodifiable form of Indianness that Americans would have been familiar with from Wild West shows and, increasingly, films. In place of traditional Ahwahneechee homes and management practices, the park imported stereotypical plains-style culture—tepees and feathered headdresses— and paid the community to perform a more easily marketable version of Indianness in the valley. This was especially visible during the park's

FIGURE 6. *(upper) The Domes of Yosemite,* 1867, by Albert Bierstadt and "Postcard depicting Yosemite Valley from Artists' Point, Calif." *(lower)* Photo by William Henry Jackson, 1898, showing the change in the valley. From Detroit Publishing Co., *Yosemite Valley from Artists' Point, Calif.* United States Yosemite Valley California Yosemite National Park, ca. 1898, https://www.loc.gov/item/2016802680/.

FIGURE 7. Chief Lemee (Chris Brown) and Supt. W. B. Lewis during Indian Field Days in Yosemite Valley, 1925. From the U.S. National Park Service, Yosemite Historic Photo Collection.

Indian Field Days of the early twentieth century where the community was put in costume and displayed for tourists, as seen in this 1925 photograph of Chief Lemee (Chris Brown).[51]

This shift was reflected in the Southern Pacific's marketing material as well. For example, their stylized promotional poster from 1921 featured an Ahwahneechee mother with a cradleboard and infant on her back. She stands before the image of El Capitan and the Three Brothers reflecting off the Merced River, draped in a yellow cloak and looking back at the viewer. This is a much more romantic image than the *Sunset* magazine cover from just sixteen years earlier and shows an evolving presentation of Yosemite's Indigenous people. The Southern Pacific also tended to feature women in their advertisement, positioning the Ahwahneechee as welcoming, domestic, and nonthreatening. In this space, the Ahwahneechee were turned into "authentic, exotic, and innocuous Indians."[52] These dual and seemingly contradictory identities served to preserve the authenticating power of Indianness while working to assimilate actual Indigenous people.

FIGURE 8. Southern Pacific Railroad advertisement, 1921.

At the same time as they performed Indianness, the Ahwahneechee were also being drawn further into a market economy through the commercialization of traditional crafts and by working as laborers in hospitality or park infrastructure development. The remaining community was moved into employee housing in 1931, known as the "new village." While these buildings were nicer, they required those who lived in them to pay rent to the park, further forcing community members to find work in the park through tourism or hospitality.[53]

Despite the power gap between their communities and the park service, the Ahwahneechee were not simply passive victims of this process. Historian Boyd Cothran describes the ways the community navigated this tourist space for their own advantage and took as much agency over their representation as they could.[54] Like the Ojibwe guides, performance was a way to reclaim at least those practices that fit into the tourist mold. These acts of agency and resistance, however, were increasingly limited as Indianness began changing from an authenticating feature to a liability under a new wilderness paradigm. As demand decreased, many Ahwahneechee "voluntarily" moved out of the park to nearby towns like Mariposa, Sonora, or Coulterville to find work. In the first decades of the twentieth century, there were still more than a hundred Ahwahneechee living and working in Yosemite, but this number dwindled as the community experienced a series of forced relocations within the park throughout the 1930s and '40s from the performative villages of the Field Days era to the "new village," eventually culminating in total removal in 1969.[55]

Frontier nostalgia and the allure of Indianness clung to American conceptions of wilderness well into the mid-twentieth century, and remnants of it still crop up today often through the nostalgic use of turn-of-the-century national park Indian-inspired design motifs. However, by as early as the 1930s and '40s, a new version of wilderness was beginning to develop, one that would forge a new settler colonial narrative, break away from any association with Indigeneity, and finally achieve the "clean wilderness" imagined and advocated for by John Muir. In the following chapter, I look at how the untrammeled wilderness we take for granted today emerged and why we have outdoor retail companies like Patagonia to thank for its present ubiquity.

SPRING 1985
THE NORTH FACE
EQUIPMENT

THE
NORTH
FACE

FIGURE 9. The North Face Equipment, spring 1985 catalog cover.

3

Wilderness Untrammeled

The way of the canoe is the way of the wilderness, and
a freedom almost forgotten.

—Sigurd Olson, *The Singing Wilderness*

n the summer of 1998, David Gotchnik, a member of the Bois Forte
Band of Chippewa, was cited for using a canoe with a small outboard
motor to reach a fishing site on Basswood Lake in the Boundary Waters
Canoe Area Wilderness (BWCA). Wilderness areas, a designation created under the Wilderness Act of 1964, ban all motorized vehicles and
mechanical means of transportation (e.g., sails, paddleboats) in order to
preserve the "wilderness character" of these areas.[1]

The BWCA borders the Bois Forte Reservation and is part of the
tribe's historic homeland. Gotchnik argued that under the Treaty of
1854, he had the right to use modern technology to access and exercise
his reserved right to fish on ceded land. As a nation-to-nation agree-
ment, treaty rights should trump other conservation regulations that
limit land-based economic activity, and indeed the act explicitly states
that no regulation in the BWCA "shall affect the provisions of any treaty
now applicable to lands and waters, which are included . . . in the wilderness," a clause that has had mixed success in legal battles.[2] In the
court case, the state acknowledged that Gotchnik had every right to
fish in the BWCA, but of course, so does everyone else. The question
in the Gotchnik case was whether modern technology could be used to

practice these usufructuary rights. The U.S. Forest Service, the department in charge of managing the BWCA, argued he did not. Rangers cited and fined Gotchnik and in the ensuing legal battle, which eventually reached the Supreme Court, the citation was upheld. The court's central argument in this case speaks both to a radical change in how wilderness was understood in the United States and to how deeply naturalized this new ideology had become by the end of the twentieth century. They argued that since a hundred thousand *tourists* fish in the BWCA each year without motorized vehicles, the ban on motorized vehicles does not actually impinge on the Bois Forte treaty rights to fish on ceded land. The argument was that Bois Forte members are fully capable of reaching remote fishing grounds by canoe, that in fact sport fishing by canoe is a central purpose of the BWCA, and that using motors would ruin the wilderness experience of tourists.

A hundred years earlier, it would have been Gotchnik's identity as an Ojibwe man, as fundamentally *not* a tourist, that would have authenticated the wilderness experience for non-Indigenous travelers. As a guide or as a random encounter, interactions with Indigenous people were part of leaving civilization. This would have been true even in a motorboat, which many guides used in the area by the early twentieth century. Yet, by 1999 the Supreme Court, the Forest Service, and the average American paddler would reduce Gotchnik's complex and sovereign political, economic, and cultural connections to the BWCA to that of a tourist. The Bois Forte Ojibwe, whose treaties guarantee access to these spaces for commercial and nonrecreational fishing, were to be treated the same as any sport fisherman. The BWCA was not an Indigenous space, or even an "Indian" space; it was a tourist space. To be there was to be a tourist.

The Bois Forte Ojibwe's Indigeneity had become illegible because of a midcentury shift in wilderness ideology from frontier wilderness to what I call, drawing from the language of the Wilderness Act, *untrammeled wilderness.* While frontier wilderness embraced a romanticized "Indianness" as it eschewed actual Indigenous people, untrammeled wilderness leaves Indigeneity out altogether. The land is represented as pristine, untouched by the hand of man, outside of time itself. Beginning with what historian Jean O'Brien calls "firsting and lasting" narratives of the disappearing Indian, evolving into the deeply mythologized stereotypes like the nineteenth-century Noble Savage and tourist attractions, and finally, removing Indigenous people completely, untrammeled wilderness is the culmination of over a century of Indigenous erasure from the story of American land.[3]

This type of wilderness should be familiar to readers since it is the primary way wilderness areas, national parks, and other outdoor recreational spaces are represented today. However, untrammeled wilderness was not inevitable and did not arise ex nihilo. It was decades of wilderness representations in marketing, storytelling, lobbying, and policy—the continual reiteration of wilderness as natural and desirable and of tourism as the only acceptable use of wilderness—that allowed the Supreme Court to uncritically make use of the concept to continue the limitation of Ojibwe sovereignty over treaty-protected land and resources. Far from the only new wilderness concept circulating in the twentieth century, it exists today as the result of a combination of social, political, and, most importantly, commercial interests that found in untrammeled wilderness a powerful ideological foundation for how they wanted public land to be managed and exploited. It was an easily sellable alternative to both the increasingly untenable frontier wilderness model and the more radical, anticapitalist or decolonial models competing for American hearts and minds at the same time.

A central piece of untrammeled wilderness's appeal and marketability is that it came with a built-in consumer: the figure of the "explorer," the imagined character drawn from a mythologizing of American history and then enacted and embodied by outdoorspeople. This figure, co-constructed with untrammeled wilderness, is a marketing archetype designed to circumvent the central contradiction of this model of wilderness—that wilderness can exist outside of human influence. By constructing human presence in wilderness as always exploration, wilderness can and must continually be represented as untouched and undiscovered, always waiting to be seen for the first time by the intrepid tourist. Like untrammeled wilderness, the explorer requires terra nullius, an erasure of Indigenous people and Indianness alike. Together, untrammeled wilderness and the explorer who traversed it formed a powerful, and sellable, story for an industry in need of a new narrative.

Indigenous Activism and the Need for a New System

Like the shift in wilderness consciousness at the end of the nineteenth century that led to the frontier wilderness mythology, untrammeled wilderness emerged alongside a major shift in federal Indian policy as well as a growing visibility of Indigenous people in American society more generally. The late nineteenth and early twentieth centuries had been defined by the U.S. government's policy of assimilation, including breaking tribal organization, privatizing collectively owned land, and suppressing traditional practices and languages. Under President Franklin Roosevelt and Commissioner of the Bureau of Indian Affairs John Collier, this policy was temporarily rolled back with the Indian Reorganization Act of 1934 and the Indian New Deal. This legislation resulted in renewed tribal self-governance and the creation of many tribal constitutions, as long as these governments followed the American constitutional model. Despite its limitations, it was a major win for Indigenous communities and, while the period was short lived, it gave Indigenous nations an important foundation of governance from which to launch more organized political resistance to later policies of termination.

This moment of self-determination was quickly reversed by the introduction of what became known as Termination Policy in the 1940s and '50s. Termination Policy was a set of laws and resolutions designed to end any special relationship the U.S. government had with Indigenous nations, abrogate all treaty rights and responsibilities, and fully integrate Indigenous people into American society as everyday citizens. Over the next two decades, over a hundred tribes were dissolved as political entities and their remaining land fully privatized.[4] This was the most devastating set of policies for Indigenous political sovereignty over land since the Dawes Act. However, while the Dawes Act resulted in Indigenous people being minimized in American culture and political discourse except as stereotypes and movie motifs, termination policy galvanized multiple generations of Indigenous activists who forced non-Indigenous Americans and politicians to *see* Indigenous people and confront the American colonial project in a way they had not had to for half a century.

Perhaps the policy with the greatest blowback on U.S. colonial aims was the Indian Relocation Act of 1956, which offered money and incentives for Indigenous people to move to urban areas in the hopes that they would assimilate into mainstream American society. While many Indigenous people took the government up on this offer, seeking better economic opportunities in regional urban hubs like Chicago or Denver, the program failed to destroy Indigenous identity. Instead, this migration led to the emergence of new intertribal political identities as individuals from many Indigenous nations were brought together and shared their common experiences and struggles. Urban Indian centers like the American Indian Center of Chicago founded in 1953 became hubs for mutual support and political activism.[5] Indigenous people founded organizations like the National Indian Youth Council and the American Indian Movement to organize direct action protests, sit-ins, fish-ins, and occupations.

While originating in cities, these movements quickly spilled over into wilderness areas as reclaiming treaty-protected land and resources became an increasingly central tenet of Indigenous activism. Indigenous nations that for decades had struggled to practice treaty-guaranteed rights as tourism and conservation took priority suddenly found they had the support of not only their own community members but vibrant intertribal coalitions who saw the fight of one Indigenous nation as the fight of all.

One of the most famous examples of this was the 1964 fish wars in the Pacific Northwest. In the preceding decades, sport fishermen had lobbied hard to not only stop Indigenous people from fishing out of season, but to abrogate the treaties altogether. The state of Washington, newly empowered by the recently passed Public Law 280, began aggressively enforcing conservation laws over treaty rights despite very little legal precedent.[6] In an unprecedented display of intertribal direct action—something the older and more conservative National Council of American Indians had intentionally avoided—hundreds of activists from the National Indian Youth Council fished out of season in support of the threatened treaty rights of the Nisqually, Puyallup, Skagit, Makah, and other Washington tribes.[7] While it took a decade to be fully successful, the Pacific Northwest fish-in galvanized similar protests on public lands and in recreational spaces including the Wisconsin Walleye Wars and the 1971 occupation of Mount Rushmore. Outdoor recreators and sportsmen were suddenly reminded that Indigenous people were still there and Indigenous sovereignty still very much existed.

The rise in Indigenous activism in the 1950s and '60s led to another pivot in U.S. Indian policy from an era of termination to one of self-determination. Termination policy, which had been so devastating to so many tribes, was reversed and Congress passed a series of new acts designed to restore and support Indigenous identity and governance.

These included the Indian Civil Rights Act of 1968, the Indian Self-Determination Act of 1975, the Indian Child Welfare Act of 1978, and, importantly for public land use, the American Indian Religious Freedom Act of 1978, which, among other things, guarantees Indigenous people access to sacred sites and the right to practice ceremony on public lands. Together, this change heightened the visibility of Indigenous people in American political discourse and drove a reexamination of the place of Indigenous people in American society. Suddenly, subservient guides, Indian princess graves, costumed performers in Hollywood headdresses, and other trappings of Indianness in the wilderness were eclipsed by the presence, voices, and actions of actual Indigenous people.

Outdoor tourists, in their zeal to reenact a mythical manifest destiny on their artificial frontiers, wanted the romance of the Indian without the discomfort of complicity in genocide. The appropriative use of Indianness to authenticate wilderness only worked if actual Indigenous people were not empowered enough to press claims or, preferably, if they were nonexistent altogether. As Indigenous activism increased and popular representations began to change, this fiction became increasingly difficult to maintain. Only in a park free not only from actual Indigenous people but also from the idea of "Indianness" altogether could recreators continue to make these claims to ownership. In the presence of actual Indigenous people, Indianness as a fantasy, once an indispensable part of wilderness, now undermined settler claims to these spaces. For settlers to reassert power over these lands, they required a new interpretation of wilderness.

Untrammeled Wilderness

Recreators found this in untrammeled wilderness. Untrammeled wilderness can be understood as a classic replacement narrative. In this new construction, Indigenous people, if they were ever there at all, are long gone and white travelers are either distant inheritors of the land or have themselves become indigenous to the spaces they traverse. In her study of replacement narratives among settlers in New England, Jean O'Brien defines a replacement narrative as "non-Indians [staking] a claim to being Indigenous," claiming indigeneity as a way to claim the land.[8] This claim to indigeneity is made possible through the narrative construction of land as untouched and pristine, as having no prior human claims whatsoever.

Wilderness scholar Roger Kaye calls the concept of untrammeled the "essence of wilderness, the source of its mystique, its otherness, and its transcendent function."[9] The word was carefully chosen and fought for by the author of the Wilderness Act, Howard Zahniser, who saw its particular and highly specific definition as key to how he perceived wilderness and how he desired for it to be protected and managed. When used today, untrammeled is often assumed to mean untrampled or undisturbed, especially when used to talk about land. However, this was not the original definition, nor the definition intended by Zahniser and other early wilderness advocates. Untrammeled, in reference to a trammel used to restrain and train a horse, means to be unhindered, uncontrolled, unmanaged. Wilderness was not meant to be a product of man's absence; it was instead to be a space outside of his control and conscious impact.[10] For Zahniser, the act of restraint by humans, forgoing control over nature, a sort of abstinence, was as important to his view of the relationship between man and the earth as the purity of the landscapes themselves. While the frontier wilderness model removed or carefully managed actual Indigenous people but held on to Indianness as an idea, the untrammeled wilderness model managed to drop the last vestiges of Indianness altogether. Untrammeled wilderness has no room for permanent human society, which, in Euro-American philosophy, is inherently about subduing and controlling the natural world. It does allow, however, visits by man "who does not remain."[11] People are observers, sojourners, explorers who watch and study the natural processes of the world. Like the cathedrals to which wildernesses are so often compared, visitors enter these sacred and pure spaces for a short time to become sacred and pure themselves, and then they leave.[12]

Zahniser was just one of the group of men most responsible for defining the language and philosophical underpinning of untrammeled wilderness. This group consisted of a who's who of environmental activists of the 1930s and included pioneering ecologists like Aldo Leopold and Sigurd Olson, National Park Association founder Robert Sterling Yard, the founder of Great Smokey Mountains National Park Bernard Frank, BWCA advocate Ernest Oberholzer, and the wilderness evangelist and philanthropist Bob Marshall. Together they founded the Wilderness

Society in 1935 to lobby for roadless areas and untouched lands to policymakers and to market these ideas to the public. As demonstrated by the ideology they so carefully articulated, these men were both deeply invested in wilderness serving as a recreational space and seem to have been unconcerned about the colonial impacts of their proposed policies. Untrammeled wilderness is and has always been deeply tied to outdoor recreation. The emphasis was on the experience of wilderness rather than any scientifically sound idea of a sustainable ecology or the intrinsic value of the spaces themselves. Most members of the Wilderness Society were avid outdoor recreators and explicitly centered their advocacy around preserving the recreational integrity of wilderness. This is most obvious in the name of one of the earliest wilderness areas, the Boundary Waters Canoe Area, which was designated a roadless area years before wilderness areas were officially legislated. The name emphasized canoeing as the primary purpose of the reserve since canoeing was seen as a primitive, close-to-nature recreational activity that fit with the wilderness model, a frontier wilderness trope.

In the 1930s, the frontier model of wilderness was still prominent and writers like Sigurd Olson often explicitly connected their canoeing and recreation to a long tradition of canoeing in the area by both Indigenous people and voyageurs.[13] Increasingly, however, these connections were less about entering a space imbued with Indianness and more about recreators becoming the inheritors of a people and culture that had disappeared. While writers like Olson viewed this as vaguely tragic, it was also clear to them that Indigenous people of the day, with their motorboats, commercial fishing, and logging contracts, no longer fit the wilderness ideal and perhaps it was best if they disappeared after all. Bob Marshall, when he served as head of forestry for the Bureau of Indian Affairs, even recommended that forests managed by the federal government on reservations be protected as wilderness areas rather than managed by the tribes themselves.[14]

They would likely have been surprised, however, at the extent to which their wilderness spaces were to be used to support commercial ventures like the multibillion-dollar outdoor industry. The men of the early Wilderness Society were decidedly anticapitalist in their positioning, with Bob Marshall even being accused of communist collusion by the infamous Dies Committee. As a space outside of civilization and incompatible with modernity, wilderness was thought to be also outside of, in fact protected from, the rampant commodification and exploitation of American natural resources. These lands, collectively owned by the American people, would be shining examples that another world was possible.

The Wilderness Society's advocacy for the creation of recreation based on the untrammeled wilderness model, which continues today, was of critical importance to the eventual passing of legislation that codified these ideas, the most important of which was the Wilderness Act of 1964, but which also included the Wild and Scenic Rivers Act of 1968 and the National Trails System Act of 1968.

Deep Ecology, Ecological Indians, and Alternatives to Untrammeled Wilderness

Despite being written into law and advocated for by the wealthy, well-connected Wilderness Society, the mainstream naturalization of untrammeled wilderness in American discourse was not a forgone conclusion. At the same time as the Wilderness Society was advocating for untrammeled wilderness, several other new environmental philosophies were beginning to circulate that would also have effectively addressed the increasingly visible contradictions in the frontier wilderness model. The two I briefly introduce here approached these contradictions in different ways, one reinterpreting how we understand the land and the other redefining America's romanticized view of Indianness.

The first and most popular of these was deep ecology, a philosophy that in many ways ran counter to the core man-versus-nature tenets of the Wilderness Society and pushed for a more biocentric interpretation of the Wilderness Act itself that would limit recreation.[15] Popularized by the writing of Rachel Carson in her 1962 landmark book *Silent Spring*, Sierra Club executive director David Brower, and Norwegian environmental philosopher Arne Næss, deep ecology argues that humans are fundamentally part of the ecosystem as an equal—though certainly not superior—member of the earth's community.[16] This is a strong departure from untrammeled wilderness, which is built on the idea that any human influence on the environment is harmful to it. Drawing on philosophers and ecologists like Baruch Spinoza, Ralph Waldo Emerson, Aldo Leopold (whose membership in the Wilderness Society demonstrates the inevitable overlap in these ideas), and of course Rachel Carson, deep ecologists call for radical sustainability—often in the form of population control and simple living—and the recognition of nonhuman life for its intrinsic rather than human value.[17] While the idea of wilderness was still at the center of deep ecologists' conservation advocacy, it was a wilderness that decentered humans in a radical way, at least when viewed from within the trajectory of western environmental philosophy. Recreation, which has long been the driver of wilderness preservation, would also have to be sidelined in favor of stricter non-interference measures. In the words of deep ecologist and wilderness advocate Francis Walcott, "the primary human benefit of wilderness is ecological."[18]

Deep ecology, while inarguably more ecologically sound, was still deeply colonial. Proponents either cherry-picked Indigenous ideas without acknowledging the specificity of place and culture where they developed or the colonial genocide that drove many of them out of practice, or they ignored Indigenous contributions altogether, wholly grounding the philosophy in western traditions. Furthermore, in its zeal to decenter humans in the biological order, it made the common error of treating all humans as both equally responsible for and equally impacted by the environmental ills of the world. Discussions of deep ecology included no engagement with the role colonialism had played in the creation of America's deeply unsustainable land systems or the possibility of creating the kind of culturally crafted landscapes shaped by Indigenous people. The wilderness of deep ecology certainly steered away from a romanticized notion of Indigenous people found in frontier wilderness, but in doing so also erased the unique political, social, and cultural claims Indigenous people in the United States have to the land, creating an ideology where we are either all indigenous or none of us are.

It is not hard to imagine why, despite being a far more environmentally healthy model, deep ecology has remained a fringe philosophy even decades into the twenty-first century while untrammeled wilderness has become the wilderness ideology of contemporary environmental activists. Deep ecology demands reduction and is antithetical to capitalism. Untrammeled wilderness, developed for recreation, is an ideology of consumption—consumption of experience and consumption of the products that support those experiences. There is simply more money to be made from land being used than land being protected.

On the other side of this spectrum, there was an attempt to take advantage of Americans' renewed awareness of Indigenous issues rather than avoid it by rebranding the Noble Savage trope that had so strongly defined early wilderness ideology into what historian Shepard Krech III calls the "ecological Indian." Krech defines the ecological Indian as "the image of the Indian in nature who understands the systemic consequences of his actions, feels deep sympathy with all living forms, and takes steps to conserve so that earth's harmonies are never imbalanced and resources never in doubt."[19] The most famous example of this is the 1971 "Crying Indian" PSA produced by Keep American Beautiful Inc. to combat highway littering. The commercial showed Iron Eyes Cody emerging from the woods dressed in stereotypical traditional clothing, looking at the camera, and shedding a single tear in response to litter being thrown from a car window. The ad plays on the trope that Indigenous people are inherently closer and more spiritually connected to nature. In the frontier wilderness model, Indians and Indianness were an intrinsic part of nature whose presence authenticated the recreational experience. The ecological Indian trope retained the close association of Indians with nature, but instead of being part of the wilderness, the Indian was now its most strident protector. The ecological Indian had internalized the untrammeled wilderness ideal that constructed wilderness as something fundamentally separate from humans, but still maintained a unique relationship to it, albeit a relationship anyone could and should replicate.

Iron Eyes Cody, the crying Indian, however, was not Indigenous at all, but an Italian actor who made his career playing Indians, and this performance encapsulates the main problem with the ecological Indian trope. Its romanticization of Indigenous relationships to the natural world is generalizing and reductive, obscuring the many and varied complex connections different Indigenous nations and people have to the environment.[20] Its close-to-nature positioning also precluded Indigenous modernity and engagement with capitalist enterprise, representing Indigenous people more as Druidic nature guardians than contemporary people fighting for concrete political sovereignty of land. All of this would have been nothing though if the ecological Indian had proved a more marketable stereotype. While effectively playing on the pathos of its non-Indigenous audience and successfully passing the responsibility of littering from corporate manufacturers to individual citizens, in the end the ecological Indian ran into the same problem as frontier wilderness did. It acknowledged competing claims to American land, potentially undermining the very foundation of the public land system. In his discussion of the rise of the Leave No Trace ethic, historian James Morton Turner describes how Leave No Trace was embraced by the outdoor industry over alternative ethics like that of woodcraft in part because it required expensive specialized gear, creating a culture where "actions in the shopping mall were the best way to save wilderness beyond."[21] The outdoor industry played a similar role not just in the ethics of wilderness use but in how Americans understand wilderness itself. The men of the Wilderness Society provided the language and philosophical foundation, but it was the outdoor industry that shaped it into the consumable product it is today. The industry embraced the untrammeled wilderness, pushing for this softer and more easily commodified version of conservation over the more radical deep ecology or the romanticized ecological Indian. They accepted and reproduced the ideology wholesale from its recreational focus to its claims of settler indigeneity and diligently forged a deep association between themselves and the public lands created under the untrammeled system. The landscapes built upon this idea had no Indigenous people past or present to challenge the explorability of the land, no human constructions to detract from its pristineness. They were custom-built arenas, perfectly designed at the taxpayers' expense to produce a market the outdoor industry was more than happy to fill and a narrative they were more than prepared to market. And if the outdoor industry became the biggest supporter of untrammeled wilderness, the implementation of untrammeled wilderness became a springboard for a massive expansion and reinvention of the industry itself, growing from $400 million in consumer spending in the mid-1970s to nearly $40 billion in 2020 on outdoor gear alone.[22] Nowhere is the deep connection between the popularization of untrammeled wilderness and the emergence of the modern outdoor industry clearer than in Yosemite National Park.

Clean Climbing

Just as Yosemite had been a stronghold of frontier wilderness, it was also the perfect place for this nascent shift in ideology to fully emerge. The legacy of John Muir gave the park a powerful origin story already deeply connected to an Edenic version of wilderness. The Ahwahneechee were in the process of being totally removed, and unlike many other western parks, there was no official treaty protecting Indigenous rights to the land.[23] And, of course, there was a growing community of outdoor recreators ready to embrace it and go on to share the gospel of untrammeled wilderness with the world.

More than Muir and the Wilderness Society, it was the ethics, fantasies, and ideologies of a small community of self-proclaimed "dirtbag" climbers that influenced mainstream ideas about wilderness in the late twentieth and early twenty-first centuries. While hardly the first community to espouse and internalize the idea of wilderness as untouched and ahistorical, Yosemite climbers of the 1950s and '60s coalesced at an opportune time—a moment of shifting environmental values and increasing radicalization of Indigenous activists—and in a fertile place—the deeply mythologized Yosemite Valley—which allowed untrammeled wilderness to take root. Even more important, however, was the afterlife of this community. Its members became outdoor mentors, writers, and, critically, businessmen. Dirtbag climbers went on to found some of the giants of today's nearly $900 billion outdoor industry including Patagonia, The North Face, Black Diamond, and Royal Robbins, into which they imbued the ethics and ideologies developed on the cliffs of Yosemite and out of which came the triumph of untrammeled wilderness.

Yosemite might not be the birthplace of rock climbing, but it is at the center of the sport in the United States and the place where it matured from a fringe activity into a mainstream one. Some of the earliest recorded first ascents in the country occurred in the valley, notably John Muir's climb of Cathedral Peak in 1869 and Scottish mountaineer George Anderson's aided ascent of Half Dome in 1875, only a few years after it had been declared unclimbable. In the early twentieth century, Sierra Club members and a few Alpine mountaineers summited nontechnical peaks, hiking and scrambling up routes that did not need specialized equipment. However, despite a handful of early twentieth-century wall climbs, including a 1934 ascent of Higher Cathedral Spire, it was not until the 1950s and '60s that climbers truly began to flock to the valley. This community lead to the development of specialized gear, the Yosemite Decimal System—the now-standard numerical system used to describe the difficulty of a climbing route—and a unique "dirtbag climber" culture.[24]

In outdoor parlance, a dirtbag is someone who pursues their outdoor sport with a single-minded passion, full time, and often with little or no money. While ubiquitous today, the term was first used to describe a dedicated and anti-establishment group of rock climbers who made Yosemite National Park their home, living in the park, usually illegally, often in vans or caves or, famously, Camp 4, a campground now listed in the National Historic Register because of its role in the history of rock climbing. These dirtbag climbers would scrounge for food, foraging or taking scraps from the garbage, making money where they could. In one famous, possibly apocryphal incident, climbers living in the park got word of a drug-smuggling plane that had crashed in the park, salvaged and sold the drugs, and used the money to fund half a dozen climbing seasons.[25]

This community began to express a sense of ownership over the valley, using the idea that public land is collectively owned to challenge government authority over their activities in the valley. If the valley belonged to anyone, the logic went, it belonged to them, the climbers who lived there and whose culture had been born from there. They set up semi-permanent squatter camps and openly defied what they considered government occupation by park rangers. This eventually led to the infamous 1970 Stoneman Meadow Riot in which rangers clashed with four hundred young people, mostly part of the dirtbag community, and an increased militarization (or remilitarization) of the park system.[26] This ironically was just a year before the American Indian Movement's occupation of Mt. Rushmore National Park, an explicit response to this kind of settler presence. Yet at the same time, this settler self-indigenization still maintained a western view toward the natural world, one predicated on an essential separation between humans and their environment. Unlike the Ahwahneechee for whom the valley was at the center of their society, the climbers considered Yosemite wilderness a space outside of society. Living in Yosemite was a rejection of mainstream culture, an intentional embrace of outsider status.

This self-indigenization of the dirtbag climbing community was happening at the same time as the government's final removals of the Ahwahneechee from the park. In the decades since Yosemite National Park forced the Ahwahneechee community into a cash economy, essentially appropriating them as park employees, the population living in the park had shrunk.[27] In 1969, the park decided to formally end even this arrangement and razed what remained of the village, located nearly adjacent to the climbers' Camp 4. Anyone not officially working for the National Park Service was forced to leave the valley as their homes were used as practice for the park's firefighters.[28]

The ethics of this niche group of climbers—their deep commitment to public land, the drive to conquer every wall, and their unshakable belief in their own right to be there—was born out of the untrammeled wilderness of Yosemite Valley. However, it did not stay isolated in the park. It turned out that some of these climbers were not as anticapitalist as their behavior would suggest. Dirtbag climbers developing and selling new climbing gear formed the basis for what would become some of the world's largest outdoor retail companies including Black Diamond, Patagonia, Royal Robbins, and The North Face. The North Face even used the shape of Half Dome as its logo. Through these companies, they would have an outsized influence on the direction of wilderness outside the valley as well as on the outdoor industry as a whole.

While deep ecologists like David Brower and Paul Ehrlich founded nonprofits and wrote compellingly about their views, the Yosemite advocates of untrammeled wilderness found themselves building corporate empires with sophisticated marketing techniques and financial investments in promoting a certain kind of wilderness experience. As Yosemite-birthed climbing companies like Yvon Chouinard's Patagonia (originally Chouinard Equipment), Doug Tompkins's The North Face, and Royal Robbins's eponymous clothing company grew, they brought with them dirtbag values, making them at once some of the most environmentally responsible corporations of their size as well as deeply complicit in the normalization of a reimagined colonial representation of land.

One example of how this played out was through the dirtbag climbers' and their companies' obsession with what was known as "clean climbing," a backlash against the kind of bolt and piton climbing of people like Warren Harding who used some eight hundred bolts in his first ascent of El Capitan. In clean climbing, artificial assistance was a last measure, and the challenge of route finding was foregrounded. This supposedly leave-no-trace method reflected the mythology of a pristine wilderness and was designed to encourage the idea of overcoming the challenges of nature as a fundamental part of the wilderness experience. While sport climbing of the 1990s rolled this back somewhat with a heavy reliance on bolting, the popularization of free-climbing over the 2010s can be seen as an extreme version of this movement.[29]

Marketing material began reflecting this ethic, portraying outdoor spaces as clean and empty, as places where the figure, usually alone, is clearly an outsider, and until very recently, as racially homogeneous. White, fit men and women clinging to denuded cliffs above and in front of majestic, untouched landscapes is among the most common motifs in images produced by Patagonia and The North Face in the mid- to late twentieth century. The wilderness was both hostile and integral to the human experience, but always fundamentally extraordinary.

Take for example the 1985 The North Face catalog cover seen at the beginning of this chapter.[30] The black-and-white photograph features a solitary climber dwarfed by the granite precipice they are ascending, white pants contrasting sharply against the dark gray stone. The valley floor, with its potential human impacts, is out of the frame, leaving only the tops of the trees and the clean cliffs in view. Even the climber's equipment is obscured. They may even be free-climbing this crevice, using no ropes or harness at all, the purest and least impactful method of climbing. In this advertisement, athleticism, the drive to improve one's skill and achieve first ascents, has replaced the drive for frontier reenactment. Instead of the need for an Indian antagonist, untrammeled explorers are pit against primeval nature itself, an outsider in a deeply nonhuman space. Marketing material like this has become ubiquitous in outdoor retail, fully eclipsing earlier mythologies by the mid-1960s and continuing virtually unchallenged through the social media upheaval of the 2010s.

Of course, untrammeled marketing is just as mythological as marketing wilderness with Indianness. Far from untouched, climbing is deeply impactful on the environment. Soil erosion and ecosystem disruption at climbing approaches, "gardening" or removing plants and lichen from the cliff wall, nest destruction, fixed anchors, and chalk residue are just a handful of the long-term impacts of climbing.[31] The erasure of both Indigenous people and Indianness from the narrative has also led to impacts like climbers ignorantly bolting over Indigenous petroglyphs and other sacred sites, believing them to be merely graffiti.[32]

The legacy of the dirtbag climbers in the evolution of untrammeled wilderness goes beyond just its colonial implications. For decades, outdoor recreation and climbing has been a particularly hostile space to women and people of color. The almost exclusively white, masculine Yosemite climbing community produced an exclusionary and fraternal group that, like representations of wilderness, was reproduced through their marketing and ideology. The racialization and patriarchal nature of this community is intertwined with their colonial ideology, an ethic of dominance over space designed to uphold existing structures of power in a moment of upheaval rather than challenging them.[33]

The Forever Explorable Wilderness

Having successfully sold the idea of wilderness to the American consumer, outdoor marketers then had to convince an ever-larger audience of its need to enter these spaces. It did this by leaning into an archetypical figure long associated with wilderness, one already culturally embedded in the collective consciousness of the nation: the explorer.

The North Face's longest running tagline is "Never Stop Exploring." The concept of exploration is the cornerstone of its brand, a call to push limits and blaze new trails (or climbing routes). Their stated mission is to "provide the best gear for our athletes and the modern-day explorer, support the preservation of the outdoors, and inspire a global movement of exploration."[34] In his seminal essay "The Trouble with Wilderness," William Cronon identifies the fundamental separation of man and nature as one of the central paradoxes of wilderness. If wilderness can only exist without humans, then any human presence inevitably destroys the wilderness.[35] Corporate marketers, however, are unconcerned with philosophical consistency and, instead of fretting over this contradiction, have appropriated an American identity that had become as closely associated with contemporary untrammeled wilderness as Indianness was with earlier paradigms. Into the untrammeled wilderness enters the explorer.

The explorer is one of the key founding figures in American settler mythology and the one most closely associated with the values and landscapes represented by the outdoor industry. It is closely tied to a romantic, and largely fictional, age of American exploration, expansion, and environmentalism—which is also to say, tied to colonialism. The character haphazardly draws from any number of real and mythical (and white and male) individuals like Davy Crockett, Kit Carson, Paul Bunyan, Edmund Hillary, and above all, the patron saint of the outdoors, John

Muir. The explorer has been consistently narrativized alongside the concept of wilderness, becoming an indispensable part of it. They are the observer who, by bearing witness to it, realizes its very existence. While the explorer is a global archetype, appearing in myths and stories throughout the world, the version most often emulated by American outdoorspeople is one that arose out of a literary trope from the nineteenth century.[36] In *Virgin Land,* Henry Nash Smith calls this literary figure the Mountain Man—a man representing "anarchic freedom" who "ranged the wilderness [fleeing] from the restraints of civilization."[37] Cooper's Leatherstocking tales, most famously *The Last of the Mohicans,* created the template for the heroic explorer figure—the white frontiersman, noble and genteel but on the margins of society, connected to nature in a special way but also always in opposition to it as the forerunner of civilization.[38] This paradox of being in the wilderness but not of it is a defining trait of the American incarnation of the explorer.

Smith aptly uses Kit Carson as his example, a man who was mythologized during his own lifetime in sensationalized stories published in dime novels and "blood and thunders."[39] Carson's real life emulates the explorer paradox. He was famous for both his close, even unseemly, connection to nature and Indigenous people—he was a famous guide and trapper and he married an Arapaho woman named Singing Grass and later a Cheyenne woman named Making-Out-Road—as well as his violent campaigns against the Navajo, the Apache, and the Kiowa. The myths about him exaggerated these exploits, making him both more noble and more violent, to the point where even Carson himself began criticizing the stories.[40]

Carson is a good example of an explorer from the hostile wilderness era of the early nineteenth century when the relationship between western culture and wilderness was one of dominance and cultivation. He was driven by the goal of subduing the wilderness, a concept that at the time extended beyond the land and resources to include the Indigenous people living there. The explorer was also the conqueror; discovery and subjugation went hand in hand. Carson's famous scorched earth campaign against the Navajo was an example of this dual assault on both land and people. To be brought into the fold of productive civilization, the desert wilderness of the southwestern United States had to be tamed. The mythologizing of living people was experienced by other recognizable names of the period as well—Davy Crockett, Daniel Boone, and John C. Fremont—in a process that continues with contemporary outdoorspeople over social media. The fact that these legendary explorers were based, if loosely, on real people only cements the explorer as a genuine identity, rather than a constructed one, in the minds of American recreators.

Indigenous people are often a part of these nineteenth-century narratives and were inextricably connected to the mythic wilderness. People like Sacagawea and Uncas authenticated the wilderness, signaling to the narrative's audience that these are indeed spaces outside civilization. Considered part of the wilderness itself, they served the same paradoxical role toward the white hero. On one side, they serve as guides and conduits for the white hero between civilization and wilderness; on the other side, they serve as his enemies, symbolic personifications of the battle between the white hero and the wilderness, something he must inevitably—if tragically—overcome. Of course, on a less metaphorical level, this is also representative of the very real systemic racism and violence perpetrated against Indigenous people by explorers like Kit Carson. The metaphorical conquering of the wilderness/Indian by explorers and their real violence against Indigenous people cannot be separated even in the reenactment of the explorer figure by contemporary outdoorspeople. Settler exploration and settler wilderness are fundamentally violent toward Indigenous people, culture, land, and sovereignty.

As the popular conceptions of wilderness began to change in the latter half of the nineteenth century from a hostile place to be subdued toward the frontier wilderness discussed in the previous chapter, the explorer figure changed along with it. However, just as the function of wilderness ideology remained the same despite a friendlier face—a background upon which to perform Americanness—the explorer also continued to function for the same purpose. Instead of domesticating the land with rifle and plow, the new explorer domesticated himself, reified his own Americanness, through encounters with an untamed wilderness. Despite still being closely associated with Indianness for much of the early twentieth century, wilderness was fundamentally about whiteness and Americanness.

The best example of this new explorer is John Muir. Muir was one of the earliest and most prominent American preservationists. Known as the Father of the National Parks and the "patron saint of twentieth-century American environmental activity," he has become a symbol of the larger American conservation and wilderness movements. Unlike many wilderness advocates of the era like Sigurd Olson and Ernest Oberholtzer who took the presence of Indigenous people in wilderness as natural, even authenticating, Muir was an early advocate of the untrammeled wilderness, a space free of all human interference. Today, his open disdain for the presence of Indigenous people, who he described as dirtying an otherwise pristine environment, is often passed over in favor of his lyrical description of beautiful, parklike Sierra Nevada or wonders of Alaska. He apparently never managed to grasp the irony that the pure and parklike landscapes of the Sierras he so admired were the result of careful management by the Nüümü, Miwok, and other Indigenous communities he disparaged.

It is this early advocacy for untrammeled wilderness that makes Muir such a potent symbol for outdoorspeople today. In contemporary society, untrammeled wilderness is naturalized, accepted as the purest form of wilderness rather than a largely late twentieth-century phenomenon. His contemporaries are not seen as merely embracing the wilderness ideology of the time, but as instead failing to grasp the true nature of wilderness. Only Muir, the myth goes, had the foresight to understand wilderness and what our relationship with it should be. His narrative is also among the most widespread of any explorer, carrying the ideologies embedded in his myth with him.

Together, the real-life exploits of these white, male explorers, their mythologizing from dime novels to Instagram pages, and over a hundred years of media reproductions of this trope have firmly established the explorer in the American collective consciousness as someone who is authentic, closely connected to the natural world, and quintessentially American.[41]

Outdoorspeople, aspiring environmentalists, and people trying to craft some kind of authentic Americanness find in the explorer an identity they can emulate. Sometimes this means adopting the aesthetic of these people—think coon-skin hat and lumberjack flannel—but more often it is about a less material sense of nostalgia, an attempt to reenact or perhaps salvage what is seen as a lost American identity. Like the origins of the American environmental movement itself, enacting the explorer is a way to recapture a sense of lost authenticity, to escape the confines of modern life, and to play with the idea of a romantic anticapitalism.[42]

While the explorer archetype has existed in our stories and myths since the founding of the United States, the emergence of modern brand culture and co-option of archetypical storytelling into consumer culture and marketing has changed the explorer from a figure people tell stories about to a figure they embody. In many ways, brands have become where much of the mythmaking in contemporary society takes place. As Sarah Banet-Weiser argues, brands are more than just the stories companies tell their customers; they meld with the personal experiences of the individual consumer, becoming "the setting around which individuals weave their own stories, where individuals position themselves as the central character in the narrative of the brand."[43]

Despite the desire of companies to speak to the individual narrative of every person, the complexities of actual human identity do not work well for marketing. Although companies have tried, it is simply impractical to personalize a product and marketing campaign to fit the identity of or to provide meaning to any one individual consumer. Marketers instead must find ways to strategically group potential consumers. With the rise of social media, many marketers began turning to big data as a solution to this problem. Social media and ad-tech software have provided marketers with more information than has ever been possible before.[44] They no longer need to rely on a handful of focus groups and surveys; they can now draw from thousands of data points from millions of people who have voluntarily—at least from a legal sense— divulged almost everything about their lives to private corporations, and then use algorithms to crunch those numbers quickly and efficiently. Basically, by designating a demographic—for example, twenty-five- to thirty-five-year-old white males who frequently use social media and work remotely—and gathering as much information about them, the idea is that you can define an average person from that demographic and develop a campaign around him. If this person is demographic X, then he will be likely to buy product Y.

However, big data has proved to be insufficient in an increasingly competitive market. It has been criticized as being too predictable, not sensitive enough, and failing to foster emotional connections between consumers and companies—that last being a key factor in brand loyalty.[45] In response to this, some brands have turned to methods in anthropology and psychology to integrate identity formation and meaning making into their campaigns. Modified ethnographic techniques like participant observation are becoming increasingly common and effective storytelling increasingly sought after. Branding archetypes, first introduced by Margaret Mark and Carol Pearson in their 2001 book *The Hero and the Outlaw,* epitomize this. Between quotes by theorists of mythology like Carl Jung, Joseph Campbell, and Johann Wolfgang von Goethe, Mark and Pearson outline twelve archetypes, or culturally embedded identities, that can be used to manage meaning in a brand. These include the lover, the hero, the everyman, and, of course, the explorer.[46]

Mark and Pearson cite the explorer as one of the most influential brand archetypes of the twenty-first century, representing individuality, nonconformity, and authenticity. Given the motto "Don't Fence Me In," by Mark and Pearson, the explorer archetype is used by brands that seek to inspire a sense of freedom and a disregard for boundaries. This is a strategy that has been embraced across industries, but no industry has used it quite as effectively as outdoor retail. Together with untrammeled wilderness, it provides the foundation for the outdoor industry's carefully crafted consumer narrative.

Untrammeled wilderness and its co-constructed explorer archetype have proved powerful wildernessing narratives for the outdoor recreation industry, which relies on the unquestioned legitimacy of public recreational spaces to support its sales and services. Expertly using print media and eventually television to disseminate its marketing, the industry had maintained a virtually unchallenged monopoly on commercial wilderness representations through the 1990s. However, beginning in the early 2000s and dramatically ramping up in the 2010s, digital and social media radically changed the way Americans consume media and how marketers produce it. In the following chapter, I look at the strategies the outdoor industry used to reproduce time-tested methods in a digital space. Taking advantage of the unique properties of social and networked media, the industry has managed to maintain and entrench untrammeled wilderness and the ethic of exploration in a new era.

‹ **4** ›

#Explore

To photograph a thing is to appropriate the thing
photographed.

—Susan Sontag, *On Photography*

Figures 10–13 are images from the September 5, 2019, home pages of
The North Face, Patagonia, Osprey, and Kathmandu.[1] In the background of the photographs is a landscape, a wilderness, pristine and
uninhabited, a forest trail, a rocky shoreline, a horizon of snowcapped
peaks. The settings are different, but each of these photographs show
the same thing—terra nullius. It is land that belongs to no one (or sometime everyone). It has no history and no culture. It is a place untouched
since the dawn of creation. It is the carefully constructed product of over
a century of wildernessing.

Through the foreground of the image moves a figure. You see them
from the back, anonymously, as they survey the landscape. From a cliff
or a hill or an outcropping of rock, the land spreads out before and below
them. They are the explorer, the adventurer, the person who enters this
space not to conquer, not even to stay, but merely to roam, to see, to
capture the light. Tread lightly. Take nothing but photos. Leave nothing but footprints. These images are designed to evoke the freedom to
roam—and hide the claiming that comes along with it.

There are as many versions of this photo as there are hikers with
cameras. It is the classic adventure photograph and is used extensively
by marketers and recreators alike, more pervasive and more powerful

than either a landscape alone or the typical tourist shot of a smiling, recognizable face. It seems innocent enough, and on an individual basis, it is. It is just a photo, to be posted, seen, forgotten, and eventually lost in an ocean of constantly changing media. However, images like these are both the result of and the impetus for a series of social and political conceptions about land, people, and their relationship to each other that are fundamentally colonial in nature and have material impacts for Indigenous people and their environments.

In the previous chapters, I described the concept of wildernessing and the ways in which the outdoor industry has influenced evolving conceptions of wilderness. In this chapter, I turn to the specific strategies the

FIGURE 10. The North Face home page, September 5, 2019.

FIGURE 11. Patagonia home page, September 5, 2019.

industry uses to perpetuate these narratives. I examine the roles social and networked media have played in naturalizing the industry's wilderness ideology within their community of consumers and the digital photographic techniques popularized on Instagram. Leaning on their influence within outdoor digital networks and employing strategies like co-creative media, immersive photography, and enclothed cognition, outdoor marketers take advantage of new technologies to redeploy old ideologies. They turn consumers into explorers who, symbolically claiming land through photography and story, go on to maintain the narrative conditions necessary for a settler colonial public land system as well as reproduce personal colonial power relationships over that land. This

FIGURE 12. Kathmandu Outdoors home page, September 5, 2019.

FIGURE 13. Osprey home page, September 5, 2019.

relationship, established in the digital collective consciousness of the outdoor community, creates the cultural conditions necessary for the actual commodification of land and continued attacks on Indigenous sovereignty.

An Old Narrative, a New Medium

In the mid 2010s, there was an Instagram account called You Did Not Sleep There (@youdidnotsleepthere) that took photographs of people camping in incredibly beautiful but also highly improbable places and called them out on it. These were either photoshopped images—a rugged mountain landscape inserted into a tent opening for example—or people who had merely set up their tent for the sake of the picture while never intending to actually stay there. These kinds of pictures are incredibly popular because they inspire awe and drive engagement, but few people who have ever camped believe these are real places one might set up a tent. While it would be lovely to wake up to the cliffside view of some alpine vista, a windy, rocky point is uncomfortable at best and dangerous or illegal at worst.

Unlike the static magazine ads that first established the iconic outdoor marketing "adventure" style, in digital advertisements, the content of these images is only a part of what is happening in these posts. Their meanings and impacts are deeply influenced by the medium in which they are shared—digital images circulating over a networked platform. Social media promotes a "curated" life. These platforms are more than simply archives; they are public history sites, art galleries, and marketing tools all rolled into one. As such, they are made to be seen, responded to, judged, and interacted with.

If adventure photography were only to appear in print or on static websites as a traditional form of ad placement, it would still contribute to the proliferation of the colonial explorer fantasy. However, the way it functions and is networked over social media magnifies this effect in several ways. The digital format of the photograph itself, and thus its acknowledged and accepted distance from reality, contributes to a breakdown between reality and fantasy. The co-productive nature of social media gives users increased feelings of ownership and participation in the creation and dissemination of these images as well as in the corporations that post them. And finally, the instantaneousness of photo sharing and the portability of mobile devices make these images less merely representations of exploration and more part of the exploration process itself, creating an insular circle of representation that moves quickly and with great impact.[2]

In response to the early popularization of digital photography, photography theorist Fred Ritchin expressed anxiety about a world where photographs will no longer be referents to the real world, but would merely be "desirents," constructed to sell a story, brand, or product rather than to represent reality.[3] While there is a good argument to be made that this has always been the case with photography, analog photography at least maintained a direct trace of light on film. In the words of filmmaker Wim Wenders, digital photography has "broken the relationship between picture and reality once and for all."[4]

Ritchin feared that the shift in photography from the documentation of reality to the construction of fantasies used to sell narratives would result in the breakdown of trust between consumers and the media. This is clearly a general trend we are seeing. A 2018 Monmouth University poll suggested that 77 percent of Americans believe major news outlets report fake news or are otherwise untrustworthy, and a 2016 study by marketing firm Olapic showed nearly 95 percent of people did not trust traditional advertisements.[5] Keep in mind, these numbers are *before* the rise of AI-generated content in 2023 and 2024, a technology primed to do to digital photography what digital photography has done to film. Consumers understand that photography and video, especially when deployed as a method of marketing, are no basis for truth.

What Ritchin could not have predicted in 2009, however, was the impact social media would have on the photograph and media landscape as a metamedia through which other media circulates. So-called natural advertisements (paid ads designed to seem like organic content) and social media influencers became media launderers, further eroding the already fuzzy distinction between marketing and personal media. In fact, according to Olapic, social media users are seven times more likely to trust the kind of user-generated content shared on Instagram than traditional forms of advertising.[6] Finding themselves in the midst of a relational and technological revolution, otherwise skeptical and savvy media consumers are suddenly at sea.

The reason for this disconnect is, of course, the result of many intersecting factors. Consumer protections have struggled to catch up to evolving technologies, leaving the door open for intentionally misleading practices. Influencer culture encourages one-way parasocial relationships, something ubiquitous in celebrity culture and mass media, but put into hyperdrive by social media. One of the key reasons, however, is the personal investment consumers have to the content they consume, largely the result of the co-productive nature of social media. Unlike the opaque, top-down nature of traditional forms of media, social media gives users a peek behind the curtain. The photos might not be unaltered, but users know how they were created because most of the time it was the users themselves who created them. Work in rhetorical studies tells us that the author is never the sole arbiter of what they produce; audiences always engage with, filter, and reimagine the meaning of work.[7] With social media, this takes on a much more literal meaning. Readers can directly and immediately respond not only to text or image but also to the author, creating a co-producing community. Author, reader, commenter, and lurker all play an important part of the production and reproduction of knowledge and representation in these digital spaces.

The idea of social media producing co-creating communities first arose out of business scholarship as a way to understand new marketing techniques and less hierarchical producer/consumer relationships, suggesting it would be a powerful marketing tool.[8] Capturing consumer investment in a marketing narrative can significantly reduce skepticism and build trust. Zwick and colleagues brought a Marxist critique and a theoretical grounding to the concept of co-creation, drawing on Foucault's writing on the dispersed and fragmented nature of power to argue that co-creation allows corporations to exploit the free creative labor of social media users. In this model, corporations build the narrative design, scaffolded upon the foundation of an outsized network influence, and allow their "community" of followers to do the unpaid work of construction, at once outsourcing costs and capturing consumer investment. While corporations do not have full control over individual user-generated content in this model—social media can be a dangerous site of potential dissent and restructuring—at scale, consumer interaction with corporate posts is easily appropriated by the larger capitalist agenda.[9]

Co-creative social media has since been taken up and explored in other fields, including political ecology. Bram Büscher uses co-creation in his theorization of Nature 2.0. Drawing on the political ecological concept of "second nature," or the idea that all nature is within the realm of human influence, Büscher looks at the construction of nature online, especially concerning conservation efforts. Users' separation from "real" nature allows users, conservation organizations, and corporations to collectively construct an imaginative natural environment that promotes real-world conservation efforts, although at the expense of further commodification of nature.[10] The integration of fully virtual natures with the heavily mediated representations of nature only serves to make consumer discernment more difficult.

In other words, co-creation and the reliance on user-generated content builds a relationship of trust between the companies and their consumers, turning consumers into digital communities. While the outdoor industry's target market, tech-savvy millennials and Gen Z, may be critical of being sold a certain narrative in a traditional marketing format, they are far more likely to accept it when the narrative is generated by real people they feel connected to and when they feel personally engaged in a community of like-minded individuals. Being an explorer is seen as less about purchasing the proper gear and more about engaging in a certain set of practices and shared cultural experiences (i.e., lifestyle branding). Outdoor corporations are not seen as just trying to sell their products, but as connectors, bringing people together. I do not want to say that this relationship is ultimately a fantasy in and of itself—Patagonia for example has become a base for political action and physical REI stores are hubs for in-person outdoor groups—but somehow outdoor products still prominently feature in the images produced by these communities.

Objectively, co-creation sounds like it could be a surprisingly democratic way for media to form and circulate. The means of media production and dissemination are widely available, far more so than under the mass media regime of the late twentieth century. However, the reality is that rather than disrupting preexisting inequities and power structures, social and algorithmic media dynamics tend to reproduce them. The rise of social media and Web 2.0 has revealed many of the limits of our digital lives and technologies.

While social media creates asymmetrical networks and parasocial relationships between people and organizations that tend to mediate content through corporations, it also creates a system that mediates content through the device and platform itself. Unlike traditional cameras, which require a delay between capturing and reproducing, with networked, mobile devices the process can be almost instantaneous.

This incorporates the camera into the process of exploration itself, an integral part of how outdoorspeople interact with the spaces they enter both physically and virtually.

One way to think about this is through Andrew Hoskins's theory of "connective memory." Hoskins suggests that collective memory is no longer a useful concept when talking about social media. He suggests the term "connective memory." Collective memory, he argues, involves human minds collectively producing memory that is then mediated or enabled through media and technology. Connective memory on the other hand suggests that social media is actively part of the memory production process forming socio-technical or cyborg relationships between user and device. Mind and technic—or the means by which knowledge is externalized—work together to produce collective meaning.[11] Instead of merely constructing a "first draft of history," a static representation, from which users can draw to create a narrative about the past, social media *produces* the narrative.[12]

In more concrete terms, this brings us to what John Urry calls a closed circle of representation. Urry argues that as tourists view images of the places they intend to visit, they are primed to see and experience the places in a specific way, so when they actually enter those places, they merely reproduce the images they have previously seen and experience the place in a prescribed way. The instantaneousness of social media photography—both in capturing and disseminating images—radically accelerates this process. Visitors will have seen a particular destination countless times on their Instagram feeds before they visit, possibly even prompting them to visit somewhere in the first place. Through their mobile devices, they will also have access to all these representations, both professional and user generated, while physically at the destination. Completing the circle, they can then take the photo that they want, often based on the images they expect to see, and immediately post their own example, contributing to the growing archive/collective understanding of the site.

This process has incredible power to reinforce certain representations. While each remediation will slightly reinterpret the otherwise reproduced representations and experiences, social media does not work like a game of telephone, each person drawing on only the last image. It is instead more of a giant mosaic, thousands of images, captions, videos, and experiences collectively creating a single narrative. Individual interpretations, with the possible exception of those with immense network influence, are lost in the overarching story. This mosaic has a powerful stabilizing force on the overall representation, with each individual tourist being continually drawn in by the whole rather than by any single representation.

Like co-creative marketing, circles of representation are not organic, democratic media landscapes, but are subject to unequal forces and power relationships within the social network. The most basic basis for a network involves nodes—in our case these are Instagram users and accounts—and edges or ties—the various connections between the nodes. Individuals, organizations, and companies are all nodes in the network with content flowing between them. Following, reposting, and commenting are all ties that produce and mediate content on Instagram. They form what Christian Pentzold and Vivien Sommer describe as "living intertexuality," where pages, documents, and users link to, draw from, and reproduce each other in a dynamic way, a far cry from the much more passive (although never totally passive) consumption of non-networked media. Pentzold and Sommer also draw on Astrid Erll's concept of "remediation," or the idea that media is always drawing on other media to describe how online media flows through different groups and settings. Content is always both remediating—being transferred from one media to another—and remediated—creating layers of mediation.[13] Each remediation revitalizes the content while also changing and reinterpreting it.

While every user may be a node within any given network, not all nodes exert the same influence on the network. Nodes with greater centrality—nodes that have more ties, stronger ties, or asymmetrical ties—are going to have greater influence and control over the network and within certain subnetworks.[14] It is impractical to take all billion-plus Instagram users as a single network, although there are certain weak ties that eventually connect them all. It is more useful to look at a specific subnetwork of users, for example, users connected to outdoor recreation. Like many subnetworks, the outdoor recreation community creates a kind of clique, where there are many strong ties between the members of this network with fewer and weaker ties to users not in this network. It is relatively insular. Within the outdoor recreation world, outdoor corporations tend to be nodes at the center of large networks of individual users. Patagonia for example has, as of August 2024, 5.4 million followers/ties. While there are a few individuals that do have comparable numbers—landscape photographer Chris Burkard has 3.9 million followers—these tend to be weaker ties. This means that while there are 3.9 million people who follow Burkard, for the most part, Instagram is their only relation to him.[15] With Patagonia and other outdoor corporations, people are not only followers; they also consume their products (a second point of connection), generate the content shared on their accounts (a third point of connection), and regularly encounter these brands in the nondigital world through more traditional marketing (a fourth point of connection). Corporations might be legal "persons," but they are not individuals, which is seen as a mark against them when it comes to consumer trust and relationship building. However, overall, they tend to have an outsized influence on networks compared with individuals with similar followings—of which there are very few. Furthermore, since networks tend to exhibit preferential attachment, or a "rich get richer" tendency, strong ties and large followings will attract even stronger ties and larger followings faster than weak ties and small followings will.

Finally, beyond power differences in the network of users on these platforms, the platforms themselves serve to disempower users. Scholars like Tero Karppi and Safiya Umoja Noble argue that inherent to these techno-social spaces is a transference of agency from individuals to algorithms, automated processes, and those who created and own them.[16] Social biases that exist in the general user population can reproduce and spread as systems learn to predict user behavior, a problem likely to grow with the growing AI-ization of digital ecosystems. Karppi further suggests that this automation produces increasingly abstracted and legible digital facsimiles of users, what John Cheney-Lippold describes as "algorithmic identities," identities that subsume individual action into marketing data.[17] Corporations, already abstracted facsimiles of "persons," benefit from this dynamic both as users of the platform—as legible, shareable products—and as buyers of advertising space. Consumers, on the other hand, are constantly fed media designed to target and reify their algorithmic identities in ways that can and do shape offline behavior.

This all means that outdoor corporations are in a position to mediate the images and representations with the largest distribution. As a result of their influence within the networks, the curatorial choices of outdoor corporations—choices that promote the wilderness ethic most beneficial to their product sale—reinforce an entire culture of exploration within a large community of people. This culture promotes specific land politics that benefit the industry and its core market at the expense of other communities, specifically Indigenous people and their land-based cultural practices and resource sovereignty.

Turning Consumers into Explorers

It is clear that outdoor retail marketers have had little difficulty transitioning into these new digital media, but thus far I have only discussed how marketers take advantage of power dynamics within networked technology itself. To further examine marketers' strategies of representation, specifically strategies that take advantage of mobile technology and social media, I want to turn to some concepts in consumer psychology and photographic theory. By operationalizing models like mediated place attachment, enclothed cognition, and adventure photography, the outdoor industry seeks to create digital environments that allow consumers to imagine themselves as explorers, crafting lifestyles that require the products they produce. Some of these strategies draw on preexisting models, especially in photography, and are more impacted by the digital turn. Others are produced by it. All serve to turn the consumer, both as an algorithmic identity and as a physical agent on the land, into an explorer, creating a demand for wilderness.

To frame this, I want to return to The North Face, which, thanks to their long-standing tagline, has tied itself closely to the idea of exploration. The company is known for sponsoring elite outdoor athletes who embody this mission. Most notably these include a host of climbers famed for their first ascents like Jimmy Chin, Alex Honnold, and Conrad Anker and skiers known for their first descents like former The North Face "team captain" Hilaree Nelson.[18] The company is not only interested in supporting the handful of athletes who are truly doing what no one had done before; they want to "inspire a global movement" of everyday people who live their lives as explorers—something they achieve by selling these potential explorers The North Face products.

The North Face products are not just about their function of keeping you warm or dry or supporting your ankles—you can find functional gear for those kind of activities for much less money elsewhere—they are about cultivating a lifestyle of exploration. If you wanted to, you could wear The North Face's high-quality, technical gear on an arctic expedition or climbing treacherous peaks in the Andes on the type of trips The North Face athletes regularly embark on. While the vast majority of consumers will not become extreme alpinists, just the fact that they could means every hike in the local state park, every climb up that hill in the middle of campus, every walk around the block with your dog is an act of exploration, an act of discovery.[19] By invoking the figure of the explorer, The North Face is tapping into a powerful archetype, fulfilling a fantasy held by many outdoorspeople to not just read about, not just see, but to actually become the hero explorer of their own life. To dress like an explorer is to become one.

How does this process actually work? How does The North Face or other outdoor retail companies get people to believe that by merely putting on the accoutrements of an explorer, they can in any way transform their identities? To answer this, I look to a concept called enclothed cognition. This is the idea that something happens when you put on a costume, that the clothes you wear give you the freedom to be someone or something else.

Social psychologists Hajo Adam and Adam Galinsky coined the term "enclothed cognition" in a 2012 study to describe this phenomenon. In their study, they had participants wear white lab coats, describing them as doctor's coats. White lab coats are familiar to most people, a common trope in pop culture, normally associated with science and medical fields, careful research, lab conditions, and higher education. Medical professionals have even instituted a "white coat ceremony," where they physically enclothe new students with a white lab coat as a way of welcoming them to medical school. The theory was that when wearing these coats, participants would act more like scientists, impacting their cognitive skill, and indeed, participants showed increased selective attention in a series of tasks while wearing the coat. Furthermore, when told it was a painter's coat rather than a lab coat, there was no difference in cognitive ability.[20] Adam and Galinsky's enclothed cognition has since been used to look at everything from the way plus-sized professional clothes impact women at work to how police uniforms impact perceptions of people in street clothes to children's behavior in Halloween costumes, all with supporting results.[21] Dressing professionally is not just about how others perceive you, although that is always an important consideration in what one wears; it seems that it may actually make you act more professionally. To some extent it is true that we are what we wear.

Based on their findings, Adam and Galinsky theorized that for enclothed cognition to occur, two conditions were necessary. The first is an established symbolic meaning of the clothes. Unless you understand the cultural symbolism of a white lab coat—that it is worn by doctors and scientists—*and* have some preconceived notion of how doctors and scientists behave, a white coat is just a white coat. Just the association is not enough. Adam and Galinsky also discovered that participants must physically be wearing a lab coat for the effect to occur. In one of the tests, they merely put in the lab coat in the same room as participants and, while participants still associated the lab coat with all the same properties, they did not associate those properties with themselves. It was not until they wore the coat that it could be internalized and they performed better on the cognitive tests. In practical terms, this would be the difference in motivation between just looking at your running shoes—a good reminder that you *should* be running—and actually putting them on and tying the laces—now you *are* a runner.

What does one become, what new character is enacted, when a person zips up that Patagonia jacket or ties those Columbia boots? While there is no inevitable answer to this question, through its choice to market toward the explorer archetype, a cultural figure already firmly established in the collective consciousness of many Americans, the outdoor industry has decided its consumers will be explorers. The problem, of course, is that the explorer is not an identity created from whole cloth by the industry. This is not a completely top-down process. Many potential consumers may have already seen themselves as explorers, have already drawn on shared cultural ideas of what an explorer is, how they act, and what they value. But by cleaving their companies so closely to this identity, outdoor retail has ensured that these would-be explorers see outdoor products as a way to realize that desire. When you wear outdoor clothes you become an explorer, a discoverer, an adventurer (a settler, a colonizer, an empire builder). The myth becomes a costume, or maybe a uniform, which the wearer is then free to enact. The outdoor industry constructs the necessary symbolic connection between their products and the explorer archetype—and its settler colonial connections—in their marketing by relying heavily on a genre of landscape photography called adventure photography.

Susan Sontag writes, "To photograph is to appropriate the thing photographed."[22] An unseen viewer reproducing a subject constructed as passive has power over the subjects' representation and dissemination and thus power over the subject itself. To some extent, this is true in any photograph. In their discussion on the relationship between tourism and photography, John Urry and Carol Crawshaw assert that photography is used to fix and appropriate what the tourist sees. It is not enough to see—an experience must be captured, collected, and, increasingly, shared for it to be real.[23] Barbara Kirshenblatt-Gimblett argues that a central goal of tourism is to transform a location into a destination and that photography is a powerful tool in this process.[24]

Adventure photography is a specific genre of tourism photography, one that makes its appropriations, its claims to land in particular, explicit in several ways. First, as a variation on American landscape photography more generally, adventure photography follows in a long tradition of using landscapes, and constructing the semiotics of landscapes through photography, as a method of settling and Americanizing the West. Second, *unlike* landscape photography more generally, adventure photography depends on the presence of the explorer—the one doing the observing and appropriating—in the photograph itself. Instead of merely the beautiful, but almost hauntingly empty, landscapes of Romanticism and early twentieth-century photography, adventure photography constructs land and wilderness as very much connected to people, but to very specific people doing very specific activities. Finally, the social and digital media in which these photographs are taken, processed, shared, and interpreted—in particular on the social media platform Instagram—reshape and rescale the power dynamics involved in photography, increasing both the ability of a photographer to shape the representation of a landscape as well as the ability of consumers or activists to push back against these representations, reappropriating them for their own purposes. In the following sections, I will look at all three of these factors in greater detail alongside examples of them functioning within the outdoor retail industry.

American landscape photography—and landscape painting before it—has long been a classic example of how appropriation through photography functions. Historian Mark David Spence describes how Thomas Cole and other romantic painters of the Hudson River School used their representation of land, in its wildness and primitiveness, as a way to claim and define Americanness. These landscapes, often historical and usually including nostalgic images of Indigenous people in line with early twentieth-century wilderness models, representationally separated the United States and its land from Europe. They were designed to lift up the continent's uncharted wilderness to the level of Europe's genteel pastoralism and deep history of "civilization."[25] They served to not just claim the continent for America, but also indigenize America to the continent. While Cole and the philosophical foundation of the Hudson River School were concerned about representation and a vague Americanness, other Romantic painters were much more concrete about their purpose. For Albert Bierstadt, landscape painting was explicitly connected to settler colonialism and manifest destiny. He would tour his paintings around the country, expounding on the wonder of America's empty, untrammeled lands and his own hope for eventual Euro-American ownership of them.[26] They were essentially, like the landscapes of Instagram today, advertisements selling wilderness, designed to attract white settlers at the expense of the Indigenous people already there.

This tradition has continued as artists transitioned from the brush to the camera. Lynne C. Manzo and Patrick Devine-Wright, for example, argue that western landscape photography has been pivotal in creating settler attachment to land.[27] Place attachment—or the bond created between people and place—is a powerful affective motivator usually developed over time through a combination of personal experiences, social interactions, and cognitive knowledge connected to a place. Landscape photographer Ansel Adams for example was explicit about his goal to use photography as a way to connect his audience to the spaces he was photographing. Not reproducing, but instead recreating nature through his own interpretation, his mission was to create shared social spaces—the national parks in particular—that brought all Americans together.[28] Although he considered his work apolitical, his photographs were actually deeply political, forming social arguments about land use and American identity.

Traditionally, scholarship on place attachment has stressed the impact of tangible interactions with place. However, scholars have begun to acknowledge the power of symbolic and mediated interactions with land in developing place attachment.[29] This embrace of mediated relationships closely aligns to the narrative turn within memory studies, especially the focus on physical media rather than simply abstract social frameworks. As media theorist José van Dijck argues, media and memory work together to shape the stories we tell about our communities and ourselves.[30] In this model, media is a powerful force because it is both a social framework—or a part of the communication process itself—and an archive for memory. These memories do not have to belong to the individual consuming the media, but can be drawn from the collective consciousness, the shared cultural understandings we have about whatever is being represented in the media. These two aspects, communication and archive, create a more pervasive and concrete collective memory or cultural memory, what Marita Sturken defines as "a field of cultural negotiation through which different stories vie for a place in history."[31]

Through the affective images produced by early photographers like Ansel Adams and stereoscope photographer Charles Zimmerman, a wide range of people, consumers of these images, were able to begin emotionally connecting to previously unseen western landscapes. They built relationships with land not through physically being in these places, living on the land, experiencing it personally and generationally, but through photographic images and collective cultural understandings others had constructed for them.[32] Unlike most people in most of human history for whom place attachment could only occur through physical presence, photography and the ability to mass-produce photographs ushered in our modern era of mediated place attachment. However, the landscapes people saw, connected to, and desired to visit and live in were only half truths, designed by the photographer to tell a particular story of the land at the expense of its complexity.

Take, for example, this image of Glacier National Park by Ansel Adams (Figure 14).[33] Commissioned by the Department of the Interior as part of a series on the national parks, the photograph represents Glacier

FIGURE 14. *In Glacier National Park.* Photo by Ansel Adams, from the National Archives, 519859, 79-AAE-4: Ansel Adams Photographs of National Parks and Monuments, 1941–1942.

through a typical untrammeled wilderness lens discussed in the previous chapter—rugged, peopleless, pristine. But it does more than just create a wilderness of the landscape; it was designed to familiarize people with these mountains, create some sort of attachment to them, and ultimately convince people to visit. Adams's multiple shades and layers draw the viewer into the scene and the careful balance of fore- and backgrounds creates a satisfying sense of completeness. Viewed as it was originally intended to be, as a mural covering an entire wall, the effect would have been powerful. One can imagine potential visitors longing to enter this space physically, to explore its untouched expanses.

These methods continue to influence vernacular landscape photography into the social media era. While scholars like Wendy Harding have illustrated how professional photographers and artists in the late twentieth and early twenty-first century have subverted the traditional western landscape image, focusing heavily on the presence of people, development, and environmental degradation, the art of photography does not always align with vernacular photography. Most contemporary photography produced and consumed is created by amateur photographers with camera phones and shared digitally over social media.[34] Landscape photography within this context overwhelmingly reproduces the wildernessing tropes pioneered by Bierstadt, Adams, and others— sometimes to the point of taking the same picture.

I am guilty of this myself. I took this photo (Figure 15) while in Glacier of the same mountains portrayed in the Adams photograph because it "seemed" like a beautiful perspective. Was I subconsciously being influenced by the images of this land I had seen, primed to see beauty in certain places?

Tourism photography has never been celebrated for its originality, but when put in conversation with place attachment and memory creation, this mimicry can have much deeper impacts. Photography is a "practice that reproduces a dominant set of visual images, at the very same time that it conceals its constructed character."[35] In other words, while photography gives a sense of realism and authenticity, it is actually being created within and influenced by larger worldviews and preconceptions. Sontag argues that photographs must work within an existing and usually hegemonic ideology. "Photographs," she contends, "cannot create a moral position, but they can reinforce one—and can help build a nascent one."[36] Urry and Crawshaw echo this with their

FIGURE 15. The author's photo of Glacier National Park, perhaps inspired by Ansel Adams.

circle of representation. They see tourist photography not so much as memory making as it is memory appropriation.[37] In other words, visitors are forming memories of a place before they physically visit it through the consumption of other people's images and experiences. Their photographs then are created to align with a "memory" of what they have already anticipated the landscape to look like.[38]

Companies selling the explorer archetype draw on these well-established methods for creating place (and product and brand) attachment. They prime potential consumers to create memories not just of the place but of *themselves* in that place and, more to the point, of themselves in the companies' products in that place. Empty landscapes may create place attachment, which, while good for the outdoor industry as a whole, do nothing for an individual company. This is where adventure photography becomes so effective. It makes use of strategies that disguise the mediating photographer, more fully immersing the viewer into the world of the photograph. It is not just being in a certain landscape that makes you an explorer; it is being a certain person in that landscape.

Adventure Photography and the Immersed Consumer

Adventure photography claims land more explicitly than traditional landscape or tourism photography. One of the key motifs of adventure photography is the presence of the explorer—sometimes the photographer themselves and sometimes an anonymous subject—in the photograph. Whether it is the presence of a limb like a hand or foot, a carefully composed shot using the camera's autotimer, or an anonymous figure facing away from the camera, the explorer makes themselves the main subject of their shot. They are usually in the foreground and often in a possessive pose—eyes gazing from a high vantage point, hand grasping a piece of the landscape, boot treading upon the ground, or body traveling through the space. If the empty landscapes of the Romantic painters and early photographers could make the land more attractive, comfortable, and settleable, adventure photography goes the next step by inserting the potential explorer/settler into the space.

Adventure photography is also a departure from traditional tourism photography in that the subject of the photograph is almost always anonymous. Typically, a tourist photograph is captured to prove that the tourist was physically in a place. Parents take pictures of their children or strangers are waylaid to take a picture of a family. Today, this usually expresses itself as a selfie, where the photographer takes a picture of themselves. These are personal photographs. They are meant to be keepsakes or shared with friends and family, people the tourist actually knows. Adventure photographs, especially those used in marketing, are meant to be widely distributed and widely relatable. Therefore, the photograph will feature the subject's feet, the back of their head, or a more distant silhouette. There will almost never be a recognizable face in an adventure photograph. The explorer they show is not some famous sponsor whose adventures are unachievable by the average person; it is not any specific person at all. The idea is that they could be you or me, that they *are* you and me.[39]

The Classic Adventure Image

The most easily recognizable version of this is what I call the classic adventure image, the type of image described at the beginning of this chapter and exemplified by the Bradley Mountain photograph (Figure 16).

FIGURE 16. Bradley Mountain advertisement, "In the Valley with the Wilder Pack," depicting the classic adventure image.

This is a landscape photograph, usually of a grand mountainscape, with no sign of human intervention whatsoever in the background. In the foreground is the explorer, their entire body, photographed from behind by presumably another hiker. This is by far the most common image posted by the outdoor corporations in my survey and is produced and reproduced in user-generated content by their followers. Through the ways the explorer's scale and movement is represented, the classic adventure shot becomes a powerful tool for companies constructing the explorer archetype for their brands.

In these images, the explorer is designed to give scale to the larger-than-life landscapes around them in an "I feel small" trope. Whether looking up at towering peaks, down at plunging canyons, or across vast expanses of water, the solitary figure is dwarfed by their environment. This is a classic throwback to Romanticism, the same strategy used by artists of the Hudson River School like Albert Bierstadt and Thomas Cole. Bierstadt in particular would intentionally exaggerate the landscapes of the American West, using light, menacing weather, and even rearranging mountains to present the land as more dramatic, and ultimately more attractive to potential settlers. The grander the scale, the more effective the advertisement is at making the consumer feel as one viewer of Bierstadt's work put it, "motivated, yet small."[40]

Adventure photography, especially in the context of outdoor retail marketing, but even with normal user-generated content, is in the same business of making outdoor landscapes as attractive to potential visitors as possible—a key aspect of selling the explorer lifestyle. As opposed to portraits or selfies where the person is the subject of the photograph, taking up most of the frame, the classic adventure pose centers the landscape as the subject, using the small figure to emphasize the grand scale of the environment. This sentiment is sometimes reiterated explicitly in the caption with the poster remarking on how small they feel in the landscape, how humbled they are, or how large or special or unique the landscape around them is, signaling to the consumer who may have not been moved by the image itself what emotion it is intended to evoke.

Again, like the Romantics, photographers make strategic use of light to increase the drama of the landscape. Sometimes referred to as "chasing the light," capturing the right light can transform an image. Photographers often seek to work at golden hour, at dawn or dusk when the sun is low on the horizon, creating dramatic shadows and casting everything in an atmospheric golden glow. For adventure photographers shooting far from roads, this means trekking at times an average hiker is unlikely to be out—in the dark, often on rough trails—to dramatic locations to get the shot they are looking for.

The landscape is then further romanticized in the post-processing phase. While photographs are generally assumed to be more accurate representations of land than the Hudson River School paintings, to assume what you see in an image is what you will see if you physically go to the location would be optimistic. You no longer need to be an expert to edit your photos. Preset filters on Instagram and other apps allow photographers to add layers over the image and quick, easy-to-use mobile editing apps give them the power to adjust light, exposure, contrast, and other aspects of the photo before posting it. These filters are integrated into the social media platforms in such a way that they are part of the posting process itself. In other words, users do not think about post-processing as a separate step or additional mediation, but rather as akin to adding a caption or geotag, a finishing touch before sharing.[41]

Instagram filters in particular seem perfectly designed to reinforce the nostalgia inherent in the explorer archetype. When the app was re-leased, it was designed to re-create the look and feel of the instant Polar-oid cameras, including requiring photos to be cropped into a square and leaning heavily on filters that reproduced the desaturated look of faded or yellowed photographs or other imperfections of analog photography. While Instagram eventually moved away from these restrictions, allow-ing rectangular photos and building more specialized editing tools, the production of authenticity at the center of the platform remained. While a photograph posted may be hypersaturated and high resolution, the very fact that it is posted on Instagram gives it an amateur and authentic pa-tina. Viewers recognize that the photograph was taken by an everyday explorer looking through the screen of their smartphone and forget that the bright and colorful landscape is not what they would in reality see.

Finally, adventure photography includes a trajectory, a sense of movement and direction. While the figure is always in the foreground, it is made clear that they are already moving through the space, an active figure on a passive backdrop. The passivity of the land is the key aspect here. The explorer's purpose is to uncover and to conquer. Or to ride a skateboard on your hands down the middle of a highway.[42]

FIGURE 17. Goal Zero advertisement, "California Desert," demonstrating trajectory through space in an adventure image.

As unrealistic as it is, this Goal Zero post is a prime example of using the adventure image to sell a product. Goal Zero is a company that sells solar-powered charging devices, but you would not know it from seeing this photograph. The photograph has all the pieces of a great adventure image: the high vantage point, the anonymous figure, the vast, empty landscape—deserts have a particularly complex history of being representationally emptied—and the subject actively moving into and through the space. By not featuring any of their products, the photograph also has the feel of user-generated content (UGC), or content created organically by someone not associated with the company. As I covered previously, UGC is far more effective in brand and trust building than traditional advertising. In reality, the photographer, Travis Burke, is a professional adventure photographer with over eight hundred thousand followers on Instagram and this image was likely commissioned. The point is that they do not need to feature their products. They are selling a lifestyle of adventure and risk taking. "Get out, stay out" is their motto. If their followers choose to pursue this lifestyle, to emulate the type of explorer figures regularly featured by the brand, they will eventually need the product regardless, not so much because they necessarily need a solar charger, but because a solar charger becomes part of the costume required of an explorer.

The Portal Image

The portal image is a variation on the classic adventure image that relies on the use of a frame within the image itself, creating a window through which the explorer, the subject of the photograph, views the landscape. Sometimes this is literally a window, often the windshield of a car, but it can be any frame that exists between the explorer and their landscape. The back of a truck and the door of a tent are the most common, but caves, arches, trees, and even taking a picture through the lens of a second camera can serve as the portals through which the explorer sees. Like in all adventure photography, a metonym of the explorer is present in the foreground, within the portal. Typically, this is the explorer's feet as he or she photographs from a lying position, but sometimes it is the entire body, a piece of gear, or a pet. The actual object does not matter as it is always representative of the explorer themselves.

In addition to the strategies employed in the classic adventure shot, the portal image reinforces the explorer archetype in new ways. First, it helps disguise the artificiality of the photograph—blurring the barriers between the physical consumer, the photographer, and the photographer as the subject/explorer. The explorer—or their feet, their guitar, their sleeping bag—becomes a conduit, a space in between, through which the consumer looking at the photograph on Instagram can more easily imagine themselves in that place. In the classic adventure photograph, the consumer is meant to identify with the anonymous explorer, but the portal image, by positioning the explorer as always already one step removed from the landscape, a viewer themselves, creates an even stronger affinity between the consumer and the explorer. Focused on the feet of the explorer, the invisible camera seems to move out into the same physical space occupied by the consumer.

Point-of-view photography like that commonly used in portal images is designed to create an environment, for the consumer, akin to virtual reality. The use of professional athletes and explorers, sponsorships, and traditional product placements is of course a powerful and proven method to get people to buy products. If an Olympic skier, a famous

FIGURE 18. Huckberry advertisement, "There are things known," demonstrating a classic portal shot, August 4, 2017.

mountain climber, or a National Geographic photographer is using a product, there must be something special about it. But all those people are proxies and aspirations for the consumer. They themselves being in the places, using the products virtually, precludes the need of those proxies and creates a much more powerful connection—the digital version of enclothed cognition.

Michele Zappavigna calls this type of point-of-view photography "subjectivity." Beyond merely seeing from the place of the photographer, the viewer "imagines oneself as being" the photographer.[43] In photographic social distance, a system developed by Gunther Kress and Theo van Leeuwen, subjectivity creates the most intimate connection between the subject and the viewer—to the point that they become indistinguishable. This indistinguishability is important when you put it in conversation with Kress and Leeuwen's system of power relationships. Kress and Leeuwen argue that a high-angle shot, which most adventure photographs use, suggests that the photographer or photographer's subject has power over the object of the photograph, in this case the

FIGURE 19. Goal Zero advertisement, "Well, you can't win em all," demonstrating another portal shot.

landscape.[44] Since in portal images, the viewer and the subject are intimately connected, the viewer is able to put themselves in this position of power before ever actually entering that space.

At the same time, as much as the portal draws you in visually, it also creates a divide between the explorer and world beyond, reinforcing the otherness of the landscape and its construction as wilderness, a barrier that protects the wilderness from the contradiction of human presence. As discussed earlier, in "The Trouble with Wilderness," William Cronon explores this contradiction, calling it the "central paradox" of wilderness. Cronon argues that "if we believe that nature, to be true, must also be wild, then our very presence in nature represents its fall."[45] The more closely associated a person is with land, the more they are immersed in it, the less the land can be considered wilderness, as something apart, something other.

The explorer, however, is antithetical to wilderness. They can only exist as a result of this separation. The portal image positions the explorer as both in the space and not in the space at the same time, harkening back to the "in, but not of" construction of the explorer. Visually, if not actually, the portal overcomes Cronon's contradiction.[46]

Road and Trail Images

Road and trail images, like the Goal Zero skateboarding picture, are another way of drawing the viewer into the landscape. Unlike portal images, in which the viewer is passive, often lying down, road images are active. They involve a person physically moving through the space, as on the skateboard, or the movement can be implied by just showing the road itself or the front of a vehicle. In the former case, these images take advantage of the anonymity I described in the classic image section where the model becomes a stand-in for the viewer. In the latter case, these images become point-of-view images in a similar move as the portal images with the viewer bypassing the anonymous stand-in model and embodying the explorer themselves.

The most important characteristic of road and trail images is that they make use of leading lines, one of the most basic techniques in photographic composition. Leading lines are designed to draw the eye of the viewer naturally in toward the main subject of the photograph. As the viewer's attention is drawn along the line, in this case the road or trail, they become more fully immersed in the image, focusing in on the wilderness scene in the background. Like the physical function of roads and trails, their function in images is not to be part of the wilderness, but to get you there in a quick and easy fashion. Sometimes road and trail images will make use of "paths" rather than leading lines. The only difference is where leading lines lead the viewer to the wilderness, often ending in the crest of a hill or a mountain, paths lead the viewer through the wilderness, a journey unto itself.

Both roads and trails also have important implicit meaning embedded in them. Paved or even gravel roads give the sense of extended possibility and have an especially affective appeal to road-trip-obsessed Americans. The appeal of the open road is practically synonymous with adventure and exploration, with some of the most iconic American stories centering on road trips like Kerouac's *On the Road* or Steinbeck's *Grapes of Wrath*. Road-trip films are a staple of American cinema. Netflix for example has coded 156 distinct categories of road-trip movies—granted categories like "Critically Acclaimed Witty Road-Trip Comedies" and "Emotional Independent Road-Trip Dramas" are pretty niche. The emergence of #vanlife on Instagram and into mainstream culture, documenting the travels and adventures of people and families who live full-time in vans or RVs, speaks to the continued fascination with exploring on the road. Road-adventure images draw on these already existing connections between road trips and more vague American ideals of freedom and exploration to connect viewers to the portrayed landscapes and products.

At the same time, roads do not always fit well into the wilderness myth. Roads are extremely unnatural, often straight features cutting mercilessly across landscapes, immediately and visibly out of place. They are also disruptive to ecosystems, creating artificial divides that can seriously damage the continuity of animal and plant habitats. Both physically and metaphorically, they are pathways that bring the outside, civilized world into the primitive wilderness. They are so antithetical to wilderness that the Wilderness Society's first definition of *wilderness* was literally a roadless area, a priority the organization continues to champion. They were instrumental in the passing of the 2001 Roadless Area Conservation Rule that governs forestry in the U.S. and the Roadless Area Conservation Act of 2021.[47]

While roads might not fit well into the wilderness ideal, trails are apparently considered completely natural. A trail photo has all the strategic imagery of a road image without the paradox having a road through a wilderness creates. Trails are crooked and winding, and seemingly naturally occurring—although they are often laboriously constructed and maintained. They are still active, but at a slower pace. They still draw the viewer into the scene, but unlike a rigid, constructed road, trails are organic, giving the traveler more agency either in the reinforcement of the trail or in breaking from the trail. This extra agency is important, especially for companies selling the explorer archetype. For marketers, the more agency a consumer feels like they have over their experience of an image, the more likely they are to forge an attachment to the subject of the image—even if the agency is a carefully crafted illusion.

The Light Shines in the Darkness

There is another genre of adventure photography showing explorers literally bringing light to dark places. In addition to having the same charac-

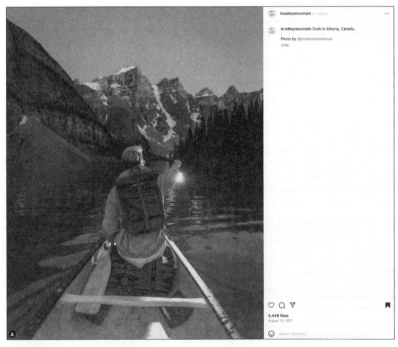

FIGURE 20. Bradley Mountain advertisement, "Dusk in Alberta, Canada," showing a light in the dark adventure shot.

teristics as other adventure photographs, they are usually at night or in a dark space like a cave, and the explorer themselves becomes less of a focus than the light they bear. A lantern held aloft, penetrating the darkness and exposing the unknown, a powerful beam connecting the explorer upward to the stars or downward to the earth. On both a symbolic and a technical level, these photographs further reinforce the explorer archetype; they are contemporary, physical manifestations of the explorer's mission to create dark places so that they might then bring them light.

From a technical standpoint, these photographs use many of the same strategies as other adventure shots including leading lines, anonymity, and the illusion of agency. It is the light that operationalizes these techniques, especially in regard to giving the viewer agency. In addition to the movement through space in these photos, the act of bringing light is an empowering one for the subject of the photograph and thus also for the viewer for whom the model is a proxy. Beyond the symbolic nature of light, it is a way to act upon and change the landscape without

FIGURE 21. Clif Bar advertisement, "That awe-inspiring moment," showing another light-in-the-darkness shot.

impacting the wilderness of the place, an attribute that of course relies on the lack of human impact. For example, in this image from Clif
Bar, the subject projects their light ahead of them into the darkness,
tethering distant wild spaces to themselves while leaving the spaces
physically untouched.[48] They are using light to extend their reach into
areas that, unlike most landscapes, remain truly unexplored. The hiker's
light merges with the light of the stars and Milky Way above them. The
symbolic gaze into outer space becomes analogous to the more physical
movement through the terrestrial landscape.

The Accoutrements of the Explorer

The final explorer image I want to highlight is the gear shot. This is a
picture from above, showing all the gear the photographer is presumably
taking with them on their voyage, meticulously styled. Again, these are
usually complete constructs, designed to evoke a fantasy of exploration
rather than an actual outdoor experience. When looking at these adventure photographs, it can be easy to forget that these are companies that
are selling products, not just stories and worldviews—especially when
they may not ever feature the products they are selling. The gear shots
flip that problem. They focus on the products, the physical stuff an explorer carries with them, but it does not take much probing to see how
the items in these photographs still contribute to the explorer narrative.
Figure 22 is from Bradley Mountain, a company that relies heavily on
shots like these, and is typical of this style. This is a busy image, but there
are a few things I want to point out.[49]

First, notice the focus on instruments of visuality. There are four
cameras, five including the one presumably taking the photo, all of them
antique. Modern cameras are lighter, more accurate, and more conve-
nient than vintage cameras, but a mobile phone camera just does not
quite capture the era of exploration the same way a 1950s Bolex 8mm
does. There are also binoculars and an additional lens. These items easily
outnumber those serving any other single purpose. This is not surprising given the centrality of photography to the outdoor adventure community, but alongside the jar of rocks, the pine cones, the antlers, the
coral, and the leather journal, it also points to the propensity of explorers
to collect and record. Collecting and recording are about the personal
memories for the individual hiker, simultaneously about nostalgia and

FIGURE 22. Bradley Mountain advertisement, "The Pine Collections," demonstrating an overhead gear shot.

authenticity, but historically they have also been critical parts of state building. In fact, the primary purpose of exploration was always to collect and record, to map and document, to make land known and legible, the vanguard to the expansion of power and authority over a previously unconquered space. Contemporary state- or corporate-sponsored explorers have maintained the need to document, usually through photography. While not necessarily intentional, that documentation and its eventual dissemination continue to play a remarkably similar role regarding who is seen to have power and control over the place recorded.

Second, let's consider the arrow. Is this person going to be hunting their own food? Where is the bow? In the context of Americans and the environment, arrows are often closely associated with American Indians, the "primitive" and natural counterpart to the more industrial firearm. However, while "playing Indian" is an American pastime, I do not think that is all that is happening here. In this case, the arrow is, like the vintage camera, signaling authenticity, a move away from modern technology. Anachronism is common in nostalgic fantasies, so the fact that firearms definitely existed throughout all of American history and would fit perfectly within any era being reenacted is irrelevant. The arrow represents a rejection of modern, technology-based interactions with the outdoors—narratively, if not actually.

Finally, the book. In this particular photograph, it is a vintage copy of C. S. Lewis's *Perelandra,* an allegorical, Christian, space exploration novel about a man from Earth who arrives on an Edenic planet whose people never experienced the Fall of Man and is the second in Lewis's Space Trilogy. Other texts that show up in Bradley Mountain's gear shots are *National Geographic* magazines, the Apollo 12 issue of *Life* magazine, and the Bible. These are really interesting choices of texts and a departure from the nonfiction nature writing of people like John Muir, Jon Krakauer, or Bill Bryson I expected to see. However, they fit the explorer narrative. Space is perhaps the only real wilderness, a truly unpeopled place that is just waiting to be filled with whatever fantasy we wish to create, avoiding all the messy realities and contradictions of earth. Furthermore, they explicitly connect exploration to Christianity, something that was often central to the explorers that outdoorspeople emulate but gets left out of most contemporary versions of the narrative. By including texts like these, Bradley Mountain is selling literal narratives along with its products.

In this chapter, I wanted to connect adventure photography and the outdoor industry's marketing strategy with the colonial archetype of the explorer, and the methods they use to promote and reproduce this representation. Drawing from a deep and long-standing fascination with the explorer figure in American culture and society, contemporary outdoorspeople inhabit this identity when they participate in outdoor adventure travel and they reproduce it in the images they share over social media. While the connection between outdoor recreation and exploration is not new, the adoption of the archetype for marketing by outdoor retailers and its proliferation over social media has created a feedback loop of representation that has further cemented the explorer as the most important figure within outdoor recreation.

This is a symbolic claiming of the land, empire through narrative control and representation. I in no way want to downplay the power of the symbolic. Symbol and myth have long been important tools in empire building and colonialism in the United States and elsewhere. From the dime novels about conquering heroes like Daniel Boone and Kit Carson to the Romantic landscapes painted in service of manifest destiny to contemporary corporations peddling the explorer to every hiker and climber to scroll through their social media feeds, it is these representations, these curated, secondhand experiences, that shape expectations, goals, beliefs, and assumed entitlement of the largely white, wealthy consumer. As these representations are produced, consumed, reproduced, reinterpreted, and re-consumed, they become part of a collective identity, accepted and, importantly, acted upon. Representation matters.

The examples are mostly drawn from Instagram as part of my digital ethnography, but I want to stress that Instagram is merely the primary home for outdoor digital marketing at this moment, and if you are reading this book five or ten years from when it was written, the platform itself may be hopelessly outdated. However, due to the strength of the collective production of these images, I would expect many of these motifs and strategies to transfer to the next image-based platform becoming prominent, and, of course, the underlying narratives of exploration and exploitation will likely remain the same for many years to come.

However, these representations do not exist in some digital void, disconnected from the material realities of people physically on the land. The culture that has developed around the outdoor retail industry, strengthened and reinforced by the industry's representation of the land as wilderness and its consumers as explorers, has created a community of people devoted to making real the fantasy they play out every day over social media. This is realized through a commitment to a set of land politics that, while consistent with traditional left-wing environmental ethics, are still deeply tied to colonial capitalism and state empire building. In the following chapter, I will break down the real-world impacts these representations have and how they contribute to the ongoing structure of settler colonialism.

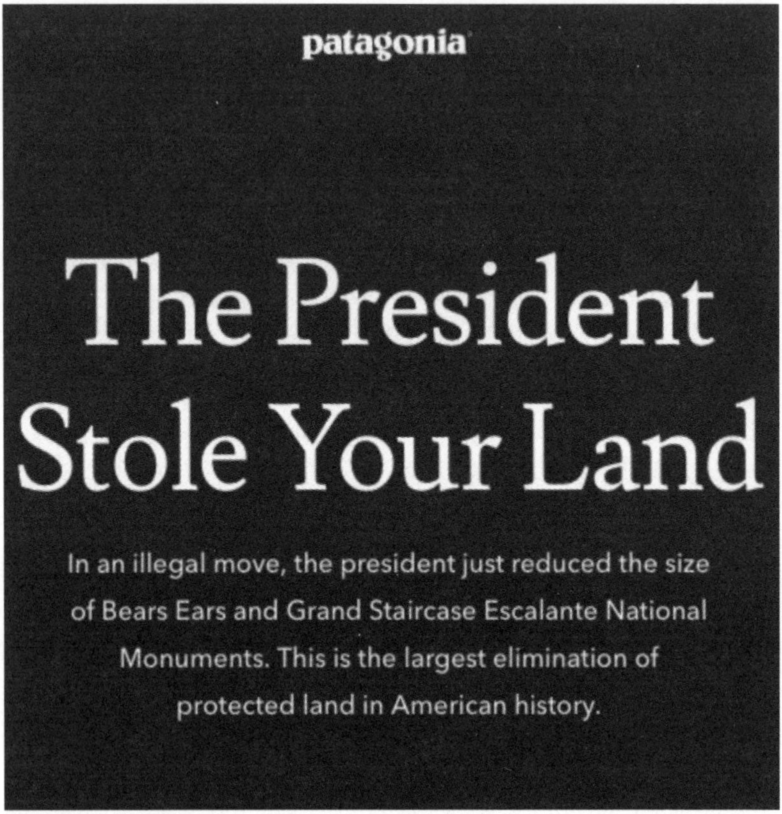

FIGURE 23. Home page from Patagonia making the political statement that "The President Stole Your Land," December 2017.

‹ **5** ›

The President Stole Your Land

This belongs to all of the people in America. It's our heritage.

—Yvon Chouinard, "Why Patagonia Is Fighting for Public Lands"

On December 4, 2017, President Trump signed an executive order to reduce the size of Bears Ears National Monument by 85 percent. Bears Ears (Shásh Jaa' in Diné) had been recently created under the Obama administration and consisted of over 1.3 million acres of important cultural and recreational sites in southern Utah. Its reduction galvanized a broad response from a diverse range of public land stakeholders, including tribes, environmentalist organizations, and outdoor corporations. From a distance, these groups seemed aligned in their purpose, brought together for the common goal of protecting the environment and thwarting the Trump administration's extraction-centered policies. A closer look, however, reveals that while the objectives of tribes and corporations might intersect at Bears Ears, their relationships to the land and long-term vision for the future of public lands remain at odds.[1] While Indigenous people sought to use the designation as a decolonizing measure, protecting sacred spaces and giving tribal governments land management power, the outdoor corporations' relationship to the land remained fundamentally extractive and colonial, centering the wilderness model of public land needed to sell their products.

While this inherent dissonance between the land ethics of Indigenous people and the outdoor recreation industry has played out repeatedly in public land and conservation conflicts over the last century and a half, previously the agency of Indigenous people had largely been reactive, acts of resistance against and strategic utilization of the dominating media and political power of the industry.[2] Bears Ears, however, marked a shift in this relationship. The monument had been proposed by Indigenous people, included full comanagement by local tribes, and centered contemporary Indigenous presence and priorities in ways no other monument previously had. This co-option of the historically settler colonial national monument system was a direct attack on the wilderness ideology of the outdoor industry, a reimagining of protected public lands as Indigenous spaces, fully integrated with contemporary communities rather than primarily recreational spaces fundamentally separate from human society.

In this chapter, I unpack Patagonia's response to the Bears Ears controversy as an example of how the outdoor industry countered this Indigenous, decolonial appropriation of the lands and policies that they had spent decades carefully cultivating for their own benefit. I describe how they turned a land conflict into a marketing opportunity and changed what could have been a transformational debate around Indigenous relationships to land into a nonthreatening one about settler—or consumer—relationships to it. Rather than directly challenging Indigenous people's rhetoric, the company presented it as simply another appendage of the larger battle against extractive industry, equivalent to the concerns of other stakeholders like climbers, runners, and western archaeologists. They sidelined contemporary Indigeneity, realigning the spectrum of the conflict from a decolonial/colonial one to a preservation/extraction one, neutralizing the threat by ensuring all possible outcomes fall within a settler colonial paradigm.

Patagonia's marketing campaign is a contemporary example of the process of wildernessing and the maintenance of an increasingly challenged wilderness ideology. Despite the media and political performance of controversy and debate, the status quo was ultimately maintained at Bears Ears, and what began with the potential to be a radical shift toward Indigenous resource sovereignty within the national monument system ended as a painfully familiar landscape of extractive wasteland and recreational wilderness, public land's dual forces of settler colonialism. Bears Ears is both a story of Indigenous resilience, organizational power, and political potential as well as an example of the adaptability of colonial power and the limits of public land's ability to serve the needs of Indigenous people.

Background on Bears Ears

The original protection of Bears Ears National Monument was the result of a coalition. The American Indian nations in the region watched for years as this rich cultural and spiritual site was pillaged by generations of graverobbers and pothunters. A long history of relatively sedentary civilizations combined with a dry climate has made the southwestern United States a popular site for pothunters since Mormon and American settlers first entered the area in the nineteenth century. Over the years, it has attracted an army of amateur archaeologists, digging haphazardly through ruined buildings and graves, searching for arrowheads, pottery shards, and, most prized of all, Indian skulls. Gravedigging became so popular that outings known as "skeleton picnics" were centered around the activity. For profit and pleasure, groups would head out into the desert armed with shovels, desecrating grave after grave in search of the valuable artifacts.[3]

With over a hundred thousand archaeological sites spread throughout its nearly two million acres—among the densest collection of sites anywhere in the United States—the Bears Ears area had been a center of much of this activity. Although, as federal land, the sites within Bears Ears were technically protected under the Archaeological Resource Protection Act of 1979 (ARPA) and the Native American Graves Protection and Repatriation Act of 1990 (NAGRPA), the primary agency in charge of enforcing these laws, the Bureau of Land Management (BLM), dedicated only a single law enforcement officer to the entirety of San Juan County. Even if controlling the acquisition and trade of American Indian artifacts were top priority for the BLM, managing such a large area with such limited resources would be impossible. Furthermore, BLM land allows for a wide variety of legal uses that threaten cultural resources including mining, grazing, and ATV use.

The Bears Ears Intertribal Coalition arose out of the need to address this issue, bringing together the Hopi, Navajo, Ute, Ute Mountain, and Zuni Nations to advocate for more formal protection of the area in the form of a national monument.[4] From the beginning, this advocacy was about protecting an Indigenous connection to the land. The coalition, setting aside historic differences, united around a shared understanding of Bears Ears as a spiritually and culturally significant space and a shared fear that, if something was not done, it could be destroyed forever. The original proposal emphasized practicing traditional art, medicine, and land management as appropriate uses and reasons for preservation. This monument was to be about protecting Indigenous pasts and decentered outdoor recreation. Except for limiting or banning ATV use, recreation and tourism were not mentioned.

On December 28, 2016, the coalition's proposal was accepted, and President Obama used his executive authority under the Antiquities Act of 1906 to create Bears Ears National Monument, including 1.3 million of the 1.9 million originally proposed acres. This was considered a major success for the tribes as it was the first national monument to be proposed by Indigenous people and the first to be equally comanaged by federal agencies and tribes. While extremely important to the tribes of the Southwest and contentious among the non-Indigenous residents of San Juan County, the newly formed Bears Ears National Monument remained largely unknown on a national level and low on the list of destinations for outdoor recreation. However, less than a year later, when the new Trump administration threatened to reduce the size of Bears Ears, this little-known monument became an unlikely rallying point in a much larger political row.

The monument's creation—which came along with tribal comanagment—was seen as a victory for both tribal resource sovereignty and environmental preservation. National monuments have typically been seen as a way to protect resources in perpetuity, and the tribes considered it an acceptable compromise since the ultimate goal of full land repatriation seemed out of reach. The National Park Service, the agency in charge of managing national monuments, has had a difficult, even violent, history with American Indians, and Bears Ears seemed to be the beginning of what could be a more productive relationship.

This turned out not to be the case. On April 26, 2017, President Trump issued Executive Order 13792 requiring the reassessment of twenty-seven large (over a hundred thousand acres) and recently created (since 1996) national monuments. Bears Ears at the time was the second largest national monument in the contiguous United States, was located in a state generally hostile to federal interference, and was deemed to have the potential for significant multiple-use management (i.e., energy extraction). It represented exactly the kind of protected land the administration sought to eliminate and was among those recommended for reduction. This announcement galvanized thousands of activists from Indigenous, corporate, and environmental groups who organized to defend Bears Ears specifically, and public, environmentally protected lands in America more generally. Despite the pushback, President Trump and Secretary of the Interior Ryan Zinke followed through on the recommendation, removing over a million acres of Bears Ears National Monument and nearby Grand Staircase-Escalante National Monument from their protective designation.[5] That area included thousands of American Indian cultural resources that the Department of the Interior deemed "not of significant scientific or historic interest."[6]

Since the decision to reassess the protected land of twenty-six national monuments was announced in the spring of 2017, President Trump and the Department of the Interior had consistently maintained that the decision was about curbing federal overreach around the Antiquities Act, making sure that the land protected reflected the original intent of the legislation. They specifically assured the country that this was in no way about oil and gas extraction in Bears Ears. However, emails secured by the *New York Times* under the Freedom of Information Act reveal a different story. Emails between Utah senator Orrin Hatch and employees at the BLM and DOI from March 2017, a month before the reassessment was announced, contained both a discussion of state-level oil and gas interests within Bears Ears and a map with redrawn boundaries resolving mineral conflicts in the area—boundaries that were eventually incorporated into the reduction later that year.

While this proved to be the smoking gun showing that oil and gas were at least considered when redrawing Bears Ears' boundaries, the documents also make clear that oil and gas were an important part of the conversation around the reassessment and likely part of the reason for the order itself. For example, soon after taking office, President Trump ordered a comprehensive assessment of oil and gas resources in national park and monument land. Bears Ears was shown to contain the potential for silver, copper, iron, salt, potash, gravel, coal, uranium, vanadium, and of course, oil and gas.[7] Emails show that gas and oil were also discussed during the conversation around Canyon of the Ancients National Monuments in Colorado—a monument that was saved largely due to public outcry by Coloradans.[8]

The correspondences between Senator Hatch and various federal agencies further reveals just how arbitrary and flexible the justifications for this kind of resource appropriation can be. Senator Hatch's initial argument against Bears Ears National Monument, stated in a December 2016 letter of dissent to President Obama, was that the designation would be harmful to the tribes in the region. He went so far as to suggest that tribal leaders had been hoodwinked into supporting the national monument with the false promise of comanagement of the monument, a promise Hatch argues is outside the DOI's authority to make and is "one of the most alarming aspects of [the] prospective action."[9] However, as described above, tribes and Indigenous activist organizations were not only in support of the monument without outside coercion but had been the central impetus for establishing the monument. If there were any doubt, the Ute Mountain Tribe made sure to send explicit letters of support for the monument after a leadership change.[10] Furthermore, comanagement and the establishment of such an arrangement is legal, does not need congressional approval as Hatch claimed, has precedent on other federal lands—although not in a national monument—and was accepted by Secretary Zinke.[11]

Undeterred, Hatch switched his focus to the impact that removing national monument protection would have on schools. In Utah, the State and Industrial Trust Land Administration (SITLA) manages and leases land to provide funding for schools—the fact that school funding is tied to extractive industries and land grants in the first place is another interesting colonial aspect of this situation, but is outside the scope of this project. When some of the land owned by SITLA was included in Bears Ears, it was very easy for Hatch to argue that by removing this land from the leasing market, it would negatively impact education. Hatch and SITLA even submitted a map with a revised border for the monument that would "resolve all mineral conflicts," which excluded from the monument the 109,000 acres of SITLA land.[12] This line of argument proved to be more successful as the map was eventually incorporated into the DOI's border revisions. It seems clear, however, that educational funding was merely an excuse, a point of argument useful in the back-and-forth between Hatch and the DOI since in the end, it was not just the 100,000 or so acres of SITLA land that was removed from the monument, but 1.1 million acres of land encompassing many of the mineral resources the BLM had identified the previous January.

More revealing than what was left out of the redrawn boundaries—the United States' valuing oil, gas, and mineral resources over Indigenous cultural heritage is unsurprising—is what the DOI chose to include in the remaining two hundred thousand acres. The two noncontiguous units, Indian Creek and Shash Jaa, contain the original monument's most celebrated climbing routes and its most dramatic and photogenic natural and archaeological sites, respectively. For the Intertribal Coalition, this was a double blow. Not only were some of the most important and endangered sites left unprotected, including Cedar Mesa, but the conversation around protection had also shifted from focusing on Indigenous resources and heritage to recreational heritage. For the outdoor industry, however, this was at worst a mixed success. They had failed to prevent the reduction of over a million acres of protected land, but the most popular recreational sites remained. More importantly, the visibility and agency of contemporary Indigenous people, an existential threat to the industry and its wilderness model, were sidelined. This outcome was the result of many factors including President Trump's energy policies, Senator Hatch's anti-federalism, and lobbying by oil and gas companies, but among them is the outdoor industry itself. In its fervor to protect public land from the threat of development by extractive energy, it closed ranks with them to form a settler colonial narrative set against the decolonial goals of the tribes and the potential of what Bears Ears could have been.

"The President Stole Your Land": The Outdoor Industry's Investment in Public Land

It should not come as a surprise that the debate around public lands is the issue that forced the outdoor industry to start flexing its political muscle. In the United States, free, accessible outdoor space is the foundation of the industry and the vast majority of this is federal and state public land. While the smaller outdoor companies may feel that it is important to stay apolitical or risk losing part of their market, the larger corporations fully understand the role public land plays in their industry. In their immediate response to the president's announcement, *Outside Magazine* stated that the industry "would not exist were it not for our public lands and the $887 billion outdoor recreation industry they help support," and in a separate article editor Abe Streep called public land the "610-million acre ballpark for gearmakers' $887 billion game."[13] Critics of the outdoor industry understand this as well, with Terry Anderson writing in the *Wall Street Journal* that public land was an "enormous subsidy from the American Taxpayer" for the "rock-climbing industrial complex."[14] In this conflict, outdoor corporations faced a double threat. On one hand, federal reduction of protected land threatened the land base for their products, but the solution being offered—increased Indigenous sovereignty that reduced the industry's control over outdoor recreation—was just as dangerous. The outdoor industry is invested in the idea and reality of wilderness-based public lands and, to use their own metaphor, is willing to go to war for them.

The original proposal for Bears Ears was entirely Indigenous centric. It was an intertribal coalition focusing on resource sovereignty, comanagement, and the protection of cultural and religious sites with no mention at all of recreation as a reason for preserving the area. However, when Bears Ears rose to national attention after President Trump's April 2017 executive order, what started with the potential to be a nuanced conversation about public lands, one that included Indigenous people and their rights, was quickly co-opted by other interests. As Bears Ears began to filter into mainstream media and gain greater attention—largely thanks to social media activism on Twitter and Instagram—the outdoor retail industry, including companies like Patagonia, REI, and The North Face, was quick to get involved.

In the year leading up to the official reduction of Bears Ears and Trump's December 4, 2017, announcement, the outdoor industry moved from strategic marketing to overt political action. Three of the largest outdoor companies—REI, The North Face, and Patagonia—dedicated the valuable home pages for their websites to public land advocacy. Patagonia went the furthest, actually replacing their normal home page with a new landing page (Figure 24). The all-black page was emblazoned with large white letters reading, "The President Stole Your Land," and in a smaller font, "In an illegal move, the president just reduced the size of Bears Ears and Grand Staircase-Escalante National Monuments. This is the largest elimination of protected land in American history."[15] They also sued President Trump.

This was a bold move for an industry that has traditionally attempted to stay out of politics and a victory of sorts for Patagonia, which had previously struggled to get the rest of the industry on board with their version of politicized corporate responsibility. The outdoor industry generated $887 billion in consumer spending, employed 7.6 million people, and contributed $412 billion to total U.S. Gross Domestic Product or about 2.2 percent of the U.S. economy.[16] Yet despite being in the economic big leagues, when it comes to political clout and power, they have barely been in the game at all. In an interview with *Outside Magazine,* Patagonia founder Yvon Chouinard called the rest of the industry "a bunch of weenies" saying they were "afraid of their own shadow" and they "suck the life out of outdoor resources and give nothing away."[17] Harsh criticism from a man who has built a billion-dollar company using these same outdoor resources, but it seemed that the threat to Bears Ears finally pushed other companies to change their tune.

REI, for example, changed their profile picture across social media to a graphic reading "We [heart] Our Public Lands" and, while still trying to take a bipartisan stance, directly called out the Trump administration as failing to serve the American people. This bipartisan approach was reflected in their associated hashtag #UnitedOutside, which argues for finding common ground in the outdoors and was used over fourteen thousand times in its first twenty-four hours. The North Face dedicated a rare nine-photo spread on Instagram to the Utah Diné Bikéyah logo with text explaining that they donated $100,000 to the creation of a Bears Ears education center. "We are all equally welcome on our nation's public land," they explain, "They need us as much as we need them."[18] Chaco Sandals posted on their website and social media that they are "Standing Strong for Public Lands," and are supporting the Bears Ears Intertribal Coalition in their protests.[19] Arc'teryx, Black Diamond, and the Outdoor Industry Association all made statements of support for Bears Ears and criticisms of the Trump decision. While most of the smaller outdoor companies did not mention Bears Ears or make political statements, many are still members of the Outdoor Industry Association, which made a strong statement and employs lobbyists fighting for public lands. The companies that did make statements command a collective social media following larger than all the other member companies combined.

While from an uncritical perspective it appeared that the outdoor industry was allying with the tribes in their fight to preserve their hard-won victory, in many ways the involvement of the outdoor industry is a backlash against Indigenous people using what was intended to be a tourist land designation to reclaim some level of sovereignty over their homelands. Increased Indigenous sovereignty over public land is a threat to the outdoor industry, potentially limiting recreational use and general accessibility, another competing interest the industry does not need. The Bears Ears situation could have been about the U.S. government's attack on an Indigenous-managed national monument or about whether public land was the right route for Indigenous resource protection at all, but the industry made sure the debate was instead about whether the proper use of public land should be recreation or extraction. Creating this false binary precluded a discussion of the land's complex history and politics, keeping all potential future uses for the land within the bounds of a settler colonial system.

The marketing strategies companies used to shape the debate mirror long-established strategies of settler colonialism like Indigenous erasure and assimilation. Many companies, for example, failed to acknowledge the tribal coalition, which has spent years fighting for the protection of this land and the right to use it at all, keeping the monument's rich cultural history completely out of the frame. This is Indigenous erasure. For others, it was used to create a false equivalency between claims on the land by Indigenous people and claims by non-Indigenous outdoor recreators. This is assimilation, eliminating the claims of Indigeneity by eliminating the difference between Indigenous and settler experiences. I expand on both of these strategies below.

The social media networks and influence these companies had carefully built, the type of network power discussed in the previous chapter, became critical tools in this new campaign. These companies posted high-quality photos of Bears Ears on social media highlighting its "untrammeled wilderness" and recreational opportunities. Companies like Patagonia, which alone commanded over five million followers on Instagram, quickly came to dominate the representation of Bears Ears, generally prepping potential visitors to see the space as an empty wilderness, the perfect place for adventure tourists to climb, run, and explore—using their products, of course.[20]

The Bears Ears campaigns put forth by these companies were couched in the language of conservation—both environmental conservation and the political conservation of a particular kind of public land system. However, for the outdoor industry, this translates into a fight for corporate profits. Fundamentally, the conservation of a public land system is also the conservation of the economic system upon which public lands rely. In a less subtle move, the extent to which the outdoor industry's interest in Bears Ears was at least as fiscal as it was environmental is revealed in the ways the companies capitalized on the publicity through marketing. Activism sells, green sells, and it did not take long to discover that Bears Ears sells.

Many companies dabbled in marketing around Bears Ears. Chaco Sandals, for example, produced a line of products around Bears Ears. Specially designed sandals, wristwraps, and T-shirts inspired by the

FIGURE 24. Chaco products from 2017 created as part of their campaign around Bears Ears National Monument.

landscape were used to raise awareness about the conflict, generate money for the monument's defense—all net proceeds for the products were donated to Diné Bikéyah and Friends of Cedar Mesa—and herald Chaco's political investment in it.[21] Wisconsin-based Wigwam Socks produced a product around Bears Ears, although apart from its name, the vaguely southwestern design has little connection to Bears Ears specifically. Other companies like Arc'teryx, The North Face, and REI also incorporated Bears Ears in their activism-based marketing.

Patagonia, emerging as the main driver of political action within the industry, took this the furthest, making the conflict a centerpiece of their marketing strategy for the year, an important appeal to its young, liberal market base. While their posts about Bears Ears make up only a small portion of their total posts—mostly appearing in spring 2017 when the monument was initially threatened and again in December when it was officially reduced—no other location or issue was featured more often or more regularly on their Instagram account. Furthermore, while most of Patagonia's posts were basic adventure shots sourced from their sponsored athletes, many of the posts featuring Bears Ears were in-house produced photographs or videos that were meant to be tied much more closely to their larger marketing campaigns, company brand, and image.[22]

Patagonia is ostensibly telling two narratives of Bears Ears through this collection of posts, both that of outdoor recreation as well as that of Indigenous cultural heritage. In reality, they are telling a single story about recreation, conflating millennia-long Indigenous connections to land with the far more ephemeral connections non-Indigenous recreators have as well as positioning recreators as inheritors of the Indigenous connections. Contemporary Indigeneity and the anticolonial, anticapitalist ideologies it represents is illegible within the extraction/protection paradigm within which public lands were designed. Patagonia is unable to recognize, let alone support, Indigenous claims independent of this paradigm without undercutting its own claims to Bears Ears and the systems upon which the company is built. Indigenous threats to colonialism are therefore neutralized by reinterpreting Indigenous claims. Instead of competing with recreational claims to land, Indigenous heritage was represented as ancestral to them.

The campaign creates a false equivalency between the way Indigenous people relate to and understand the land and the way athletes and

FIGURE 25. Two Patagonia Instagram posts demonstrating how the company represented Bears Ears National Monument in their marketing campaign. "Two Friends Meeting Up," March 8, 2017, and "A Room with a View," June 10, 2017.

explorers do, suggesting that both groups have a preternatural relationship to the environment. However, while the climbers, runners, and cyclers are represented as contemporary actors fighting to protect this space for future generations, Indigenous heritage is represented as a "living museum," fighting to protect a quickly disappearing past. The fight to preserve the ruins, rock art, and sacred spaces of Bears Ears became less about an expression of resource and cultural sovereignty for the five nations of the tribal coalition and more about showing that Americans, *all* Americans, have long had a deep, noncommercial relationship to this place, a relationship that is worth preserving.

Two representative Instagram posts from March 8, 2017, and June 10, 2017, respectively, are examples of this. In the first, on March 8, 2017, Patagonia posted an image from the Indian Creek unit of Bears Ears, a section that was not eventually removed from the monument.[23] The image shows rock climber Brittany Griffith high on a cliffside within the Bears Ears landscape, including the twin namesake buttes, and a caption reading, "@brittany_griffith and Scarface, two old friends meeting up for a classic climb. #DefendBearsEars Photo: @andrew_burr." This photograph falls into the category of adventure photograph discussed in the previous chapter. It places the subject, in this case the climber, in a physically high position, actively moving through the landscape. The only human impact visible is the slight whitening of the stone along the rock from years of climbing chalk rubbing off the hands of explorers. The landscape otherwise is pristine, rugged, and remote, exactly the type of landscape valued by extreme climbers and, therefore, worth preserving. This style of image was described in detail in the previous chapter and in and of itself is not very interesting beyond how it conforms to the adventure photo archetype. However, the caption and the photograph's place within the context of the larger campaign adds a critical affective layer, revealing an established relationship between cliff and climber. The great peril for Bears Ears, implies the caption, is not just that the landscape or the environment could be threatened by a change in designation, but that this relationship could also be destroyed.

The establishment of a relationship between the explorer and landscape is one of the key points in Patagonia's Bears Ears campaign. As discussed in previous chapters, Patagonia and other outdoor companies had already invested heavily in helping their consumers inhabit the identity of explorers. Drawing on this established connection, the company's athletes become easy stand-ins for the general market. This relationship is largely emphasized in the ideas of heritage or legacy, that public lands like Bears Ears are part of an American heritage, our inheritance as American citizens. For example, a May 5, 2017, post quotes a letter written by Patagonia CEO Rose Marcario to Secretary of Interior Zinke where she argues that Bears Ears represents a "vital part of our nation's heritage—a legacy that belongs not just to us but to all future generations."[24] The language of heritage and legacy turns up again in their television commercial, quoted in full later in this chapter, and is referenced multiple times throughout the series of virtual reality videos the company created for the campaign. Ironically, a key strategy for this aspect of the campaign is the creation of an equivalency between the athlete's relationship to the land and Indigenous relationships to the land.

Breaking from the wilderness mold by showing the ruins of a cliffside building, Patagonia's June 10, 2017, post shows one of the ways this false equivalency is established. The photographer Josh Ewing is a climber and environmental advocate as well as the executive director of Friends of Cedar Mesa, one of the main advocacy groups for preserving Bears Ears. In many ways, the image follows the rules of an adventure photo, with the person being replaced by a structure. The cliffside ruins are in the foreground, situated far above a vast, unpeopled landscape. While the ruin itself is passive, the caption, "A room with a true view," makes it a site of activity. This activity, the viewing of the landscape from the ruin, could refer to the ruins as a site of Indigenous heritage, a reference to people who lived in this area and used it as a functional space, not a tourist site—and to some extent, it does. However, it is also a clear reference to outdoor recreation.

The post suggests parallel experiences between the unknown Hopi ancestor who built the structure and the contemporary climber who took the picture. Both are looking at the same unchanged landscape from the same unchanged space, both have a relationship with the cliff, are in fact physically attached to the cliff, and both have created something there, a legacy for those who come after. For the builder, the climber is the one who has received the legacy and therefore has a responsibility to preserve it. For the climber, you and I and Patagonia's five million followers and anyone who sees this image are the beneficiaries of his legacy, charged in turn with its preservation. While I think it is safe to assume that the builder of this structure likely looked upon the landscape in a very different way than a non-Indigenous climber would have, the post sets up the two worlds as analogous, separated only by time.

This equivalency is furthered in a series of videos created by Patagonia for the Bears Ears campaign. The site that hosts the videos, bearsears.patagonia.com, organizes them in three volumes—Culture, Sport, and Take Action—consisting of "chapters" that can be "explored." "Explore" becomes more than a metaphor here. All these videos are virtual reality optimized, which allows any viewer with something as simple as a smartphone and a Google Cardboard headset to become fully immersed in the spaces shown, to freely look around and move through the spaces with the narrators. Even the 360-degree, interactive videos on the web version are far more suggestive of a first-person experience than traditional video. The 360-degree video, where the viewer has the power to look in all different directions as the video plays, creates the illusion of agency and embodiment. The user can theoretically "break" the intended narrative of the video by looking away from the intended subject in what is known as "narrative paradox."[25] For marketers, the increased depth of engagement between the user and the environment, or, in the case of Patagonia, the creation of a mediated place attachment, is more important than the simple narrative they are telling. At the same time, however, although users feel like they have agency, that they can engage and move through the space in a natural way, the entire environment is still carefully constructed by the marketer, hiding the intense mediation behind the illusion of a firsthand experience.

The first volume focuses on the American Indian cultural heritage of the monument. This is of course the reason the land was protected in the first place, although Patagonia does not mention this history. The videos feature elders, archaeologists, and tribal leaders from the five tribes of the coalition. The narrators lead the viewer through Bears Ears, telling the stories of their communities' connections to the land. The land is described as *a place of refuge* where the Navajo went to escape Kit Carson's campaign against them, *a space of distinction* as a "living museum" that shows the deep historical presence and stewardship of the Hopi, and *a sacred space* where the Zuni traditionally prayed for life-giving water. These narrators use the language of heritage and legacy as well, explaining their hopes that the protection of Bears Ears would safeguard the heritage entrusted to them by their ancestors and, through that protection, their relationships and covenants with the land itself.

These videos fail to address the numerous ways this land has been threatened and damaged by recreation, the outdoor industry, and American conservation policy, and they do not draw the connections between companies like Patagonia and the overt government conquest of the land, which I explained in previous chapters. The dark irony of Bears Ears being a place of refuge for Indigenous people from the threat of early explorers like Carson and now being preserved for explorers is especially jarring. That these abuses were perpetrated by the same government upon which they are now depending for protection is made easy to ignore. However, I want to emphasize that these videos do successfully show powerful stories of resilience and cultural survival in the face of systematic attacks on both people and place. Unfortunately, the compelling nature of these stories is what makes them such powerful tools for the subsequent arguments Patagonia uses them to craft.

The voices of these Hopi, Navajo, Zuni, Ute, and Ute Mountain leaders and the stories they tell as you virtually walk with them through these spaces—the strength and conviction of their message—create a narrative foundation and framework of heritage upon which Patagonia can then build its own story, which comes through in the second volume, Sport. The chapters of Sport are narrated by professional athletes—climbers, cyclers, and runners—who describe their own relationship to the land. They explain their relationship to Bears Ears in nearly identical terms as the Indigenous elders did. It is described as *a place of refuge*, an escape from modern society where the worries of everyday life can be momentarily left behind; *a space of distinction*, the site of some of the nation's most unique and difficult climbing routes; and *a sacred space* that reminds us what it means to be free, what it means to be American. This space, they explain, is a legacy for future generations. From these athletes, it is the audience who is then entrusted with the protection of this space.

Watching these videos back-to-back, it is easy to see the parallels Patagonia is constructing. Both the Indigenous people and the outdoor athletes experience the land in the same ways. Both have deep, intimate relationships with the cliffs and canyons. Both are fighting to preserve the land in order to preserve their cultures. There is one important difference, however. The focus of the Culture section is on the past—history, ancestors, and tradition—and the Sport section on the future—descendants and legacy. And of course, it is an outdoor corporation that paid for, produced, and distributed the videos.

The implications of this argument are twofold. First, these largely superficial similarities, which consist mostly of language and narrative framing rather than actual content, suggest much deeper connections that do not exist. The goals, rights, and worldviews of the five tribes and the outdoor athletes may intersect at this one point, but they are far from parallel and in many cases are irreconcilable. Second, the athletes are set up as the moral inheritors of the land and its heritage. The tribes' story is powerful but is from a past time. This is no longer sovereign land; it is public land, it belongs to all of us. Indigenous people are the stewards of the past, but it is the athletes—the young, fit, white consumers of Patagonia's products, with their intimate connections to land and environmental advocacy—who are the stewards of the future. This erases both the colonial history that made this situation possible and the contemporary colonial condition of public land.

This entire narrative is then reinforced by the medium in which it is presented. The 360-degree video format immerses the viewer into the Bears Ears landscape, creating the illusion of a firsthand experience. This means that the videos are fundamentally about the experience of the user, not the subjects being portrayed. Consumers bring their identity, experiences, and worldviews with them into this virtual space, shaping the way they understand the message. For the largely white, middle-class, recreation-focused consumer base for Patagonia, the white, middle-class, outdoor recreationist identity is going to be the one centered even in the videos that feature Navajo, Zuni, or Hopi people and culture. These are the very identities that had been prepped, developed, and reinforced as wilderness explorers in the types of marketing discussed in previous chapters. How then are they going to see their relationship to the real place of Bears Ears?

The third section, "Take Action," consists of just one chapter entitled "Defend." Here Patagonia points viewers to resources and concrete ways they can work to protect Bears Ears from reduction. The page lets you enter your information and have Patagonia automatically send a note to your representative in Congress telling them you agree with Patagonia's message (and also adds you to their mailing list). The rhetoric reinforces the messages they have already put forth with the concluding line, "Defend the land you have left," again suggesting collective ownership and a shared experience of loss.

The last piece of Patagonia's campaign I want to dissect is the company's first and to date only television commercial. It succinctly encapsulates the themes established in the social media campaign. The commercial begins by following Patagonia founder Yvon Chouinard walking through white sage toward a stream with fly fishing equipment and continually returns to him sitting on a fallen log narrating the below text.

> I can be a pretty cynical guy. The one thing that really keeps me going are these wild places that are the real soul of the country. A great part of my life I've been climbing and fishing and hunting on public lands. I've been a successful businessman because of the lessons I learned in the outdoors. My business was built on having wild places. Public lands have never been more threatened than right now 'cause you have a few self-serving politicians who want to sell them off and make money. Behind the politicians are energy companies and big corporations that want the use of those natural resources. It's just greed. This belongs to us. This belongs to all of the people in America. It's our heritage. I hope my kids and my grandkids will have the same experiences that I have. Our Secretary of the Interior Zinke has said he believes in public lands. Let's hold him to it. Let's not let him back down on that.[26]

Interspersed between images of Chouinard are images of recognizable national parks—Yosemite, Glacier, and the Grand Canyon—along with more general wilderness images of slot canyons, fog-covered forests, and silty river deltas. There are also images of the ravages of industry—giant tree stumps, scarred landscapes, and oil derricks. All humans in these scenes, of course, are wearing Patagonia gear. The commercial ends with a call to action. In the company's now-signature white text on a black background, it tells viewers to "Text DEFEND to 52886."

Broadcasted to an audience across Montana, Utah, and Nevada—all states with significant public lands—and hosted on social media and

YouTube, the commercial was Patagonia's widest appeal in its campaign. As you look through the text from the commercial (and I encourage you to watch the commercial as well), you will notice the arguments that come through: the focus on wild places—especially national parks and monuments as representative of this wilderness—as central to what it means to be American, the connection between the business and these wild places, the difference between Patagonia's ethics and the greed of extraction companies, and the claim of collective ownership over these places. The company heavily leans into the very traditional idea of wilderness and its connection to America (discussed in Chapter 1) and describes a broad, corporate-backed attack on public lands in general, one aided and abetted by corrupt politicians.

This is a description that, while a generally accurate representation of the situation in Bears Ears, is not true for most of the parks the company shows in the commercial, including Yosemite and Glacier National Parks. These parks are much more developed than Bears Ears—although the wilderness myth is extremely adaptable and can easily be warped to encompass even the most developed national parks. More importantly, these parks are much more well known, with which many people have already established place attachment, and are institutionalized to the extent that they are in far less danger of being opened for extraction than somewhere like Bears Ears.

By using these images behind Chouinard's commentary and alongside the Bears Ears landscape, Patagonia creates another equivalency. The company does not need to go through all the work of forging new connections between their consumers and Bears Ears specifically; it can borrow previously established connections with more well-known parks and link them to Bears Ears. All of a sudden, an attack on Bears Ears is not just about a remote, desert monument previously almost unknown; it is an attack on Yosemite and Glacier and all the beloved national parks so central to the popular understanding of the American public land system.

Patagonia's investment in this campaign helped make the company's name synonymous with the entire coalition working against the reduction of Bears Ears and with public land activism in general. Their activism had an impact far beyond their own company, pushing the entire industry to become more politicized and actively involved in public land advocacy. This impact is most clearly seen in the company's successful campaign to move Outdoor Retailer, the industry's largest trade show and conference, from Utah to Colorado. While the reduction of Bears Ears was a federal decision, much of the initial impetus for it came from the state of Utah. Home to six national parks, popular climbing sites, and some of the most iconic western landscapes in the country, Utah has become an important center for outdoor recreation. At the same time, they are a state that heavily relies on ranching and extractive industries like mining. Extraction companies based in the state were unwilling to allow over a million acres of leasable land to be removed from their economy. State leadership—in particular Representative Rob Bishop, who chaired the House Committee on National Resources and had been advocating for opening more land for oil, gas, and uranium exploration for years—sided with the extraction industry.

In response to Utah's stance, Patagonia founder Yvon Chouinard and Black Diamond CEO Peter Metcalf called for the Outdoor Industry Association (OIA) to boycott Utah by moving Outdoor Retailer away from Salt Lake City to a state friendlier to the industry. Initially, Utah saw this as an empty threat, citing a history of good relations between the state and the OIA, but Patagonia's call quickly gained support from other member companies, eventually exerting enough pressure to force the move to Denver.

Finally, in December 2017, Patagonia's very contentious—and very profitable—year of advocacy marketing culminated in the filing of their long-promised lawsuit against President Trump and Secretary Zinke around the decision to reduce the size of Bears Ears.[27] While the relocation of Outdoor Retailer showed Patagonia's growing influence within the outdoor industry, the rhetoric around this lawsuit illustrated the company's influence within public land policy more generally, the growing power of its brand, and the investment of both the media and courts in the narrative Patagonia was spinning. While this was just one of three lawsuits filed simultaneously in response to Bears Ears, each representing different stakeholders and different impacts of the decision, the Department of Justice chose to consolidate the cases as they were all challenging the same aspect of the Antiquities Act.[28]

Consolidation of these lawsuits means that a judge would hear them together as a single case, making a decision collectively rather than considering the individual merit of each argument. The central question the case would decide is whether the Antiquities Act allows the president to unilaterally reduce the size of a national monument in the same way they can create one.[29] Although technically representing the grievances of all involved groups, from a media and public relations perspective, this case became, in the words of the *New York Times*, "Patagonia v. Trump," a moniker that revealed the tilt of public perception.[30] (*GQ* called the case "Patagonia vs. Evil," which is another interesting insight into public perception.) In the eyes of the media, this was not an Indigenous issue but a corporate one.

The first lawsuit, known as *Hopi Tribe v. Trump,* was brought by the five tribes of the Bears Ears Intertribal Coalition—the Hopi, Navajo, Ute, Ute Mountain, and Zuni Nations—the same group responsible for the initial push for Bears Ears' creation. Like the other suits, their case makes the argument regarding presidential overreach of the Antiquities Act. However, unlike the other suits, *Hopi Tribe v. Trump* was not dealing with generalities of preservation or recreation, but the specificities of Bears Ears itself as a culturally and spiritually important space. They explained that some ceremonies require items that can "*only* be harvested from Bears Ears" and that "Bears Ears is in every way a home to the Plaintiff Tribes."[31] The complaint made clear that the importance of Bears Ears is in neither its recreational value nor its environmental value, but in its value as an ancestral and contemporary home for Indigenous people, and its reduction was another act by a colonial government in a long history of state actions targeting American Indian culture, people, and sovereignty.[32]

The second suit was filed by a coalition of environmental advocacy organizations including the Sierra Club, the Wilderness Society, and the National Parks Conservation Organization. While the lawsuit cited the protection of archaeological artifacts as its main reason—an argument tailored toward the Antiquities Act—these organizations saw this as an explicitly environmental issue, an attack on the public land conservation system they had been carefully constructing since the Sierra Club was founded by John Muir a century ago. The Wilderness Society's suit was not really about Bears Ears at all, but instead was about the importance of public lands and national monuments in general.

The final lawsuit, the suit that garnered headlines and social media clout, was the one brought by Patagonia Works, the parent company of Patagonia Inc. Ostensibly about the protection of public land, cultural resources, and challenging presidential overreach on the Antiquities Act, the language of the complaint made it clear that the area was of corporate interest to Patagonia and the damages were financial. While this lawsuit was actually a broad coalition of organizations including the Indigenous-run organization Utah Diné Bikéyah—the primary name listed on the suit—and environmental and cultural organizations like Friends of Cedar Mesa, it was bankrolled by Patagonia and represented in media as primarily a corporate lawsuit.[33]

Among the company's arguments for having standing to bring the suit at all was its special interest in the region based on its "long history in the Bears Ears area," specifically citing its connection to the area's rock-climbing assets.[34] Patagonia argues that its employees, athletes, and consumers have long used the area for "product testing, marketing, professional training, fitness, education, recreation, and spiritual and aesthetic enjoyment" and they need the monument in which to "climb, run, and explore."[35] While the company's "long history" is inconsequential beside the language of "time immemorial" used by the tribes in their complaint, it was a further attempt to create an equivalency between industry claims and Indigenous claims, between Bears Ears as a site of recreation and Bears Ears as a home.[36]

For the self-branded "Activist Company," it makes sense to think about this lawsuit as part of their months-long Bears Ears marketing campaign. In many ways, it is reminiscent of their famous 2011 Black Friday campaign "Don't Buy This Jacket." Featuring a full-page image of a fleece jacket, the ad's copy described the cradle-to-grave environmental impact of producing the jacket and gave suggestions for repairing and buying used. On one hand the advertisement is a genuine expression of Patagonia's commitment to sustainability. Patagonia does have a thriving used gear market and does actively seek ways to reduce its environmental impact as a Public Benefit corporation. On the other hand, it certainly did not stop selling the jacket and through its earnest and transparent discussion continued to build its long-term loyal consumer base. The advertisement proved to be the beginning of eight years of incredible growth for the company, launching what had been a niche brand for professional climbers into a much broader market.

The Patagonia lawsuit was as genuine as its commitment to sustainable clothing. The company committed real time and resources to the legal battle in addition to the millions of dollars in grants to Bears Ears advocacy organizations in the years leading up to it. No doubt their team cared deeply about public land access. However, the battle has raised their profile to hitherto unreached levels including being featured on late night shows, having multiple *New York Times* stories, and potentially having a landmark Supreme Court case named for it—name recognition that cannot be bought any other way.

As a result of sitting at the center of a number of competing and deeply held ideologies, public lands like Bears Ears have become important spaces—both physically and narratively—in which conflicts over these ideologies play out. Bears Ears is a powerful example of the ways the ideological complexities of preservation, extraction, and colonization function in the political sphere as well as on the ground. The particularly tense political context in which the conflict erupted resulted in exaggerated and relatively clear-cut responses. It is not, however, a unique situation.[37] Bears Ears took the national stage, but these types of conflicts not only happen all the time but are inherent parts of the contradictions embedded in the very premise of American public lands. Are they public or private, oppressive or opportunistic, for production or for protection?

The fact that the tribes had comanagement over the area, that it was created through Indigenous activism, and that the protections were originally put into place explicitly and exclusively to protect American Indian cultural resources and sacred sites was unprecedented. When Patagonia took control of the narrative, Indigenous voices, from Instagram posts up to court case consolidation, were marginalized. The goals Patagonia had for Bears Ears may appear similar to those of the tribes in the area, but they will never be perfectly aligned, and controlling the land's narrative is integral to controlling its future. The legal protections around public lands and structures of corporate activism are simply not designed to do what Indigenous activists are asking them to do.

Despite the tireless work of tribes and Indigenous advocacy groups, this has become Patagonia's fight. The company has and will continue to center outdoor recreation as the primary and most important use for Bears Ears and public land in general. The lawsuits were moot in response to President Biden's restoration of the monument, but from a marketing perspective the lawsuit was a success. It was a victory for the outdoor recreation-industrial complex, cementing the idea that the tribes' connections to Bears Ears and what they have to lose from its reduction are equal to those of the industry, just another stakeholder along a firmly colonial spectrum of public land management ranging from wilderness to wasteland.

FIGURE 26. Tsé Nít'i' Éí Baa Nidajina'—"Walls Are Meant for Climbing" in Navajo, satire of the North Face advertisement posted by Len Necefer, August 28, 2019.

Indigenizing Instagram

Tsé Nít'i' Éí Baa Nidajina'
—Len Necefer, *Natives Outdoors*

I n December 2018, the outdoor travel website The Outbound Collective (@theoutbound) posted a picture on Instagram of its upcoming Pursuit Series, an event billed as summer camp for grown-ups, featuring an encampment of tepee-inspired tents.[1] For its mostly white, wealthy, West Coast audience, the imagery chosen by the San Francisco–based outdoors organization apparently raised no red flags. These "conical tents" were likely chosen because of the connotative power of this architectural form, which, through many iterations of appropriation and meaning making, has come to represent explorer values of freedom, exploration, and adventure. For The Outbound, the form was whimsical, evoking an experience combining the nostalgia of Boy Scouts with the hippie spirit of festivals like Coachella or Burning Man—all organizations that likewise draw heavily from romanticized American Indian imagery. Filtered through these similarly appropriative organizations, the outdoor industry's deep and layered history of the appropriation of American Indian culture was hidden, allowing The Outbound to present the tepee as an ahistorical and universal symbol.

However, in the age of social media, events like these no longer exist in echo chambers, where companies can remain blissfully unaware of the histories and impacts of their own industries. Shortly after

The Outbound Collective's original post, Nüümü activist Jolie Varela called them out via a repost to her account Indigenous Women Hike (@indigenouswomenhike). "Native Culture is not for sale," she wrote, "We are not your backdrop."² She went on to explain in the post why appropriation is detrimental to Indigenous communities, alluding to the way Indigenous culture has historically been used by the outdoor community at the same time as much of this culture was still banned by the government in Indigenous communities themselves.³ This post did not just speak to a void, but gained traction among outdoor activists on Instagram with fifty-three comments and numerous shares, resulting in concrete change on the part of The Outbound. Varela was able to open a dialogue with the organization, prompting them to remove the post, commit to not using tepees in the future, and begin the process of including land acknowledgments. Furthermore, her post facilitated important conversations in the comments, bringing in the voices and the intellectual labor of other outdoor activists on the platform to help her address the well-meaning, and not so well-meaning, responses to her post.

Following in a long tradition of Indigenous environmental activism and building on a more recent foundation of political and racial justice activists on social media, Varela and her community of Indigenous activists and allies imagined new and adaptive methods of digital intervention that uphold grounded community values and goals while at the same time navigating fast-paced and rapidly changing online environments. This group of activists argued that the recognition of Indigenous connections to land and political sovereignty over land demanded a reimagining of the relationship between outdoor recreators and the land upon which they hike, climb, paddle, and run. They worked to overcome the inherent problems of social media—its biased algorithms, capitalist positioning, and reproduction of colonial power relations—to push for a deeper historicization of outdoor recreation, environmental conservation, public land, and the connections among them. In doing so, they have added important new methods to the ever-growing infrastructure of digital activism.⁴

Instagram in particular was molded through the labor and investment of these activists into an important site of intervention in outdoor marketing and representation. It provided a space for individuals and organizations committed to environmental justice to have conversations,

theoutbound •••

PURSUIT
SERIES

indigenouswomenhik • Following •••

indigenouswomenhike @theoutbound
Native Culture is not for sale. We are
not your backdrop. We are not your
trend. We are not your mascots. Our
culture does not exist to sell tickets to
your outdoor events. You mock us and
you encourage our erasure. The United
States government has barely granted
us the "freedom" to celebrate our
identities and practice our ceremonies
and traditions. You exploit us and
encourage the idea that we no longer
exist. And if we do we exist as the
Disney Pocahontas or Tonto. You are
harmful to our Indigenous
communities, to our future
generations. We all celebrate and hold
reverence for the land. Have respect

Liked by indigenousgeotags and
576 others

DECEMBER 18, 2018

Add a comment...

FIGURE 27. Jolie Varela's commentary on The Outbound's appropriative use of tepees, December 18, 2018.

share ideas, and begin building partnerships that exceed the platforms themselves.[5] This intervention was more than a passive effort with a whole community of new accounts actively inserting Indigenous people and histories into the story of public lands. Indigenous-run accounts like Natives Outdoors, Indigenous Women Hike, and Native Women's Wilderness challenged both followers and the industry at large to grapple with the history of these lands and rethink what and who is meant by the word *public*. These accounts reimagined the explorer-centric version of outdoor recreation, prying it from its historical ties to settler colonialism and instead engaging with it as a way for Indigenous people to reclaim their homelands, advocated for Indigenous-centered environmental protection, and forced non-Indigenous outdoor recreators to confront a different perspective on public land and conservation.

This chapter begins by looking at the history of Indigenous social media activism, tracing transnational connections among Indigenous activists and analyzing their hybrid digital/physical methods. I then return to the conflict over Bears Ears National Monument, the event that precipitated this movement, and the outdoor industry's investments in colonial narratives about the monument and public lands in general. However, I argue that the decolonial social media response catalyzed by Bears Ears exceeded its original connection to that event and became a sustaining Indigenous-led community working toward a radically different kind of relationship between outdoor recreation and the environment, one structured by relational, decolonial values rather than the extractive, capitalist ones of the outdoor industry.

Finally, within this context, I call attention to the work of several Indigenous-run activist accounts on Instagram. Among the first groups of Indigenous activists heavily using Instagram, the models with which this group experimented—methods like culture jamming of a Patagonia advertisement, the appropriation of the concept of brand ambassadors, and the subversion of the corporate model itself—can provide a road map for activists addressing other environmental and social justice issues in an increasingly digital world.[6]

Indigenous Social Media Activism

Social media platforms and other forms of digital interfaces before them have always been fraught sites for activism, with much of the scholarship on digital activism focused on how activists must engage with and overcome many of the same barriers they face in nondigital struggles. Early on, these platforms were portrayed by digital optimists as spaces of nearly unlimited potential, post-racial "new frontiers"—an overtly colonial position that is still used excessively in marketing publications—that could cut through the rigid hierarchies of the nondigital world. Digital theorist Lisa Nakamura argues that this neutral positioning of the internet, stemming from the political moment of the mid-1990s when the internet became increasingly accessible to a larger (white, urban) public, hides the way in which long-standing racial, gender, and class hierarchies are both reproduced and reinforced in digital space.[7]

Nakamura points out that a large part of this early internet inequity stemmed from a simple disparity in access and ownership and that this disparity fell along similar lines to other resource disparities. She states that "people of color, women, youths, and working to middle class users have never owned the means to produce cultural texts on the Internet in the same way the more technically skilled and better capitalized users have."[8] Internet access is far more widespread in the 2020s, although still not universal. However, as scholars like Marisa Duarte, José van Dijck, and others have pointed out, gaining access, far from correcting this early divide, merely revealed the ways that ownership of digital capital— both economic and social—and the design of the platforms themselves reflected nondigital colonial systems off the web.[9]

As discussed in more depth in Chapter 4, social media has revealed just how deep these power systems can penetrate. In particular, the atomization of human activity and experience, and the systems and mechanisms used to observe and collect these experiences, is a danger for activists seeking to use social media as a tool of resistance. Sociologists like Nick Couldry and Ulises A. Mejias appropriate the metaphor of colonialism to describe how human life and experience is extracted, abstracted, and sold for profit by those with digital capital.[10] Similarly, media theorist Shoshana Zuboff calls this system "surveillance capitalism," describing it as "a new economic order that claims human experience as free raw material for hidden commercial practices of extraction, prediction, and sales."[11] These models theorize private digital platforms as a new and more encompassing version of capitalism's expansionist need to commodify the world. They posit that all activity on social media, no matter how radical, is exploited as data for the enrichment of the platforms themselves.

These critiques of social media use are necessary cautions to keep in mind, valid observations of the power of established political and economic systems to appropriate resistance activity. They are possibly more pertinent to the kind of activist work I talk about here than among social media use in general.

And yet, despite these unequal power dynamics, social media has also facilitated large-scale resistance movements—most notably the Arab Spring and Black Lives Matter.[12] Both movements spurred new theories of digital social resistance to explain how social media platforms, despite their grounding in hegemonic systems of power, could still enable this kind of radical change. Yousri Marzouki and Olivier Oullier, for example, present the idea of a "virtual collective consciousness" that arises out of social media's fast-paced information exchange and targeted media creation to explain the emergence of these bottom-up, seemingly leaderless revolutions.[13] Others speculated that the decentralized nature of social media was a way to circumnavigate state authority and information control.[14] Scholars looking at Black Lives Matter emphasized things like the ability of social media to engage youth in political activism or the role Black Twitter played in creating the infrastructure necessary for the movement to take off.[15]

While overlapping in many ways with movements like the Arab Spring and Black Lives Matter, Indigenous social media activism is also unique, often drawing from grounded Indigenous theory and navigating social, political, and digital barriers specific to Indigenous communities. Nishnaabeg scholar and poet Leanne Betasamosake Simpson argues that the stories, experiences, and grounded practices of Indigenous people *are* Indigenous theory, that they are both community specific and applicable to a broad spectrum of contemporary social and political experiences.[16] The application of Indigenous-grounded theory to digital spaces and experiences, the indigenization of this fundamentally colonial technology, has been an adaptable tool of resistance for Indigenous activists. It echoes on-the-ground methods of resistance Indigenous people have long used to survive and push back against colonial impositions.

One way to think about this is to extend Zuboff's use of surveillance and Couldry and Mejias's use of colonization as conceptual metaphors for understanding the ways digital spaces reproduce nondigital power structures, because, in a not-at-all-metaphorical way, state surveillance, colonization, and the annexation of Indigenous land and bodies into a capitalist system are exactly the structures Indigenous resistance strategies were developed to evade. These scholars' arguments that social media and digital economies represent a new and more pervasive era of capitalism could use greater historicization. The use of surveillance by both the state and corporations to force people into cash economies, the reduction of complex human actions and experiences into quantifiable data that can be given a dollar amount, and the commodification of bodies are all long-established capitalist strategies, existing at a different scale and speed in digital space, but not as fundamentally different processes. Methods like becoming intentionally illegible to state systems, appropriating imposed assimilation policies as ways to maintain otherwise outlawed cultural practices, and occupying spaces designed for Indigenous erasure all have digital counterparts that can be used to harness the power of social media, imperfect and exploitative as it is.

The reinscription of nondigital racial politics onto digital media means that Indigenous people, who are so often represented as always outside of modernity or as a vestige of the past, are perpetually unexpected in digital spaces like social media. Their presence, like their presence in settler colonial states, is itself an act of resistance.[17] But more actively, the use of Indigenous theory means that activists are often using social media in ways that are not just counter to their designed function but crosswise to them, making them both more useful to activists and less legible to the colonial companies, states, and powers activists are working against.

An example of this is the Maori e-whanaungatanga. New Zealand scholars Joanne Waitoa, Regina Scheyvens, and Te Rina Warren describe how Maori activists have used Facebook to create e-whanaungatanga, or an electronic version of traditional relationships and networks, which in turn has led to digital tino rangatiratanga, or political self-determination.[18] While far from a perfect system, Facebook has allowed for the creation of a space where Maori activists and communities can come together in ways not always possible in colonial New Zealand politics to spread Maori political consciousness within the structure of traditional values and culture. Similarly, scholars like Oliver Froehling and, more recently, Marisa Duarte (Yaqui/Chicana) have looked at how the Zapatista movement for land sovereignty in Mexico drew on Indigenous networks to create new digital organizing techniques in the 1990s. As the internet, like the colonial state, became more centralized and increasingly used as a tool of surveillance, the Zapatistas could draw on the lived experience and methods of resisting colonization on the ground to develop decentralized digital systems that augmented and spread awareness for their nondigital activities as well as disseminate a narrative of Indigeneity and Indigenous liberation counter to that put forth by the Mexican state.[19] Unlike theorizations of the Arab Spring that credited decentralization to the design of social media, the Zapatistas adapted existing decentralized organization to a pre-social media digital space.

While e-whanaungatanga and the Zapatista movement created digital structures to support on-the-ground movements, more recent movements have become increasingly hybridized. During the protests against the Dakota Access Pipeline at Standing Rock in 2016, water protectors created a hybridization of alternative news sources, blogs, and user-generated content collected and disseminated over social media. These replaced mainstream media sources as the primary way stories and information about the protest reached people across the country. The hashtag #NoDAPL, an inherently digital term derived on social media, even came to be associated with the physical camps and the entire movement, digital and physical alike.[20] Graffiti of the hashtag #NoDAPL on physical walls represents an overlap and merging of the digital and nondigital worlds. As Nick Estes demonstrates in *Our History Is the Future*, this movement was clearly part of a long history of Lakota resistance, drawing on culturally specific practices to inform this new kind of battle.[21] But it also marked an important shift in Indigenous digital activism and coalition building, especially around environmental issues and social media. Access to this connective medium was as critical to the breadth of the movement as on-the-ground organizing, labor, and commitment was to its depth. Furthermore, the fact that what was fundamentally a radical anticapitalist movement could be facilitated through the use of private corporate networks, platforms, and servers is indicative of the ability of activism based on grounded Indigenous practice to subvert capitalist, colonial infrastructure for their own purposes. The movement, for example, included activists from around the world using Facebook to digitally check in to Standing Rock Reservation in order to disrupt police using Facebook to document who was physically there.[22] A technology of panoptic surveillance was used as a tool of resistance.

The #IdleNoMore movement in Canada is another important example of this power, taking advantage of social media in ways that did not just replicate or augment on-the-ground organizing as earlier movements had, but created a truly digitally born movement, one that helped set the stage for contemporary social media activism. In response to Canadian Prime Minister Stephen Harper's attack on Indigenous water and resource sovereignty in 2011, #IdleNoMore brought together environmentalists, feminists, and other activists across Indigenous and non-Indigenous communities to challenge state violence against the land and against Indigenous women. They used hashtags to spread and index ideas under the single Idle No More movement and were able to use their relatively frictionless digital networks to rapidly organize physical demonstrations.[23] This movement was made possible in part by the organizers' innovative use of technology, but also by their application of established Indigenous practices and grounded theory to that technology. Social theorists Terry Wotherspoon and John Hansen, for example, argue that #IdleNoMore drew on Indigenous ideas of justice and inclusion in its organization principles, and Vincent Raynauld, Emmanuelle

Richez, and Katie Boudreau Morris contend that #IdleNoMore was a departure from earlier political social media movements in that its information flows placed a strong emphasis on Indigenous culture and land-based concerns.[24] Its bottom-up, coalitional digital organizing also served as a rejection of colonial recognition and categorization.[25] While critics of these kinds of social media movements suggest they are just examples of clicktivism, or the performance of effortless online support in lieu of grounded, change-making activism, there is little evidence that social media is preventing activists who would otherwise be participating in other direct action from doing so. Furthermore, movements like #IdleNoMore, far from neutralizing other activist efforts or being appropriated by liberal state rhetoric, established strong networks that rallied to support otherwise local movements like the Wet'suwet'en occupation and led to political interventions like the Missing and Murdered Indigenous Women and Girls Inquiry.[26]

Finally, as redundant as it seems to emphasize, the greatest strength of social media is its networked nature. These platforms are social networking sites and are as much about the networks as the media itself. For Indigenous activists, these digital networks can help overcome several different barriers faced by on-the-ground movements. One of the most important functions is expanding and strengthening peer-to-peer connections. For example, in a recent discussion about how she views her digital work, Métis scholar and social media activist Chelsea Vowel argued that social media has become a powerful tool for Indigenous activists to quickly address damaging representations or actions against Indigenous people and land. Where at one time, these challenges would largely circulate locally, person to person, taking a long time to reach the critical mass to make change—if they ever did—social media has allowed for immediate and widespread responses, radically changing the possibilities for young activists.[27] Community issues can quickly become national issues as in the response to the 2016 murder of Colten Boushie of Cree Red Pheasant First Nation in Saskatchewan. This tragedy, which in another era may have become just another isolated example of violent racism in rural Saskatchewan, was instead propelled to a national level largely through the activity of Indigenous social media networks.[28] First Nations Canadians called for #JusticeForColten and connected the murder to the much larger story of casual and deeply embedded racism on the Canadian prairie and across the nation. Furthermore, because some of the racist discourse and responses by white Canadians happened on Facebook, Indigenous activists could see and expose speech otherwise hidden in homes and among isolated communities and warn others about what was going on, flipping the script on digital surveillance.

It is hard to imagine contemporary Indigenous activists like Jolie Varela gaining the traction they have without the increased public awareness and development of methods these earlier movements established. Movements like #IdleNoMore and #NoDAPL showed what motivated activists can do with social media, providing adaptive methodology and theory on which to build. However, when it comes specifically to activism around public lands and serious engagement with the outdoor industry, it makes more sense to trace its origin to the conflict around Bears Ears National Monument as a point when Indigenous activists began using social media to discuss their relationship critically and publicly with these outdoor spaces and systems. It is also where digital activism became increasingly independent of specific nondigital causes. The #SaveBearsEars movement was itself, like #IdleNoMore, a coalition of Indigenous and non-Indigenous environmental groups responding to the threat to the monument and growing out of years of on-the-ground labor by the Bears Ears Intertribal Coalition. It followed many of the tried-and-true methods discussed above and was, initially at least, deeply based in grounded Indigenous practice coming from the intertribal coalition. It was this movement that led to physical demonstrations in Salt Lake City on the day of Bears Ears' reduction and partially drove the previously discussed consolidated court case *Patagonia v. Trump*.

However, the Indigenous activism emerging around issues of public land, representation within the outdoor industry, and outdoor recreation more broadly is different; not necessarily in its theoretical basis or decolonial goals, but in the way it has deployed those goals through social media technology. It clearly grew out of Bears Ears activism, as a response to Patagonia, but the organizations like Indigenous Women Hike, Native Women Wilderness, and Natives Outdoors were fundamentally digitally born, created to address larger issues in outdoor recreation that were not tied to a single on-the-ground conflict. The values driving these accounts were still local and community based, drawn from a long heritage of Indigenous public land activism in general, and reflected political commitments to land and the environment based upon an Indigenous understanding of sovereignty. However, the physical, on-the-ground work these people and organizations did and continue to do is the result of first building digital platforms and communities, mostly over Instagram, and then taking those relationships and goals to the land—digital first, physical second.

Challenging the Narrative of Recreation

In the previous chapter, I analyzed how Patagonia and the outdoor recreation industry co-opted the defense of Bears Ears from the tribal coalition, using their marketing power to transform land that was originally protected to preserve the five tribes' cultural and spiritual sites into a space defined by its recreational resources. Here, I want to show how this co-option was contested by Indigenous activists like Varela and non-Indigenous allies who used the same powerful social media platforms to negotiate and challenge the meaning of Bears Ears.

While Bears Ears was not the first reduction of National Park Service protected land, alongside the contemporaneous reduction of Grand Staircase-Escalante National Monument, it was by far the largest and most public, signaling to the outdoor industry that the type of protected land they relied on to sell their products, and their wilderness narrative, could no longer be taken for granted. In the wake of Trump's announcement, outdoor retail giant Patagonia posted on its Instagram page the provocative words, "The President Stole Your Land." A space normally reserved for colorful, active images of hikers braving the mountains or climbers on sheer cliffs was instead filled with stark white letters emblazoned on a black background, a visual dissonance designed to grab the attention of the company's nearly four million followers. The post explained, "In an illegal move, the president just reduced the size of Bears Ears and Grand Staircase-Escalante National Monuments. This is the largest elimination of protected land in American history."[29] The statement and design also replaced the company's landing page on their website, daringly disrupting the consumer experience with a political message.

The bold post was almost universally applauded in the outdoor recreation community, the simple black-and-white design becoming the standard for political statements by the industry. It also drew comparisons with Patagonia's famous 2010 Black Friday advertisement where the company told its consumers to not buy its products (possibly contributing to its 30 percent sales increase the following year).[30] The minimalist design of simple white text on a solid black background—or the reverse—quickly became the standard for political statements not just by Patagonia, but by other companies throughout the industry as well. The examples in Figures 28–30 are from REI and The North Face with statements in support of the 2019 Climate Strike, and from Columbia making a statement about the 2018–19 government shutdown and its impacts on National Parks.[31]

However, it also sparked a serious backlash in a community Patagonia may have not expected. The company's use of the word "your" and its uncritical defense of public land as collectively owned managed to completely ignore the complex and difficult history public land and conservation advocates have with Indigenous people, an especially painful omission considering the centrality of tribal activism to the original creation of Bear Ears. This lack of awareness should not be surprising, but considering the Indigenous focus of the original monument proposal and the company's at least cursory engagement in the communities, it seems like a significant oversight on the part of the company's marketing team.

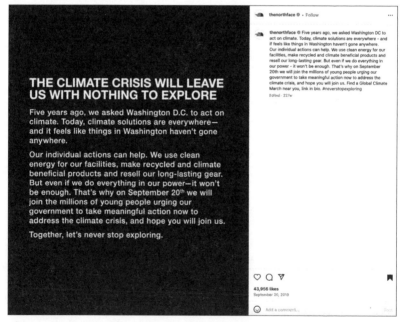

FIGURE 28. The North Face political advertisement, "The Climate Crisis," September 20, 2019.

Indigenous members of the outdoor community, however, were quick to address this misstep, and within hours of the original post, several new annotated versions began to circulate. For example, Varela (@indigenouswomenhike), added the word "modern" to remind followers that Patagonia's claim that this was the "largest elimination of protected land in American history" is ahistorical, ignoring the thefts

MAKE AMERICA'S PARKS OPEN AGAIN.

Walls shouldn't block access to parks, and federal workers shouldn't be left out in the cold. Work together to open our parks.

-Tim Boyle, CEO

FIGURE 29. Columbia's political advertisement, "Make America's Parks Open Again," January 11, 2019.

The message is loudest when we share the mic.

FIGURE 30. REI political advertisement, "The Message Is Loudest," September 16, 2019.

that created them. Varela includes a thoughtful caption, calling out these corporations, acknowledging the potential benefits of their protest, and admonishing them to "step up and step back," using their influence to create a platform for Native voices.[32] Similarly, Gregg Deal (@greggdeal), a Pyramid Lake Paiute artist known for his activism, also reinterpreted the post. Using red, hand-drawn words, he replaced "Your" with "Indian" and added "From 1776—Present Millions of acres have been taken from Indigenous communities by the U.S. Government. Know your history. THIS IS INDIAN LAND!"[33] Like Varela, Deal acknowledges Patagonia's good intentions but stresses the need for Native voices, reminding his followers that Bears Ears was originally about the tribal coalition and their desire to preserve sacred sites.

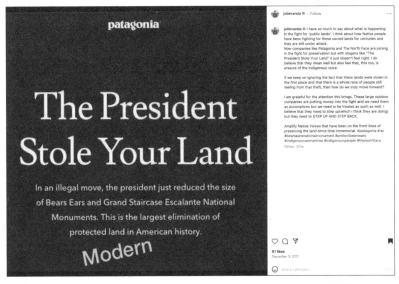

FIGURE 31. Varela's response to Patagonia's statement, December 5, 2017.

FIGURE 32. Gregg Deal's response to Patagonia's statement, December 5, 2017.

Not everyone was so gracious to Patagonia, however. Diné activist Larissa Nez (@canoecanoa) reposted the original Patagonia post with a caption beginning, "ARE YOU KIDDING ME? FUCK YOU @patagonia." She goes on to call the company "complicit in the ongoing genocide of Indigenous people," accuses them of using environmentalism as a cover for capitalistic gain, and argues that their campaigns "serve no purpose except to center the privilege and entitlement of settlers."[34] In expressing her anger and dismay toward Patagonia, Nez's words, through a repost by Terra Incognita (@terraincognitamedia), were able to provoke a conversation about what the role of Patagonia and other outdoor companies could be in these types of Indigenous-centered environmental issues as well as conversations about what an Indigenous approach to public lands might need. For example, Len Necefer (@nativesoutdoors) responded in a comment that acknowledged the importance of Nez's critique, while also challenging her to consider priorities and the potential alliance with Patagonia in the face of larger issues. Likewise, African American outdoors activist Teresa Baker (@teresabaker11) defended Patagonia's post, arguing that, while of course it was problematic, they were still one of the only companies pushing back against the reduction of Bears Ears.[35]

This type of intervention can be seen as a form of détournement or culture jamming, "turning expressions of the capitalist system and media culture against itself."[36] Détournement traditionally uses well-known symbols or memes—logos for example—and re-presents them in ways that force viewers to think about them in new, often subversive contexts. Deal taking the Patagonia post and adding his edits to it in order to challenge the assumptions in the text easily falls into this definition, but I am applying it more broadly here to include the subversion of larger systems and concepts used by the outdoor industry and social media marketers. In the example at the beginning of this section, when Varela, as an outdoor recreator herself, refused the position of the passive consumer of The Outbound's media and instead pushed back, placing herself in a position of power over that media and when and where it was distributed, she participated in an act of détournement, upsetting and sabotaging the smooth functioning of Instagram as a tool of consumerism and reimagining it as a tool of Indigenous resistance. The form of détournement used by these activists also strongly foregrounds Indigenous theory, especially stressing the need to balance tribally specific experiences with intertribal concerns and positioning decommodified relationships to land at the center of their critiques.

This can be seen in Native Women's Wilderness (NWW), an account run by Diné photographer Jaylyn Gough. Gough organized her page around her NWW ambassadors. The term *ambassador* or *brand ambassador* is one used by the outdoor industry to describe influencers on social media who have a relationship with the company to endorse them over a period of time or posts. Influence, and compensation, on Instagram is usually determined by follower count, with ambassadors with a hundred thousand or more followers commanding thousands of dollars a post for sponsorship.[37] Most brand ambassadors are what is known as micro-influencers, however, having fewer than ten thousand followers and promoting companies in exchange for product. On Instagram, ambassadors exist in a place of both seller and consumer, and they are often integral to the widespread reinforcement and reproduction of companies' narratives.

Using the term *ambassador,* Gough nods to the presence of this culture on Instagram, but she undermines its purpose by using the position to serve the ambassadors themselves rather than the organization. For Gough's ambassadors, the platform is a way to share their stories and love of the outdoors as Indigenous women. For example, in her November 3, 2017, post, ambassador Lydia Jennings (@llcooljennings) of the Yaqui and Huichol Nations describes how her Indigenous identity informs and strengthens her love of the outdoors and adventure sports.[38] While the outdoor corporation narrative has centered the environment as the victim of mining and pollution, in the caption to an image of her running on a mountain trail, Jennings centers Indigenous people, reminding her followers that protecting these spaces is not just an environmental issue but also a justice issue. And while the image follows the common theme in outdoor photography of an athlete foregrounding a wilderness landscape, the post's inclusion of the names of the tribes who lived in this space implicitly challenges the idea of an untouched wilderness put forward by Patagonia's representations. Where the typical brand ambassador is the height of late capitalist absurdism, with layers of commodification that turn the ambassador herself into both a narrative to be sold and an apparatus of the marketing process, Jennings's challenge is fundamentally about *decommodifying* land and her presence on it.[39] Gough's ambassadors are representatives of recreational interactions with land that are outside of the framing the outdoor industry has created and thus also a challenge to it.

An even clearer example of Indigenous détournement on Instagram is Necefer's remix of a recent advertising campaign from The North Face. First introduced in August 2015, The North Face created a new tagline, "Walls Are Meant for Climbing" with a further caption reading, "Some people build walls. Other people climb them."[40] The graphic makes use of plain black letters on a white background, signaling a political statement in addition to a larger marketing push. The campaign did not initially reference President Trump's plans to build a wall on the U.S.–Mexican

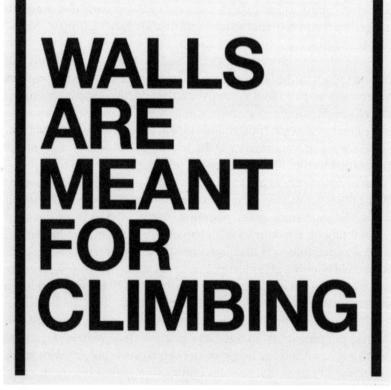

FIGURE 33. The North Face advertisement, "Walls Are Meant for Climbing," August 2019.

border—although, considering the timing, it was likely a response to this policy. It instead focused on overcoming barriers to rock climbing in underserved communities. However, reposting the image in January 2019, during the government shutdown over funding for Trump's wall and adjacent to a post quoting Trump made the connection explicit.[41] Then, on July 10, 2019, for World Climbing Day, they released a version in several other languages.

This campaign has been an important political intervention from the company that, unlike Patagonia, is a subsidiary of a large, publicly held holding company with less corporate agency. Inclusive as they are, "Walls Are Meant for Climbing" struck a nerve for Indigenous people

FIGURE 34. The North Face advertisement, "Los Muros son Para Escalarse," August 2019.

trying to address illegal and irresponsible climbing in sacred spaces, especially in the Southwest in and around the Navajo Reservation. This is not a new problem. Climbing in sacred spaces like on Devil's Tower or Shiprock has always been controversial among tribes and many spaces now have total or partial bans on climbing.[42] Social media, however, has helped this issue resurface—Necefer has a feature in *Climbing* magazine on the topic—and reach a wider audience of climbers who have been both receptive and resistant to constraints on their right to climb. This is a complex debate involving land jurisdiction, treaty rights, and climber identity, one The North Face managed to step right into the middle of.

In an attempt to nuance The North Face's claim about the universal good of rock climbing, Necefer played on their own campaign. He redid The North Face's Half Dome logo as "The Ship Rock," a reference to an important monolith in Diné culture and once-popular climbing location on the Navajo Reservation, and translates "Walls Are Meant for Climbing" into Navajo as "Tsé Nít'i' Éí Baa Nidajina'."[43] He posted it adjacent to a similar "The Ship Rock" post in English reading, "Shiprock is not meant for climbing." Necefer, a climber himself, is deeply invested in coalition building with both outdoor corporations as well as non-Indigenous climbers, but is also using his platform to encourage followers to pause and spend time examining the underlying goals of campaigns by companies like The North Face (and the social media platform on which the campaigns run).

Necefer's page Natives Outdoors takes this subversion of media production to a larger scale by organizing Natives Outdoors itself as a corporation. Started in March 2017, Natives Outdoors is organized as a Benefit Corporation (B Corp), a corporate model that commits a company to consider its code of ethics equally with profits when making decisions. However, being a B Corp alone is not enough—Patagonia is also organized as a B Corp—Natives Outdoors' corporate status is designed to open doors that allow Necefer to more directly challenge the outdoor industry to rethink how we understand public land. By featuring Indigenous hikers and climbers and sharing their stories and connections to these places, this account presents Indigenous people as integral members of the contemporary outdoor community and as allies to many of the goals pursued by the outdoor industry and environmental activists. At the same time it reminds followers that the "our" in "our land" comes with a much more complex history than is presented in the mainstream

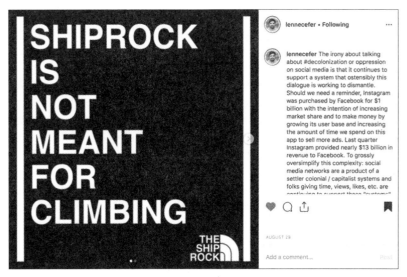

FIGURE 35. "Shiprock Is Not Meant for Climbing," satirical riff on The North Face's "Walls Are Meant for Climbing" campaign, August 28, 2019.

conversation. Natives Outdoors is also dedicated to moving beyond just critiquing public land for its colonial past and is actively working with public policy and outdoor corporations to find collaborative solutions.[44]

Compare this to the way Patagonia covered the same issue on their account.[45] While Natives Outdoors fills Bears Ears with thousands of years of cultural history, Patagonia posted an image making a similar call to action on May 5, 2017. Showing the two characteristic buttes of Bears Ears behind a red desert shrubland, the image presents the space as a wilderness, void of human presence, contemporary and historical. The caption reinforces the image by evoking the collective-ownership narrative—"our public lands," "a legacy that belongs ... to all future generations"—and the geotag locates the park within the "U.S. Department of Interior," marking the space as American rather than Indigenous. As I described previously, for Patagonia, presenting land as pristine and untouched makes economic sense. It both caters to their market, for whom the aura of wilderness is central, and makes a political case for environmental preservation. Presenting it as American is an important political move, reifying the corporate-state complex that underlies the public land system. It is also, however, wildernessing, a strategy of erasure, a way of claiming

Bears Ears for its mostly non-Indigenous consumer base. The company's aggressive social media campaign pushes visitors, and more importantly policymakers, to see Bears Ears as a commodified tourist space—a settler space—rather than an Indigenous one.[46]

Despite the commitment of individuals like Varela, Necefer, and Gough to work more or less productively alongside the outdoor industry on their organizational platforms, they have also expressed a more restrained enthusiasm, articulating their trepidation about allying with corporate entities and questioning the outdoor industry's commitment to working for the benefit of Indigenous communities. Their comments address the complexities and challenges of engaging with an industry that is at once complicit in the environmental injustices experienced by Indigenous people while at the same time a potentially powerful ally in combating blatant environmental harm at a larger policy level. For example, in a comment on a February 2, 2018, post on the account Indigenous Geotags (@indigenousgeotags), Varela articulated her tendency to rely on the moral obligations of these companies until she remembers that, no, these are not people, they are corporations. "They're out to make money," she wrote, "and if the land is compromised they stand to lose their profit . . . bottom line the land needs to be cared for because it is SACRED. So if teaming up with corporations means preservation of then OK. That's what we do, because these are our creation stories."[47] She went on to outline what she believes the outdoor industry needs to do in order to truly support Indigenous people. These suggestions included having Native American liaisons and employees at all levels of the corporation and industry support for youth programs and food sovereignty.

In a comment on the same post, Necefer laid out exactly why he believed this coalition can work and would be mutually beneficial, arguing that the outdoor industry brings the platform and economic power while tribes bring legal standing and political experience dealing specifically with protected lands. In a political and legal system that is heavily influenced by both money and public opinion, he would agree with the "step up and step back" model of corporate involvement expressed by Varela earlier, and he has been working hard to create "serious structural changes" in the industry.[48] However, at the same time he expresses his discomfort with having to approach this partnership though a corporate model. Despite the obvious benefits of organizing Natives Outdoors as a corporation including greater political latitude and a "seat at the same table," he also recognizes the drawbacks, writing, "I will be the first to acknowledge that I am completely uncomfortable working within the confines of capitalism through the company as I see it being the source of all our environmental issues at hand today."[49] Necefer's apprehension about working within and even toward a system of capitalism is at the heart of the instability of this relationship: as commenter Sophie Bowley-Aicken (@anarchopixie) wrote, "I honestly don't think justice and profit will ever be compatible."[50]

In openly expressing their apprehension and sometimes outright rejection of working alongside the outdoor industry on Instagram, Indigenous outdoor activists are adapting the platform to work for their own purposes. Instagram is itself fundamentally a corporate entity, supporting and supported by these powerful outdoor corporations. Using the platform to challenge these corporations and push for Indigenous-based, decommodified relationships to land bends the platform to serve a purpose for which it was never intended and a user group for which it was never imagined. In turn, the manipulation of the platform allows for a greater level of intervention in this narrative than would be possible in a nondigital environment.

In the years following the reduction of Bears Ears, the increasing influence and presence of these accounts, even as the social media and political landscapes continually changed, showed the strength of the activist infrastructure they constructed in the wake of that moment. Activists like Varela, Necefer, and Gough continued to keep the pressure on outdoor corporations and the culture of outdoor recreation in general, including doing more work in nondigital spaces. New media scholars Jennifer Earl and Katrina Kimport call early forays into digital activism "collective action with connective capacity," referring to the way in which movements like the Zapatistas that started on the ground utilized digital resources to augment their work.[51] This new cohort of activists has flipped that script, creating a connective, digitally born movement that addresses a culture and industry that increasingly exists in these digital spaces, and utilizing on-the-ground work to both augment their digital platforms and put into practice the alternative visions of outdoor recreation they argue for online.

Varela for example has led hiking trips on the Nüümü Poyo, physically entering a space that is emblematic of the white, outdoor recreation culture and documenting her presence and experiences over social media.[52] Her presence on the trail forces non-Indigenous hikers to rethink their assumptions about whose land they are on. Furthermore, by choosing to hike without permits, the group rejected the identity of tourists, of people who visit but do not remain. They are exercising their dual identity as both Indigenous women and outdoor recreators. Although participating in the same activity as non-Indigenous hikers, the Indigenous women hiking are claiming a fundamentally different relationship to the land, one that rejects the legacy of colonialism in this space. While there is some irony in using social media to make such a physical and embodied statement, it speaks to the contemporary state of Indigenous social media activism as both a grounded, localized practice as well as a flexible, digital structure.

It is too early to tell what impact these interventions will have or even what success for this movement would look like. On one hand, there is some movement in the right direction. The Outbound pulling the tepees from their event and being willing to open a dialogue about appropriation and land acknowledgment is a small, but positive, step. Patagonia has also increasingly invested money and resources into Indigenous communities and causes, some of which has certainly been in response to Necefer's involvement and the companies' experiences with the Bears Ears conflict.[53] On the other hand, outdoor companies are still unwilling to address the underlying ideologies about public land and wilderness that have historically driven Indigenous land and resource dispossession. Their profits continue to depend on their consumers having a fundamentally colonial relationship to land, treating space as explorable and consumable, and until this changes, outdoor corporations will only ever be half-hearted allies at best.

What is evident is that, regardless of corporate response on the specific issue of outdoor recreation, these accounts have helped establish a new kind of Indigenous social media activism, one that is able to harness the flexibility and networked nature of social media to rapidly respond to the political and social needs of the moment while still remaining grounded in Indigenous theory. This was clearly seen in the wake of the June 2020 mass protests surrounding the murder of George Floyd when, as social media sites including Instagram became inundated with politically driven, activist content, this already established Indigenous community of Instagram users was able to quickly and cogently insert Indigenous perspectives and critiques into the larger conversation. While it is clear that these activism efforts are more than ineffectual clicktivism, social media companies, as private, marketing entities, are adept at neutralizing radicalism and transforming discontent into simply content. For activists, remaining effective in their change-making efforts and illegible to the corporate social media machine will demand constant adaptation and, perhaps, a willingness to pivot across networks or abandon them altogether as technology and software continue to advance. Social media activism will need to continue to navigate a world where the digital and nondigital aspects of people's lives become increasingly inseparable. Despite the hierarchical power dynamics and colonial systems that remain deeply embedded in social media, the work of Varela and other Indigenous activists shows the power of Indigenous-based social media activism to meet these ongoing challenges.

Conclusion

The Earth Is Our Shareholder

I n the fall of 2022, Patagonia founder Yvon Chouinard announced that "the earth is now our only shareholder." Embedded in this statement is a series of values about Chouinard's relationship to the environment, his corporate ethics, and, somewhat grandly, his vision for the future of green capitalism. "Hopefully," Chouinard said in a *New York Times* interview, "this will influence a new form of capitalism that doesn't end up with a few people rich and a bunch of people poor."[1] Chouinard had long been deeply conflicted about his role as the owner of a multibillion-dollar business, a retail clothing store that inevitably has significant environmental impacts and relies on the capitalist imperative of over-consumption. Despite, or perhaps because of, marketing campaigns telling consumers not to buy their products and successfully branding the company as one of the most environmentally and ethically responsibly corporations on the planet, Patagonia's sales and infrastructure have grown rapidly in the last few years. The forty-year-old company was valued at a billion dollars for the first time in 2018, and in only four years it has tripled that value.

Nearing retirement, the billionaire was concerned about whether the company would maintain its standard of ethics after he was gone and worked with lawyers to create a system that guaranteed that the company's profits—currently around $100 million a year—would be invested in the environment. Ninety-eight percent of the company would be transferred to a nonprofit, while the voting shares would be held by a trust controlled by the family. In a statement release with the announcement, Chouinard summed up the deal by saying, "Instead of extracting value from nature and transforming it into wealth for investors, we'll use the wealth Patagonia creates to protect the source of all wealth."[2]

The nuts and bolts of this deal, this gift of a $3 billion corporation to the planet and its systems of life, are firmly affixed to financial structures available under U.S. law, and the power and decision-making remain firmly in the hands of the Chouinard family. The newly created non-profit organization The Holdfast Collective is organized as a 501(c)4, or a social welfare organization, a designation that lets them earmark up to 50 percent of their expenditures explicitly toward political causes, with the rest going to environmental and climate organizations. No doubt this will help fund important environmental causes, ameliorating the negative impacts of capitalist wealth production caused by Patagonia and other companies. Naming the earth as its shareholder, as both a point of personal ethics and a savvy marketing move, was lauded by environmentalists as an important and innovative step toward a greener and more just form of capitalism. What it says to me is that even the most liberal approach in this system is a failure when seen through the lens of Indigenous justice and ecological sovereignty.

Patagonia's new $100 million system of political lobbying and wilderness creation serves to further entrench a set of land values and physical landscapes that prop up the outdoor industry, perpetuating narratives and policies that favor recreational use but conflict with Indigenous treaty-guaranteed rights over cultural, spiritual, and natural resources. However, one lesson I hope readers have taken away from this book is that wilderness as we know it was not inevitable and is not set in stone. It is the result of interacting social, political, and economic decisions and it is in a constant state of reinvention. While the power dynamics of the different stakeholders involved—the state, outdoor corporations, tribes, individual recreators, social media platforms, and others—are deeply unequal, these actors all played a role in shaping the current relationship among public lands and those who engage with them. Their actions and advocacy will continue to shape these relationships and ideologies into the future.

The Future of Wilderness

The past few years have shown that we may be at another turning point in wilderness representation. Shifting power dynamics in media created by digital outlets, a rise in outdoor-specific Indigenous activism, and diversity, equity, and inclusion rhetoric are forcing companies and the public at large to rethink how they authenticate their wilderness experience. At the same time, dramatic impacts of climate change, rapid growth in outdoor tourism, and the rollback of environmental protections are making it increasingly difficult to uphold the fiction of truly untouched natural spaces. I want to use the rest of this conclusion to think about what the future of wilderness might look like should the untrammeled system begin to fray.

One possibility, one I see already taking place, is an adaptation of settler colonial structures through the corporate and state co-option of diversity activism. This strategy would allow outdoor corporations and recreators to hold on to the treasured idea of wilderness in a form that caters to a more diverse recreation community (and larger market) than the largely white, male, middle- and upper-class demographic previously envisioned, without addressing the underlying injustices inherent in the colonial system. The important shift toward a multicultural, if not decolonial, form of recreation has already been gestured toward by scholars and activists invested in an outdoor recreation environmental justice. Scholars like Carolyn Finney, Lauret Savoy, and Sarah Jaquette Ray show how access to outdoor recreation, or lack thereof, reflects and reinforces the larger power structures of white supremacy and patriarchy.[3] They move beyond the dominant conversations in environmental justice around how toxicity and degradation impact communities to look at the opposite—how lack of access to clean and restored environments also has cascading effects. These conversations around environmental justice and outdoor recreation clearly resonate with many previously underserved groups and are even more vibrant among activists working on the ground and over social media with figures like Pattie Gonia (@pattiegonia), who addresses LGBTQ representation; Teresa Baker (@teresabaker11), who works on removing barriers to African American access to National Parks; and numerous accounts on Instagram organizing around getting traditionally underrepresented communities outside.[4] Many of the conversations facilitated by these accounts cut directly to the heart of these historical wrongs, calling out problems when they see them and making connections between their personal experiences and systemic inequalities.

This is critical work that carefully draws out the intersections among race, gender, sexuality, ability, and class, how these identities shape one's relationship to the outdoors, and how the outdoors has been used to shape the power dynamics among them. However, this work still tends to follow the dominant narrative about public land as a universal good, rather than interrogating the underlying injustices at the base of the very existence of recreational space, and is thus easily appropriated by corporations invested in the same ideas seeking to expand their market. More often than not, the diversity in the outdoors movement does not address colonialism, or at least does not engage in what seriously addressing colonialism might mean for public land. Many groups lean into the outdoor industry's narratives about public land, seeing outdoor companies' Diversity, Equity, and Inclusion (DEI) programs as a way to rectify inequality and overcome institutional barriers.

It is beyond the scope of this project to go into a deep analysis of DEI marketing and programming by the outdoor industry, but it is clear that efforts by outdoor access activists are making an impact. Advertisements previously showing almost exclusively young, fit, white men and women are increasingly representing non-white and queer recreators of various ability. In the short term, this is good! Numerous studies have shown the importance of access to green space, and if public lands are going to be used to subsidize outdoor corporations at the expense of Indigenous sovereignty, they should at least be serving the broadest spectrum of Americans possible. But when companies sell access to the outdoors, they are also selling all the ideologies undergirding these spaces—whiteness, class power, and a particular style of American masculinity. The explorer archetype idealized in outdoor marketing, even if reenacted by a person of color, is still an investment in white colonial power. Sarah Jaquette Ray argues that "privileging wilderness protection over social justice explains why environmentalism often fails to build coalitions across lines of class, race, gender, and even nation and ability," but I argue that the problem is not privileging wilderness: it is including wilderness in the equation at all.[5] Without also challenging settler colonialism, without addressing the land's history and contested political status, true diversity in the outdoors cannot be achieved. Efforts will only serve the purpose for which wilderness was originally designed—the reinforcement of a set of very American values designed to exclude certain kinds of people—and further enrich the companies that rely on it.

On the other hand, we may see a fundamental challenge to the idea of wilderness itself. Scholarship on the Anthropocene, the idea that the age of humans has left a geological imprint on the planet, shows that even places we consider unmanaged or untrammeled are deeply impacted by human activity. Microplastics have infiltrated the food chain, acid rain far exceeds industrial points of origin, and human-influenced global climate change effects every ecosystem no matter how remote. There is no pristine, there is no untouched; there are only places more or less visibly impacted by the activities of people—sometimes for better, but mostly for worse. Wilderness has always been a fantasy, a beautiful Edenic refuge from the grease and grime of modern urban society, actively and aggressively maintained through marketing, policy, and on-the-ground land management. The fantasy is faltering and at some point may be impossible to uphold.

I can see the abandonment of wilderness as a useful principle going in several different directions. The worst would be the industrial exploitation of currently preserved areas' natural resources and the conversion of wilderness-designated spaces into extractive landscapes. The prevention of this kind of transformation has always been the best argument for wilderness. The need for untouched spaces (for recreation or otherwise) is a bastion against the ever-present need for economic growth based on the conversion of nature into concrete wealth. Chouinard's new green capitalism is designed to enshrine the wilderness system for this explicit purpose. Wilderness, by virtue of its primeval nature and all the cultural capital that comes with that idea, generates wealth through recreational use and, while not as immediately lucrative as wholesale mineral extraction, is a legible use within a capitalist system.

But what if these landscapes are *already* polluted? What happens to Eden after the Fall? The danger here is that extractive industries that are invested in getting to previously politically inaccessible resources will capitalize on these spaces so recently fallen from grace. They could easily, to draw from Traci Brynne Voyles, wasteland the landscapes, leaning into the nihilistic idea that preserved areas are already degraded to the point that they can no longer be called wildernesses and thus exploiting them is business as usual rather than a sacrilege.[6] Wilderness preservation allows for this because it is an all-or-nothing concept and thus easily destroyed, leaving no room for middle ground. While the reality is, of course, that human impact greatly varies within areas designated as wildernesses or other recreational spaces, under the ideological basis upon which political decisions are often made, there are no degrees of wilderness. It is or it is not.

The middle ground is the adoption of a more pragmatic approach to outdoor representation and relationality that essentially reflects how land management and outdoor recreation currently function in a practical sense. Instead of an idealized version that places certain spaces on a pedestal, then shapes landscapes to fit that vision, this approach looks at how land is being used, how it is being managed, successfully (according to the standards of the managers) or not, and then builds a marketable ideology from the ground up. This is a deeply unradical idea, and from a research and government land agency perspective, it already exists. We acknowledge the spectrum of human influence on public land; the social, political, economic, and ecological drivers of different kinds of land designations; and the competing stakeholder interests, of which federally recognized tribes are just one of many.

The status quo, minus the wilderness framing, remains a precarious system for both tribal sovereignty and environmental protection. Stakeholders and competing interests are inseparable from America's systems of power, systems that remain invested in managing public land for private interest, increasing the commodification of natural resources, and generally, as Chouinard eloquently points out, the transformation of nature into wealth. Our current system of land management and the values and ideologies undergirding them will result in the continued chipping away of protected lands, which, despite their failings, remain one of the strongest defenses against total ecological collapse.

If we can imagine worst-case scenarios, however, then we can also imagine better futures. A third possibility stemming from the rejection of wilderness is the embrace of a healthier and more balanced inclusion of humankind as a fundamental part of ecological systems. This would involve an understanding of ecological sovereignty, not as political ecologist Mark Smith defines it as state sovereignty over the natural world, but as nature's sovereignty over itself.[7] It would mean living sustainably and, importantly, reciprocally in community with other-than-human beings, respecting their agency and right to exist.

Within a western, Christian worldview, imagining this kind of ideology can be difficult enough—although there are many Indigenous and non-western models to emulate. Practically realizing it through policy, management, and behavior will be even harder. One path supporters of this idea have pursued is to work within existing legal systems and paradigms of human rights, in particular the jurisprudential theory of the

"Rights of Nature," which advocates for legal personhood for ecological spaces in the same way corporations have legal personhood. A 2021 study identified over four hundred rights-of-nature initiatives in thirty-nine countries including within the United States. New Zealand, for example, has famously given personhood to the Whanganui River, one of several rivers globally to have their rights recognized.[8] In the United States, a 2017 case was filed on behalf of the Colorado River, seeking similar recognition, but was dismissed by a federal court, and in 2020 Toledo, Ohio, sought to give Lake Erie a bill of rights in a law that was struck down by the Ohio Supreme Court.[9] From a generous perspective, Patagonia making the earth its only shareholder can be seen as drawing on this concept, building a legal basis for nature to be a corporate owner. An expansion of these laws could provide a legal and political basis for ecological sovereignty.

At the same time, this technique has drawbacks. The fight for legal personhood for nonhumans, at least in the United States, draws on the idea of corporate personhood, possibly entrenching the very capitalist systems that it seeks to disrupt. The language of personhood, in its appeal to legal legibility, continues to center humans, bringing nonhumans into legal and political systems designed to treat them as objects and property rather than working to reimagine what true multispecies justice could look like. Finally, as scholars like Zoe Todd and Erin Fitz-Henry remind us, ecological sovereignty without decolonization and serious consideration for Indigenous sovereignty risks simply overlaying the inequities and injustices that exist among human persons onto the natural world.[10]

This brings us to what an Indigenous-centered deconstruction of wilderness might look like. And this means, first and foremost, talking about land repatriation. There is no version of a politically just environmental future that does not include some level of restored land sovereignty for Indigenous people in the United States. This could take many different forms, but the only truly decolonial approach would be returning land, along with political, economic, and resource sovereignty over it, to Indigenous nations.[11] There is some precedent for this on very small scales including with American public land, like the Biden administration's restoration of the National Bison Range to the Confederated Salish and Kootenai Tribes; from private land, like a 2018 donation of farmland to the Ponca Nation in Nebraska; and through nonprofit agencies, like the Western Rivers Conservancy's donation of redwood forests to the

Esselen Tribe of California.[12] However, for any significant land transfers, the United States' policy can still be summed up by former Secretary of the Interior Zinke's statement that they are not in the business of giving away land.

In a 2021 article in *The Atlantic,* David Treuer made a case for the repatriation of all eighty-five million acres of National Park land, to be stewarded by a coalition of tribes for the benefit of Americans at large instead of by the federal government.[13] This eminently sensible transferal has some global precedence in places like New Zealand and would come with the kind of use covenants required to make it politically feasible, though they would be a limit on sovereignty. I would argue, however, that this proposal does not go far enough. It is both reasonable and ecologically necessary to assess all eight hundred million acres of public land for repatriation potential, with lesser models like full or comanagement the minimum option, rather than the vague consultation clauses that most public land charters include. The restoration of historic connections to land is critical to managing a post-wilderness system in a relational and responsible manner.

This is a position increasingly held by Indigenous activists in the #LandBack movement. This loose collection of mostly digital organizers is an example of a group recognizing and taking advantage of the current shift in land relationships and management models. They uncompromisingly advocate for, unsurprisingly, the return of land, in all its forms, to Indigenous people. Just as previous moments of Indigenous activism presaged the collapse of the frontier wilderness model and the adoption of the untrammeled model, #LandBack may be driving a new paradigm, one that cannot ignore Indigenous people any longer.

On the repatriation of private land, all I will say is that property is not inherent. It is a philosophical idea. We as a human community have the ability and responsibility to define our relationship to earth and each other in new and more just ways while still acknowledging and addressing the realities of this history and how it continues to impact different people in different ways.

On a more individual level, as outdoor recreators and as people living in a settler colonial nation, one way it might be useful to begin centering Indigenous sovereignty and just futures in our relationship with the natural world is to remember that all of us, Indigenous and non-Indigenous, are party to the treaties used by the United States to acquire land from

Indigenous nations to begin with. Treaties are often talked about as only pertaining to Indigenous people, but non-Indigenous people not associated with any federally recognized tribe, myself included, are equal parties to these agreements. The U.S. government made these agreements on our behalf and, whether we agree with them or not, it is not unreasonable to see ourselves as still responsible for upholding treaty responsibilities, even those the government has reneged on. How might it change your perspective on public land, knowing you have an ongoing personal investment in the difficult histories that created them? How might it change your behavior?

Untrammeled wilderness and the corporations that depend on it may be more resilient than I anticipate, and the wildernessing marketing strategy may continue to flourish far into the future, in one form or another. Patagonia's pledge may be an isolated incident rather than a sign of a more systemic turn. However, the history of wilderness reveals its instability, a deeply naturalized concept, in every sense of the word, being reinvented to serve the shifting needs of settler colonialism. And every shift is an opportunity for disruption and a chance to imagine futures that today may seem radical but tomorrow may be made real.

When I was working on and regularly posting to @indigenousgeotags, I created content that challenged established ways of recreation and standard histories of public lands. Followers had many different reactions to these narratives, but a common one was a form of paralysis, an understanding that current behaviors and systems were not working without knowing what the next step could be. The answer I gave to one of these commenters represents one of my earliest attempts to work through this issue and articulate some of the ideas that would eventually make it into this book. I think it is still relevant and so I want to end by including it here and encouraging readers to consider how they would respond themselves.

Question: *We can't turn back the clock on colonization, so what does moving forward look like?*

Answer: This is a really important question, so thank you for asking. I probably don't have a satisfying answer to it, but I want to try. I think the focus needs to be less about stewing on past wrongs and more about how to justly move forward. The pervasiveness and long history of colonization, however, doesn't mean the consequences of these actions don't still impact different groups of people today, and the inability to perfectly restore things to how they were doesn't absolve us of the responsibility to justly address these past wrongs. In some instances, this can mean addressing specific past events—like in the United States, we could uphold specific legally binding treaties that have been broken or pay for known thefts of land and property (Fourth Amendment takings for example). But you are also right that this is not possible everywhere and cannot address longer histories of colonialism and genocide. So, instead of just accepting this and saying, "I guess this is the way things are now," we move forward justly.

What I mean by justice here is that we work to restore right relationships among different groups of people, and yes—to your point about taking land from animals—between people and the natural world. Right relationships are built on respect, reciprocity, equality, and self-determination. While this seems easy, just an "everyone be nice and love each other" kind of thing, the problem is that it is actually pretty radical. It's radical on an individual level with people, especially white people like myself, having to address internalized racism and colonial worldviews, and it is radical on a political and social level—how would American society have to change if we seriously accepted the ideas that all people are inherently valuable and nonexploitable and the natural world is not a commodity but a partner to us that we need to respect and give to as much as we take from?

With regard to repatriation, sometimes this means land back in a western, property ownership way; other times it means political jurisdiction, as in the recent Oklahoma case; sometimes it means full co-management like at Bears Ears.[14] But in all cases on all land, it means a fundamental realignment of our relationship with land and with each other from a colonial one that treats land as a commodity to be owned and exploited to one that treats land, animals, and humans as a connected community. You ask, "What is the solution?" The answer is that there isn't a great one under our current political, economic, and social systems because these systems are built on the exploitation of land and people. I see public lands as places where we can begin rebuilding relationships and trust, but it has to start by addressing this history, acknowledging the contemporary consequences of it, and working together to imagine what a more just future looks like.[15]

Acknowledgments

We are taught to think of a book as a personal accomplishment, the culmination of years of individual, and often isolating, labor. It is, after all, a single authored work of scholarship written alone at a desk—or in my case a coffeeshop table. The reality is that this is a collaborative endeavor, that the writing of a monograph is holistic and is influenced and inspired by all parts of life and all kinds of people. It is only possible with the intellectual, emotional, and financial support of our communities both inside and outside the university. Far more people than I can mention here have been part of this support system for me, but I would like to take a minute to acknowledge at least a few of them.

This project was first and foremost shaped by my community at the University of Minnesota. I would like to especially thank my advisers Kevin Murphy and Jeani O'Brien, without whose guidance and support this would have been a very different book, as well as my generous mentorship of Kat Hayes, Vince Diaz, and Margaret Werry. I am grateful for the years of support from my American Studies cohort, Christine Bachman-Sanders, Jen Doane, and Lei Zhang, who have been nothing but a positive force at every point on the process. And most importantly, I'd like to acknowledge the members of American Indian and Indigenous Studies Workshop, who not only read and gave feedback on much of my work but also kept me accountable and drove me to think in broader and more critical ways about all aspects of my writing. Thank you to Katie Phillips, Mike Dockry, Amber Annis, Sasha Suarez, Kasey Keeler, Akikwe Cornell, Bernadette Perez, Kai Pyle, and Sam Majhor for being incredibly generous mentors and colleagues. Thank you to Hana Maruyama for being my coffeeshop writing companion, sounding board, and cheerleader when I doubted I would finish; to Rose Miron for being a constant inspiration for over a decade and my example for what it looks like to do meaningful, ethical research; and to John Little and Megan Red Shirt-Shaw for being like family to me.

In Chicago, thank you to the Chicagoland NAIS scholars Kelly Wisecup,

Teresa Montoya, SJ Zhang, Hayley Negrin, Matthew Kruer, and, once again, Rose Miron for their support and community and for becoming my flock during a hard, Covid-era transition.

This interdisciplinary book was only possible as the result of financial and scholarly investment from several interdisciplinary humanities institutes. I would like to thank the Institute for Advanced Study at the University of Minnesota, especially director Jennifer Gunn and my Interdisciplinary Doctoral Fellowship mentor Colin Agur; the Alice Kaplan Institute for the Humanities at Northwestern University, especially director Jessica Winegar and the incredibly supportive staff manning a nearly empty building and Doug Kiel for serving as my mentor; and the Mahindra Humanities Center at Harvard University, especially Steven Biel and Suzannah Clark. I am also deeply grateful to my Harvard colleagues Kessie Alexandre, Julio Aguilar, Meg Perret, Katerina Korola, and Jordan Kinder. Their feedback and conversation were a crucial part of my final writing and revisions.

I want to thank all those involved in the Summer Institute on Global Indigeneity where this project coalesced. I am grateful to Vince Diaz, Tony Lucero, Chad Allen, and Hokulani Aikau for their guidance and insight, which has continued far beyond the institute, and to Lydia Heberling for the many conversations that have helped shape my work and myself as a scholar.

This book wouldn't have been possible without the support of my family and friends outside academia. Thank you to my parents, Kent and Trudi, and siblings, Sarah, Ellie, and Max, for encouragement even when they weren't quite sure what I was actually writing; to my Aunt Marisa whose home became my summer writing retreat; and to many friends, especially Jenna Anderson, Amanda Kogle, and Ryan and Callie Leichty, all of whom inspired me to bring new perspectives and creative approached to my work.

I'm grateful to the reviewers for the University of Minnesota Press and to Jason Weidemann for guiding me though the editorial process.

Finally, I would like to thank and acknowledge all the dedicated activists on Instagram who have been teachers and inspirations to me throughout this project. In particular, thank you to Jolie Varela and Autumn Harry for their unceasing work to fight for a more Indigenous outdoor community and Len Necefer for his work challenging the outdoor industry from the inside. This book is dedicated to the work they all are doing to re-Indigenize the outdoors.

Notes

Introduction

1. A note on terminology: I largely use the term *Indigenous* throughout the book because, while I focus mostly on American Indian people in the United States, it is an issue that also impacts Alaska Natives, Pacific Islanders, and Canadian First Nations people. However, I use *American Indian* when referencing people specifically impacted by U.S. laws, policies, or government agencies where *Indian* remains the official term and not *Indigenous people* in general.

2. For more on this duality, see William Cronon, "The Trouble with Wilderness," in *The Great New Wilderness Debate,* ed. J. Baird Callicott and Michael P. Nelson (Athens: University of Georgia Press, 1998), 471–99.

3. Traci Brynne Voyles, *Wastelanding: Legacies of Uranium Mining in Navajo Country* (Minneapolis: University of Minnesota Press, 2015), 59.

4. Patrick Wolfe, "Settler Colonialism and the Elimination of the Native," *Journal of Genocide Research* 8, no. 4 (December 2006): 387–409.

5. Lorenzo Veracini, *Settler Colonialism: A Theoretical Overview* (New York: Palgrave Macmillan, 2010); Walter Hixson, *American Settler Colonialism: A History* (New York: Palgrave Macmillan, 2013). It is also incredibly important to point out that while *settler colonialism* as a field and term may have come from the writings of settler scholars in the late 1990s and early 2000s, the ideas expressed have been articulated by Indigenous activists and political actors for decades. See J. Kēhaulani Kauanui, "'A Structure, Not an Event': Settler Colonialism and Enduring Indigeneity," Forum: Emergent Critical Analytics for Alternative Humanities Issue, *Lateral* 5, no. 1 (2016); Tracey Banivanua Mar, *Decolonisation and the Pacific: Indigenous Globalisation and the Ends of Empire* (Cambridge: Cambridge University Press, 2016).

6. Joanne Barker, "For Whom Sovereignty Matters," in *Sovereignty Matters: Locations of Contestation and Possibility in Indigenous Struggles for Self-Determination,* ed. Joanne Barker (Lincoln: University of Nebraska Press, 2005a), 1–32; Kevin Bruyneel, *The Third Space of Sovereignty: The Postcolonial Politics of U.S.–Indigenous Relations* (Minneapolis: University of Minnesota Press, 2007); see also Taiaiake Alfred, *Peace, Power, Righteousness: An Indigenous Manifesto* (New York: Oxford University Press, 1999);

Mark Rifkin, *The Erotics of Sovereignty: Queer Native Writing in the Era of Self-Determination* (Minneapolis: University of Minnesota Press, 2012); J. Kēhaulani Kauanui, "'A Structure, Not an Event': Settler Colonialism and Enduring Indigeneity," Forum: Emergent Critical Analytics for Alternative Humanities Issue, *Lateral* 5, no. 1 (2016).

7. Kyle Whyte, "Settler Colonialism, Ecology, and Environmental Justice," *Environment and Society* 9, no. 1 (2018): 137; Heather Davis and Zoe Todd, "On the Importance of a Date, or Decolonizing the Anthropocene," *ACME: An International Journal for Critical Geographies* 16, no. 4 (2017): 761–80.

8. Kyle Powys Whyte, "On Resilient Parasitisms, or Why I'm Skeptical of Indigenous/Settler Reconciliation," *Journal of Global Ethics* 14, no. 2 (2018): 285; Amitav Ghosh, *The Great Derangement: Climate Change and the Unthinkable* (Chicago: Chicago University Press, 2016); Davis and Todd, "On the Importance of a Date," 761–80; Michael Dockry and Kyle Whyte, "Improving on Nature: The Legend Lake Development, Menominee Resistance, and the Ecological Dynamics of Settler Colonialism," *The American Indian Quarterly* 45, no. 2 (Spring 2021), 95–120.

9. Nick Estes, *Our History Is the Future: Standing Rock Versus the Dakota Access Pipeline, and the Long Tradition of Indigenous Resistance* (New York: Verso, 2019); Melanie Yazzie, "The Red Deal," *The Red Nation*, September 22, 2019, https://therednation.org/2019/09/22/the-red-deal/.

10. Mark David Spence, *Dispossessing the Wilderness: Indian Removal and the Making of the National Parks* (Oxford: Oxford University Press, 1999); William Cronon, *Changes in the Land: Indians, Colonists, and the Ecology of New England* (New York: Hill and Wang, 1983); Karl Jacoby, *Crimes against Nature: Squatters, Poachers, Thieves, and the Hidden History of American Conservation* (Berkeley: University of California Press); Dorceta E. Taylor, *Toxic Communities: Environmental Racism, Industrial Pollution, and Residential Mobility* (New York: NYU Press, 2014).

11. Todd Wilkinson, "The Question that None of Greater Yellowstone's Conservation Groups Are Willing to Confront," *Mountain Journal,* August 7, 2020, https://mountainjournal.org/conservation-groups-in-greater -yellowstone-are-missing-in-action-on-growth-issues.

12. Deborah Berman Santana and Patrick Novotny, "Where We Live, Work, and Play: The Environmental Justice Movement and the Struggle for a New Environmentalism," *Contemporary Sociology* 31, no. 1 (2002): 63.

13. David Naguib Pellow, *What Is Critical Environmental Justice?* (Cambridge: Polity Press, 2018).

14. For examples, see Naomi Klein, *This Changes Everything: Capitalism vs. the Climate* (New York: Simon & Schuster, 2014), Julie Sze, *Environmental Justice in a Moment of Danger* (Berkeley: University of California Press, 2020); Robert D. Bullard, *Dumping in Dixie: Race, Class, and Environmental Quality* (New York: Routledge, 2000); Charles Mills, "Black Trash," in *Faces*

of Environmental Racism ed. Laura Westra & B.E. Lawson (Lanham, MD: Rowman & Littlefield, 2001), 73–91; Clyde Woods, *Development Arrested: The Blues and Plantation Power in the Mississippi Delta* (New York: Verso, 1998); and Dorceta E. Taylor, *Toxic Communities: Environmental Racism, Industrial Pollution, and Residential Mobility* (New York: NYU Press, 2014).

15. "17 Principles of Environmental Justice," *Environmental Working Group,* October 2, 2007, https://www.ewg.org/enviroblog/2007/10/17-principles-environmental-justice.

16. Wolfe, "Settler Colonialism and the Elimination of the Native," 387–409.

17. Glen Sean Coulthard, *Red Skin, White Masks: Rejecting the Colonial Politics of Recognition* (Minneapolis: University of Minnesota Press, 2014), 13.

18. Melanie Yazzie Estes, "The Red Deal," *The Red Nation,* September 22, 2019, https://therednation.org/2019/09/22/the-red-deal/.

19. Tracy Voyles, *Wastelanding: Legacies of Uranium Mining in Navajo Country* (Minneapolis: University of Minnesota Press, 2015); Pellow, *What Is Critical Environmental Justice?;* Winona LaDuke, *The Winona LaDuke Chronicles: Stories from the Front Lines in the Battle for Environmental Justice* (Halifax: Fernwood Publishing, 2017).

20. Voyles, *Wastelanding,* 26; Also see Yen Le Espiritu, *Home Bound: Filipino American Lives across Cultures, Communities, and Countries* (Berkeley: University of California Press, 2003), 47.

21. Voyles, *Wastelanding,* 59.

22. "Instagram by the Numbers: Stats, Demographics & Fun Facts," *Omnicore,* January 26, 2020, https://www.omnicoreagency.com/instagram-statistics/. As of March 2023, there were two billion monthly users.

23. "Social Media Fact Sheet," *Pew Research Center: Internet & Technology,* June 12, 2019, https://www.pewresearch.org/internet/fact-sheet/social-media/; Facebook is currently under a federal antitrust law investigation for monopolistic practices with social media.

24. "Instagram by the Numbers."

25. Jo Middleton, "How Fashion Brands Are Harnessing the Power of Instagram," *Digital Marketing World Forum,* February 12, 2016, https://www.digitalmarketing-conference.com/fashion-brands-harnessing-insta/.

26. "The State of Influencer Marketing 2019: Benchmark Report," *Influencer Marketing Hub,* May 28, 2019, https://influencermarketinghub.com/influencer-marketing-2019-benchmark-report/; "Projected Revenue of Instagram from 2017 to 2019," *Statista,* January 2019, https://www.statista.com/statistics/271633/annual-revenue-of-instagram/.

27. Gretchen Fox, "The Outdoor Industry vs. the Digital World," *Forbes,* December 4, 2019, https://www.forbes.com/sites/gretchenfox/#314fb7586092; Annette McGivney, "Power in Numbers," *snews,* June 26, 2018, https://www.snewsnet.com/news/social-media-panel.

28. "High Visitation, Low Funding and Staff Jeopardizing Parks," *National Parks Conservation Association,* March 1, 2018, https://www.npca.org/articles/1762-high-visitation-low-funding-and-staff-jeopardizing-parks.

29. See Robert V. Kozinets, "On Netnography: Initial Reflections on Consumer Research Investigation of Cyberculture," *Advances in Consumer Research* 25 (1998): 366–71; Jeffrey Lane, "The Digital Street: An Ethnographic Study of Networked Street Life in Harlem," *American Behavioral Science* 60, no. 1 (2016); Zizi Papacharissi, *A Networked Self: Identity, Community, and Culture on Social Network Sites* (New York: Routledge, 2011); Daniel Miller and Don Slater, *The Internet: An Ethnographic Approach* (Oxford: Berg Publishers, 2001); and Samuel Wilson and Leighton Peterson, "The Anthropology of Online Communities," *Annual Review of Anthropology* 31 (2002): 449–67.

30. API stands for Application Programming Interface and refers to the functions that simplify access to data and features of a program or application like Instagram. Access to API is necessary to make the most of the data.

31. Netnography seems to be winning out as the most popular term in business research and is entering academic research; it seems to be the only one to definitively originate in a specific published paper with specific methodological parameters. Despite this, it is still used to describe methods not exactly what Kozinets seemed to have intended and is becoming increasingly encompassing and vague. Also, I really hate the term *Netnography* because it is unclear whether it is a portmanteau for *internet* or *network,* which implies different things, and it deeply evokes 1990s internet culture, which makes it feel dated. It is also less flexible for Web 2.0 and Web App research. Robert V. Kozinets, "Management Netnography: Axiological and Methodological Developments in Online Cultural Business Research," in *The SAGE Handbook of Qualitative Business and Management Research Methods,* ed. Catherine Cassell, Ann L. Cunliffe, and Gina Grandy (Thousand Oaks, CA: SAGE Publications, 2017).

32. Kozinets, *Netnography: Redefined* (London: SAGE Publications, 2015).

33. José van Dijck, *The Culture of Connectivity: A Critical History of Social Media* (Oxford: Oxford University Press, 2013), 28–43.

34. Mark Andrejevic, *Infoglut: How Too Much Information Is Changing the Way We Think and Know* (New York: Routledge, 2013), 1–18.

35. In reality, these things impact everything a user does on these platforms, but that is a different book that is more concerned with the platforms themselves than with the businesses using the platforms.

36. van Dijck, *The Culture of Connectivity,* 25–29.

37. Bruno Latour, *Reassembling the Social: An Introduction to Actor-Network-Theory* (Oxford: Oxford University Press, 2005); Indigenous studies presents several important critiques to Latour and ANT, most notably suggesting that questions about nonhuman agency should be drawn from an Indigenous intellectual genealogy that predates western posthumanism.

However, because I'm basing my methodology on van Dijck's preexisting models that draw from Latour, I feel like it is important to stay with this citation.

38. Donald Horton and Richard Wohl, "Mass Communications and Para-social Interaction: Observation on Intimacy at a Distance," *Psychiatry* 19, no. 3 (1956): 215–29.

39. Kjerstin S. Thorson and Shelly Rodgers, "Relationships between Blogs as EWOM and Interactivity, and Parasocial Interaction," *Journal of Interactive Advertising* 6, no. 2 (March 2006): 5–44; Leslie Rasmussen, "Parasocial Interaction in the Digital Age: An Examination of Relationship Building and the Effectiveness of YouTube Celebrities," *The Journal of Social Media in Society* 7, no. 1 (2018): 280–94.

40. Rachel Elizabeth Cargle, "Decolonize Intellect," Instagram, January 7, 2019. https://www.instagram.com/p/B6_4bi-n_tD/.

1. This Land Is Our Land

1. Len Necefer, Q&A after screening of *Welcome to Gwitchyaa Zhee* (St. Paul, Minnesota, March 11, 2019).

2. Glen Sean Coulthard, *Red Skin, White Masks: Rejecting the Colonial Politics of Recognition* (Minneapolis: University of Minnesota Press, 2014), 13.

3. Mark Allen Jackson, "Is This Song Your Song Anymore? Revisioning Woody Guthrie's 'This Land Is Your Land,'" *American Music* 20, no. 3 (2002): 251.

4. Jordan Marie Daniel (@_NativeInLA), "I cringe when I hear 'This land is your land,'" Twitter, January 20, 2021, https://twitter.com/_NativeInLA /status/1351947874616049664; Jolie Varela (@indigenouswomenhike), "This Is Native Land," Instagram, January 20, 2021, https://www.instagram.com /p/CKRmVVSl9m-/.

5. Kaitlin Curtice (@KaitlinCurtice), "This land was made . . . ," Twitter, January 20, 2021, https://twitter.com/KaitlinCurtice/status /1352065689415254024; @kat_jefferson, "Changed the Lyrics," TikTok, January 21, 2021, https://www.tiktok.com/@kat_jefferson/video /6920125942820097286.

6. "2022 Outdoor Participation Trends Report" (Outdoor Recreation Association, September 19, 2022), https://outdoorindustry.org/resource /2022-outdoor-participation-trends-report/#:~:text=Share%3A,2021%20 to%20164.2M%20participants.

7. Carol Hardy Vincent, Laura A. Hanson, and Carla N. Argueta, "Federal Land Ownership: Overview and Data" (Congressional Research Service, March 3, 2017), https://fas.org/sgp/crs/misc/R42346.pdf.

8. R. Jeff Teashley, John C. Bergstrom, H. Ken Cordell, Stanley J. Zarnoch, and Paul Gentle, "Private Lands and Outdoor Recreation in the

United States," in *Outdoor Recreation in American Life: A National Assessment of Supply and Demand Trends*, ed. by H. Ken Cordell (Urbana, IL: Sagamore Publishing, 1999), 202; This is also probably mostly about not wanting hunters on their land, rather than hikers, but this survey does not differentiate, and I would be very surprised if nonacquaintance hikers are trying to hike on private land.

9. Bureau of Land Management, *Public Land Statistics 2017*, Volume 202 (June 2018), https://www.blm.gov/sites/blm.gov/files/PublicLandStatistics 2017.pdf.

10. Although this is changing.

11. Mark David Spence, *Dispossessing the Wilderness: Indian Removal and the Making of the National Parks* (Oxford: Oxford University Press, 1999); William Cronon, *Changes in the Land: Indians, Colonists, and the Ecology of New England* (New York: Hill and Wang, 1983); Karl Jacoby, *Crimes against Nature: Squatters, Poachers, Thieves, and the Hidden History of American Conservation* (Berkeley: University of California Press); Dina Gilio-Whitaker, *As Long as Grass Grows: The Indigenous Fight for Environmental Justice, from Colonization to Standing Rock* (Boston: Beacon Press), 91–110.

12. Carol Hardy Vincent, Laura A. Hanson, and Carla N. Argueta, "Federal Land Ownership: Overview and Data" (Congressional Research Service, March 3, 2017), 1, https://fas.org/sgp/crs/misc/R42346.pdf; National Wilderness Institute, "Public Land Ownership by State" (Natural Resource Council of Maine, 1995) https://www.nrcm.org/documents/publiclandownership.pdf; While federal land is officially held in trust—as in owned collectively by all Americans and managed for them by government agencies—state land is owned directly by the states, and the level of state resident involvement in decision-making and revenue varies from state to state.

13. The Dawes Act of 1887 or the Allotment Act broke up collectively owned reservation land, distributing allotments to individual tribal members, then opened the remaining reservation land up for settlement. "OSE Statistics and Facts" (Office of the Special Trustee for American Indians, 2020), https://www.doi.gov/ost/about_us/Statistics-and-Facts; Indian Trust Land is technically included in the public land numbers and is administered under the Bureau of Indian Affairs within the Department of the Interior. It is held in trust specifically for individual federally recognized tribes and, despite how it has sometimes been treated, not for Americans in general.

14. Frederick Jackson Turner, "The Significance of the Frontier in American History" (Madison: State Historical Society of Wisconsin, 1894).

15. Mark David Spence, *Dispossessing the Wilderness: Indian Removal and the Making of the National Parks* (Oxford: Oxford University Press, 1999).

16. Herbert Hoover, "Death Valley National Monument—California, 1933, Proclamation 2028 of February 11, 1933." 47 stat. 2554 (February 11, 1933); Gilio-Whitaker, *As Long as Grass Grows*, 106; United States vs. Confederated

Tribes of Colville Indian Reservation, United States Court of Appeals, 9th Circuit, 2010; Jacoby, *Crimes against Nature.*

17. Held in trust essentially means that the land is owned by the American people but is managed and controlled by the government on their behalf.

18. Extractive industry and leasing are also on behalf of the American people with money going to the federal budget. These are far from all the conservation- and recreation-based designations, with twenty-eight designations in the National Park Service alone, but they are the most common.

19. Patagonia, "The President Stole Your Land," Instagram, December 4, 2017, https://www.instagram.com/p/BcTKr6Xl6I8/.

20. "Wilderness Act of 1964," PL 88–577 (1964); U.S. Forest Service, "Wilderness," *Managing the Land,* 2018, https://www.fs.fed.us/managing -land/wilderness.

21. Cronon, *Changes in the Land.*

22. David Garcia (@mapmakerdavid), "The US-Settler Colonial Model of Conservation," Twitter, March 8, 2021, https://twitter.com/mapmakerdavid /status/1369059207589154816.

23. Mark Dowie, "Clash of Cultures: The Conflict between Conservation and Indigenous People in Wild Landscapes," *The Guardian* (June 2, 2009), https://www.theguardian.com/environment/2009/jun/03/yosemite -conservation-indigenous-people.

24. Coulthard, *Red Skin, White Masks,* 13.

25. Giorgio Agamben, *State of Exception* (Chicago: University of Chicago Press, 2008).

26. As Mark Rifkin points out in his essay "Indigenizing Agamben: Rethinking Sovereignty in Light of the 'Peculiar' Status of Native Peoples," reservations themselves can be seen as the result of the United States attempting to deal with the "exceptional" status of Indians. Mark Rifkin, "Indigenizing Sovereignty in Light of the 'Peculiar' Status of Native Peoples," *Cultural Critique,* 73 (Fall 2009): 88–124.

27. Barry Pritzker, *Native Americans: Southwest—California—Northwest Coast—Great Basin* (Santa Barbara: ABC-CLIO, 1998), 32.

28. Environmental Protection Agency, "Environmental Assessment: Dakota Access Pipeline Project, Williams, Morton, and Emmons Counties, North Dakota," EPA, https://www.scribd.com/document/323278826/ACOE -Dakota-Access-Report.

29. Traci Brynne Voyles, *Wastelanding: Legacies of Uranium Mining in Navajo Country* (Minneapolis: University of Minnesota Press, 2015).

30. Seth King, "Carter Signs a Bill to Protect 104 Million Acres in Alaska," *New York Times,* December 3, 1980, https://timesmachine.nytimes.com /timesmachine/1980/12/03/111319482.html?pageNumber=20.

31. Greg Balkin and Len Necefer, *Welcome to Gwichyaa Zhee* (Patagonia,

Inc., 2018). Not to mention the formation of Alaska tribes into corporations that directly encourage this kind of environmental resource exploitation under the Alaska Claims Settlement Act of 1971.

32. "Executive Order 13795 of April 28, 2017, Implementing an America-First Offshore Energy Strategy," *Code of Federal Regulations* 82 (2017), 20815–20818, https://www.federalregister.gov/documents/2017/05 /03/2017-09087/implementing-an-america-first-offshore-energy-strategy.

33. Maya Wei-Haas, "Trump Just Remade Ocean Policy. Here's What That Means," *National Geographic,* July 13, 2018, https://www.national geographic.com/environment/2018/07/news-ocean-policy-indigenous -sustainability-fisheries-industry-economy-marine/.

34. "Executive Order 13940, Ocean Policy to Advance the Economic, Security, and Environmental Interests of the United States," *Code of Federal Regulations* 83 (2018), 29431–29434, https://www.federalregister.gov /documents/2018/06/22/2018-13640/ocean-policy-to-advance-the -economic-security-and-environmental-interests-of-the-united-states; Maya Wei-Haas, "Trump Just Remade Ocean Policy. Here's What That Means," *National Geographic,* July 13, 2018, https://www.nationalgeographic .com/environment/2018/07/news-ocean-policy-indigenous-sustainability -fisheries-industry-economy-marine/.

35. Kroner et al., "The Uncertain Future of Protected Lands and Water," *Science* (2019): 881–86.

36. "Statement from Secretary Zinke on the National Bison Range," Department of the Interior Press Release, April 13, 2017, https://www.doi .gov/pressreleases/statement-secretary-zinke-national-bison-range.

37. Jackson, "Is This Song Your Song Anymore?," 249–76.

38. Jackson, 250.

39. The North Face, "The North Face | This Land | Chris Burkard," YouTube, February 8, 2015, https://www.youtube.com/watch?v=5UaHljP1ar4.

40. This is itself an alternate version of this verse that is watered down. The original version reads, "There was a big high wall there that tried to stop me; Sign was painted, it said private property," lines that would not have had the political salience in 2014 that they would have even a year later at the beginning of Trump's Build the Wall campaign.

41. Pete Seeger, *Where Have All the Flowers Gone: A Singalong Memoir* (New York: W. W. Norton, 2009), 144.

42. Jackson, "Is This Song Your Song Anymore?," 271.

2. The Frontier Wilderness

1. "Labor Day Fire Destroys Historic Indian Princess Grave," *Cook County News Herald* (Grand Marais), October 6, 1960.

2. Philip J. Deloria, *Playing Indian* (New Haven, CT: Yale University Press, 1998), 5.

3. For more on this construction of wilderness, see William Cronon, "The Trouble with Wilderness: or Getting Back to the Wrong Nature," in *The Great New Wilderness Debate,* ed. J. Baird Callicott and Michael P. Nelson (Athens: University of Georgia Press, 1998), 480–81.

4. U.S. Congress. (1964). Wilderness Act. *Public Law, 577*(4), 1131–36.

5. *Oxford English Dictionary, s.v.* "Wilderness," accessed November 2, 2019; WILD Foundation, "What Is a Wilderness Area?" https://www.wild.org/how-we-work/policy-mgmt/defining-wilderness/, accessed May 2, 2019.

6. Nahnahnahnahnaah, "Wilderness," *Urban Dictionary,* September 2, 2009, accessed November 2, 2019, https://www.urbandictionary.com/define.php?term=Wilderness.

7. Roderick Frazier Nash, *Wilderness and the American Mind* (New Haven, CT: Yale University Press, 1982).

8. Alexis de Tocqueville, *Democracy in America,* ed. Phillips Bradley (New York: Alfred A. Knopf, 1945), 2, 74.

9. Mark David Spence, *Dispossessing the Wilderness: Indian Removal and the Making of the National Parks* (Oxford: Oxford University Press, 1999), 11.

10. Spence, *Dispossessing the Wilderness,* 11.

11. Nash, *Wilderness and the American Mind,* 46–47.

12. *Titus Lucretius Carus on the Nature of Things,* trans. Thomas Jackson (Oxford, 1929), 155 from Nash, *Wilderness and the American Mind,* 10.

13. Henry David Thoreau, "Walking," in *Excursion, the Writings of Henry David Thoreau,* Riverside Edition (Boston, 1893), 275.

14. See Charles Dickens, "The Noble Savage," https://web.archive.org/web/20100521073634/http://www.readbookonline.net/readOnLine/2529/.

15. Thoreau, *The Maine Woods* (Project Gutenberg, 2013), https://www.gutenberg.org/files/42500/42500-h/42500-h.htm.

16. Charles Lanman, *A Summer in the Wilderness: Embracing a Canoe Voyage up the Mississippi and around Lake Superior* (Project Gutenberg, 2015), Ch. 17, https://www.gutenberg.org/files/49506/49506-h/49506-h.htm#c17.

17. John Muir, *My First Summer in the Sierras* (New York: Penguin Publishing Group, 1987), 277.

18. Phoebe Young, *Camping Grounds: Public Nature in American Life from the Civil War to the Occupy Movement* (Oxford: Oxford University Press, 2021).

19. Frederick Jackson Turner, *The Significance of the Frontier in American History* (Madison: Wisconsin Historical Society, 1894); Theodore Roosevelt, *The Wilderness Hunter: An Account of the Big Game of the United States and its Chase with Horse, Hound, and Rifle* (New York: G. P. Putnam's Sons, 1893), 13.

20. While skirmishes continued until 1924, the official end of the Indian Wars, Wounded Knee symbolically closed that chapter of American history. Jeffrey Ostler, *Surviving Genocide: Native Nations and the United States from the American Revolution to Bleeding Kansas* (New Haven, CT: Yale University Press, 2019).

21. An Act to Provide for the Allotment of Lands in Severalty to Indians on the Various Reservations (General Allotment Act or Dawes Act), Statutes at Large 24, 388–91, NADP Document A1887; Brenda Child, *Boarding School Seasons: American Indian Families 1900–1940* (Lincoln: University of Nebraska Press, 1998).

22. Karl Jacoby, *Crimes against Nature: Squatters, Poachers, Thieves, and the Hidden History of American Conservation* (Berkeley: University of California Press), 99–120.

23. The first time was during the Mariposa Campaign in 1851; John Bingaman, *The Ahwhahneechees: A Story of the Yosemite Indians* (Lodi, CA: End-Kian Publishing, 1966), http://www.yosemite.ca.us/library/the_ahwhahneechees/chapter_3.html.

24. Deloria, *Playing Indian*, 5.

25. Spence, *Dispossessing the Wilderness*, 10–12.

26. These are not designed to be hard distinctions, but rather generalizations to help understand a long period of changing representations and ideologies.

27. Deloria, *Playing Indian*, 5.

28. Deloria, 110–11.

29. Jake Gallagher, "Remembering Abercrombie & Fitch for What It Was," *A Continuous Lean*, January 13, 2014. https://www.acontinuouslean.com/2014/01/13/remembering-abercrombie-fitch/.

30. Abercrombie & Fitch, "Abercrombie & Fitch, 1913," *USU Digital Exhibits*, accessed August 29, 2022, http://exhibits.lib.usu.edu/items/show/22439.

31. For more on replacement narratives, see Jean M. O'Brien, *Firsting and Lasting: Writing Indians out of Existence in New England* (Minneapolis: University of Minnesota Press, 2010).

32. It could also arguably be the Adirondacks where Abenaki guides were common throughout the nineteenth century or Maine where Penobscot or Maniseet guides were employed at least through the 1920s.

33. For example, the Treaty of 1854.

34. Chantal Norrgard, *Seasons of Change: Labor, Treaty Rights, and Ojibwe Nationhood* (Chapel Hill: University of North Carolina Press, 2014), 108–27.

35. Melissa Rohde, "Living and Working in Enchanted Lands: American Indian Tourism Labor, Development, and Activism, 1900-1970," PhD diss., University of Illinois at Urbana-Champaign, 2010.

36. Rohde.

37. Norrgard, *Seasons of Change,* 122.

38. Hal K. Rothman, *Devil's Bargains: Tourism in the Twentieth-Century American West* (Lawrence: University of Kansas Press, 1998).

39. Many scholars have deeply examined the ways Indigenous people navigated the tourist experience of this era. In particular, Chantal Norrgard, *Seasons of Change: Labor, Treaty Rights, and Ojibwe Nationhood* (Chapel Hill: University of North Carolina Press, 2014) and Rohde, "Living and Working in Enchanted Lands," look at Ojibwe guides in this region and many of these anecdotes come from their excellent work. Additionally, see John Troutman, *Indian Blues: American Indians and the Politics of Music, 1879–1934* (Norman: University of Oklahoma Press, 2009); Paige Raibmon, *Authentic Indians: Episode of Encounters from the Late Nineteenth Century Northwest Coast* (Durham, NC: Duke University Press, 1985); Clyde Ellis, "Five Dollars a Week to Be 'Regular Indians': Shows, Exhibitions, and the Economics of Indian Dancing, 1880–1930," in *Native Pathways: American Indian Culture and Economic Development in the Twentieth Century,* eds. Brian Hosmer and Colleen O'Neill, 194–208; Larry Nesper, *The Walleye War: The Struggle for Ojibwe Spearfishing and Treaty Rights* (Lincoln: University of Nebraska Press, 2002); Tina Loo, "Of Moose and Men: Hunting for Masculinities in British Columbia, 1880–1939," *Western Historical Quarterly* 32, no. 3 (Autumn 2001): 296–319; and Katrina Phillips, *Staging Indigeneity: Salvage Tourism and the Performance of Native American History* (Chapel Hill: University of North Carolina Press, 2021).

40. Rohde, "Living and Working in Enchanted Lands," 108.

41. Rohde, 108.

42. Norrgard, *Seasons of Change,* 123.

43. Loo, "Of Moose and Men," 296–319.

44. *Sunset* magazine, May 1904 Issue Cover, painting by Chris Jorgensen, in *Geographies of Wonder: Origin Stories of America's National Parks, 1872–1933,* The Huntington Library, Art Collections, and Botanical Gardens.

45. Montgomery Ward's 1929 Catalog features Mt. Rainier as an interesting counterexample to this, but was likely in celebration of the National Park's thirtieth anniversary.

46. Rebecca Solnit, *Savage Dreams: A Journey into the Hidden Wars of the American West* (Berkeley: University of California Press, 1994), 221.

47. This is, however, only thirteen years after Major John Savage's 1851 massacre of the Ahwahneechee—the first of four eventual evictions of the tribe from the valley—so there must have been considerable tension regardless of park policy.

48. Spence, *Dispossessing the Wilderness,* 126.

49. Albert Bierstadt, *The Domes of Yosemite,* 1867, oil on canvas.

50. Eric Michael Johnson, "How John Muir's Brand of Conservation Led to the Decline of Yosemite," *Scientific American* (August 13, 2014), https://blogs.scientificamerican.com/primate-diaries/how-john-muir-s-brand-of-conservation-led-to-the-decline-of-yosemite/?redirect=1; Detroit Publishing Co., Copyright Claimant, and Publisher Detroit Publishing Co, Jackson, William Henry, photographer. *Yosemite Valley from Artists' Point, Calif.* United States Yosemite Valley California Yosemite National Park, ca. 1898. Photograph. https://www.loc.gov/item/2016802680/.

51. Spence, *Dispossessing the Wilderness,* 120; Alfred Runte, "Indian Field Days, 1925. Yosemite Superintendent Washington B. Lewis poses with Chief Lemee (Chris Brown), while a large crowd gathers along the racetrack in the background. First held in 1916, Indian Field Days won Park Service endorsement as a means of boosting Yosemite visitation," in Alfred Runte, *Yosemite: The Embattled Wilderness* (Lincoln: University of Nebraska Press, 1990), https://www.nps.gov/parkhistory/online_books/runte2/contents.htm #illustrations; https://npgallery.nps.gov/AssetDetail/5bbdbb7a1c034a0 187ce56459d5af335?.

52. Boyd Cothran, "Working the Indian Field Days: The Economy of Authenticity and the Question of Agency in Yosemite Valley," *American Indian Quarterly* 34, no. 2 (Spring 2010): 195.

53. John Bingaman, *The Ahwahneechees: A Story of the Yosemite Indians* (Lodi, CA: End-Kian Publishing, 1966). http://www.yosemite.ca.us/library /the_ahwahneechees/chapter_3.html.

54. Cothran, "Working the Indian Field Days: The Economy of Authenticity and the Question of Agency in Yosemite Valley," *American Indian Quarterly* 34, no. 2 (Spring 2010): 195.

55. Spence, *Dispossessing the Wilderness,* 130.

3. Wilderness Untrammeled

1. Unless, of course, needed to access private land, preexisting mineral claims, or motorboats where they were historically used.

2. *Mille Lacs Band of Chippewa Indians v. Minnesota,* 861 F. Supp. 684 (D. Minn. 1994); "Wilderness Act of 1964," PL 88–577 (1964); "Boundary Waters Canoe Area Wilderness Act," PL 95–495 (October 1, 1979).

3. Firsting and Lasting refers to a settler colonial narrative strategy where the "last" of an Indigenous group is replaced by the "first" of a settler group, despite on the ground reality not reflecting these stories. See Jean M. O'Brien, *Firsting and Lasting: Writing Indians Out of Existence in New England* (Minneapolis: University of Minnesota Press, 2010).

4. Many of these tribes regained land and recognitions in subsequent decades after the reversal of termination policy.

5. Sasha Suarez, "Gakaabikaang: White Earth Ojibwe Women and the

Creation of Indian Minneapolis in the Twentieth Century" (PhD diss., University of Minnesota, 2020).

6. Public Law 280 delegated certain federal responsibilities toward American Indians to certain states.

7. Bradley Shreve, "'From Time Immemorial': The Fish-In Movement and the Rise of Intertribal Activism," *Pacific Historical Review* 78, no. 3 (2009): 403–34.

8. O'Brien, *Firsting and Lasting*, xv.

9. Roger Kaye, "The Untrammeled Wild and Wilderness Character in the Anthropocene," *International Journal of Wilderness* 24, no. 1 (April 2018), https://ijw.org/the-untrammeled-wild-and-wilderness-character-in-the-anthropocene/.

10. Kevin Proescholdt, "Untrammeled Wildness," *Minnesota History* 61 (2008): 114–23. http://wildernesswatch.org/pdf/Untrammeled.pdf.

11. "Wilderness Act of 1964," PL 88–577 (1964).

12. The flaws in this model have been extensively discussed by environmental historians including Cronon, Jacoby, and others.

13. Sigurd F. Olson, *The Lonely Land* (Minneapolis: University of Minnesota Press, 1997).

14. Theodore Catton, *Inhabited Wilderness: Indians, Eskimos, and National Parks in Alaska* (Albuquerque: University of New Mexico, 1997), 142.

15. James Morton Turner, "From Woodcraft to 'Leave No Trace,'" in *The Wilderness Debate Rages On: Continuing the Great New Wilderness Debate,* ed. Michael P. Nelson and J. Baird Callicott (Athens: University of Georgia Press, 2008), 146.

16. See Rachel Carson, *Silent Spring* (Boston: Houghton Mifflin, 1962); and Arne Næss, "The Shallow and the Deep, Long-Range Ecology Movement: A Summary," *Inquiry: An Interdisciplinary Journal of Philosophy* (1973): 95–100.

17. George Sessions, *Deep Ecology for the Twenty-First Century: Readings on the Philosophy and Practice of the New Environmentalism* (Boston: Shambhala Publications, 1995).

18. Turner, "From Woodcraft to 'Leave No Trace,'" 151.

19. Shepard Krech III, *The Ecological Indian: Myth and History* (New York: W. W. Norton, 1999), 21.

20. Krech, *The Ecological Indian,* 23–24.

21. Turner, "From Woodcraft to 'Leave No Trace,'" 162.

22. Approximately $3 billion adjusted for inflation. Tucker, "From Woodcraft to 'Leave No Trace,'" 156; Margaret Walls and Matthew Ashenfarb, "Efficiency and Equity of an Outdoor Recreation Equipment Tax to Fund Public Lands," Working paper through Resources for the Future (2020).

23. The Ahwahneechee are not federally recognized and therefore

struggle to claim the rights laid out in the American Indian Religious Freedom Act. New park agreements as of 2018 allow for some limited traditional Ahwahneechee activity in the park; Jake Bullinger, "Yosemite Finally Reckons with Its Discriminatory Past," *Outside Magazine,* August 23, 2018, https://www.outsideonline.com/outdoor-adventure/environment/yosemite -national-park-native-american-village-miwuk/.

24. Joseph E. Taylor III, *Pilgrims of the Vertical: Yosemite Rock Climbers & Nature at Risk* (Cambridge, MA: Harvard University Press, 2010).

25. This story is part of the oral history of the climbing community and there appears to be at least one associated arrest for the looting of a downed plane in the park, but whether climbers truly salvaged and sold five tons of marijuana is unclear. Peter Mortimer and Nick Rosen, *Valley Uprising* (2014; Sender Films); Glynn Washington interviewing Dale Bard, "Lake Chronicopia," on Snap Judgment, *NPR,* August 14, 2015, https://www.npr .org/2015/08/14/432233826/lake-chronicopia.

26. Robert A. Jones, "National Parks: A Report on the Range War at Generation Gap," *New York Times,* July 25, 1971.

27. John Bingaman, *The Ahwahneechees: A Story of the Yosemite Indians* (Lodi, CA: End-Kian, 1966), http://www.yosemite.ca.us/library/the _ahwahneechees/chapter_3.html. The last Ahwahneechee park ranger, Joe Johnson, retired in 1996.

28. Mark Dowie, *Conservation Refugees: The Hundred-Year Conflict between Global Conservation and Native Peoples* (Cambridge, MA: MIT Press, 2011), 10.

29. Michael Sammartino, "To Bolt or Not to Bolt: A Framework for Common Sense Climbing Regulation," The American Bar Association, August 24, 2020, https://www.americanbar.org/groups/environment _energy_resources/publications/plr/20200824-to-bolt-or-not-to-bolt/.

30. The North Face, "The North Face, Spring 1985," *USU Digital Exhibits,* accessed September 23, 2022, http://exhibits.lib.usu.edu/items/show/20916.

31. Sammartino, "To Bolt or Not to Bolt."

32. Sammartino.

33. Jennifer Wigglesworth, "The Cultural Politics of Naming Outdoor Rock Climbing Routes," *Annals of Leisure Research* (August 2021).

34. The North Face, "About Us," TheNorthFace.com, accessed October 30, 2019.

35. William Cronon, "The Trouble with Wilderness: or Getting Back to the Wrong Nature," in *The Great New Wilderness Debate,* ed. J. Baird Callicott and Michael P. Nelson (Athens: University of Georgia Press, 1998), 485.

36. For example, see Joseph Campbell, *The Hero with a Thousand Faces* (Novato, CA: New World Library, 2008).

37. Henry Nash Smith, *Virgin Land: The American West as Symbol and Myth* (Cambridge, MA: Harvard University Press, 1950), 81.

38. Shepard Krech III, *The Ecological Indian: Myth and History* (New York: W. W. Norton & Company, 1999).

39. Smith, *Virgin Land,* 81; See also Hampton Sides, *Blood and Thunder: The Epic Story of Kit Carson and the Conquest of the American West* (New York: Anchor Books, 2006).

40. Sides, *Blood and Thunder*; Smith, *Virgin Land,* 85.

41. Maurice Halbwachs, the founder of memory studies, contended that group identity is mediated through collective, and constructed, understandings of the past. The ways shared experiences are told and retold create social frameworks through which individuals within a group, in this case outdoorspeople, remember their experience and understand their relationships to each other. For Halbwachs, the past is a product of the indivisible interactions of discourse, representation, and memory. Maurice Halbwachs, *On Collective Memory* (Chicago: University of Chicago Press, 1992).

42. See Iyko Day, *Alien Capital: Asian Racialization and the Logic of Settler Colonial Capitalism* (Durham, NC: Duke University Press, 2016).

43. Sarah Banet-Weiser, *Authentic™: The Politics of Ambivalence in a Brand Culture* (New York: New York University Press, 2012), 4.

44. Ad-tech refers to the big data technology side of the marketing industry—essentially software and programs that gather massive amounts of user information based on website views, clicks, and other activity and the associated algorithms used in analysis.

45. Utpal M. Dholakia, "The Perils of Algorithm-Based Marketing," *Harvard Business Review,* June 17, 2015, https://hbr.org/2015/06/the -perils-of-algorithm-based-marketing.

46. Margaret Mark and Carol S. Pearson, *The Hero and the Outlaw: Building Extraordinary Brands through the Power of Archetypes* (New York: McGraw-Hill, 2001), 71–87.

4. #Explore

1. The North Face, "Homepage," https://www.thenorthface.com/, accessed September 5, 2019; Patagonia, "Homepage," https://www .patagonia.com/home/, accessed September 5, 2019; Osprey, "Homepage," https://www.osprey.com/us/en/, accessed September 5, 2019; Kathmandu Outdoors, "Homepage," https://www.kathmanduoutdoor.com/, accessed September 5, 2019.

2. Carol Crawshaw and John Urry, "Tourism and the Photographic Eye," in *Touring Cultures: Transformations of Travel and Theory,* ed. Chris Rojek and John Urry (New York: Routledge, 1997), 183.

3. Fred Ritchin, *After Photography* (New York: W. W. Norton, 2009), 31–32.

4. Ritchin, *After Photography,* 67.

5. Christiano Lima, "Poll: 77 Percent Say Major News Outlets Report

'Fake News,'" *Politico*, April 2, 2018, https://www.politico.com/story/2018/04/02/poll-fake-news-494421; Olapic, "Consumer Trust: Keeping It Real—A Look at Consumer Usage and Attitudes toward User-Generated Visual Content," *A Global Report by Olapic* (Q4 2016), http://visualcommerce.olapic.com/rs/358-ZXR-813/images/wp-consumer-trust-survey-global-FINAL.pdf.

6. Lima, "Poll"; Olapic, "Consumer Trust."

7. Sara L. McKinnon, Robert Asen, Karma R. Chávez, and Robert Glenn Howard, *Text + Field: Innovations in Rhetorical Method* (State College: Penn State University Press, 2016).

8. C. K. Prahalad and Venkat Ramaswamy, "Co-creation Experiences: The Next Practice in Value Creation," *Journal of Interactive Marketing* 18, no. 3 (2004): 5–14.

9. Detlev Zwick, Samuel Bonsu, and Aaron Darmody, "Putting Consumers to Work: Co-Creation and New Marketing Govern-Mentality," *Journal of Consumer Culture* 8, no. 2 (2008): 163–96.

10. Bram Büscher, "Nature 2.0: Exploring and Theorizing the Links Between New Media and Nature Conservation," *New Media & Society* 18, no. 5 (2016): 726–43.

11. Andrew Hoskins, "Digital Network Memory," in *Mediation, Remediation, and the Dynamics of Cultural Memory,* ed. Astrid Erll and Ann Rigney (Berlin: De Gruyter, 2009), 91–108; Also, interestingly, while feminist theorists like Donna Haraway have used the cyborg as a metaphor for breaking down identity barriers, this much more literal cyborg figure serves to maintain and reinforce them—something I look closer at in the final chapter.

12. José van Dijck, "Flickr and the Culture of Connectivity: Sharing Views, Experiences, Memories," *Memory Studies* 4, no. 4 (2010): 401–15.

13. Christian Pentzold and Vivien Sommer, "Digital Networked Media and Social Memory: Theoretical Foundations and Implications," *Aurora* 10 (2011).

14. Paul McLean, *Culture in Networks* (Hoboken: John Wiley & Sons, 2016).

15. Although, Burkard is a great example of how multiple ties can translate into stronger ties. He directed the commercial I analyzed in Chapter 1 and works on non-social media projects that tie back in to his digital community.

16. Tero Karppi, *Disconnect: Facebook's Affective Bonds* (Minneapolis: University of Minnesota Press, 2018); Safiya Umoja Noble, *Algorithms of Oppression: How Search Engines Reinforce Racism* (New York: New York University Press, 2018).

17. Karppi, *Disconnect*, 21–22.

18. The North Face, "Our Athletes," TheNorthFace.com, https://www.thenorthface.com/about-us/athletes.html, accessed October 30, 2019; First ascents refer to the first person to climb a particular route on a mountain

or wall, and first descents refer to the first person to ski a particular route or mountain; Hilaree Nelson tragically died in a skiing accident in the Himalayas in 2022.

19. "'You can take a backpack to school but you feel like you're in Yosemite just because it says North Face,' Dean Karnazes told me one afternoon in San Francisco. 'I think that aspirational element is really big.'" Marisa Meltzer, "Patagonia and The North Face: Saving the World—One Puffer Jacket at a Time," *The Guardian,* March 7, 2017, https://www.theguardian.com/business/2017/mar/07/the-north-face-patagonia-saving-world-one-puffer-jacket-at-a-time.

20. Hajo Adam and Adam Galinsky, "Enclothed Cognition," *Journal of Experimental Social Psychology* 48, no. 4 (July 2012): 918–25.

21. Hannah Gnegy and Deborah Christel, "Enclothed Cognition: Professional Clothing Symbolism among Plus-Size Women Ages 18 to 24," *International Textile and Apparel Association Annual Conference Proceedings* (2016), 102; Ciro Civile & Sukhvinder S. Obhi, "Students Wearing Police Uniforms Exhibit Biased Attention towards Individuals Wearing Hoodies," *Frontiers in Psychology,* 8 (February 2017); Rachel E. White, Emily O. Prager, Catherine Schaefer, Ethan Kross, Angela L. Duckworth, and Stephanie M. Carlson, "The 'Batman Effect': Improving Perseverance in Young Children," *Child Development* 88, no. 4 (2016): 1563–71.

22. Susan Sontag, *On Photography* (New York: RosettaBooks, 2005), 1–2.

23. Crawshaw and Urry, "Tourism and the Photographic Eye," 181.

24. Barbara Kirshenblatt-Gimblett, *Destination Culture: Tourism, Museums, and Heritage* (Berkeley: University of California Press, 1998), 167.

25. Mark David Spence, *Dispossessing the Wilderness: Indian Removal and the Making of the National Parks* (Oxford: Oxford University Press, 1999), 11–14.

26. Brooklyn Museum, "Caption to *A Storm in the Rocky Mountains, Mt. Rosalie,*" The Brooklyn Museum, https://www.brooklynmuseum.org/opencollection/objects/1558, accessed March 8, 2018.

27. Lynne C. Manzo and Patrick Devine-Wright, *Place Attachment: Advances in Theory, Methods and Applications* (New York: Routledge, 2014), 17.

28. Daniel L. Dustin and Kelly S. Bricker, "Life as Synecdoche: Ansel Adams and the Expanding Liberal Democratic Tradition," *Leisure/Loisir* 35, no. 1 (2011): 7–17.

29. Setha Low and Irwin Altman, "Place Attachment: A Conceptual Inquiry," in *Place Attachment,* ed. Irwin Altman and Setha M. Low (New York: Plenum Press, 1992), 1–12.

30. Courtney Hopf, "Social Media Memory," *Alluvium* 1, no. 6 (2012): n. pag. Web. November 1, 2012; José van Dijck, *Mediated Memories in the Digital Age* (Stanford: Stanford University Press, 2007).

31. Marita Sturken, *Tangled Memories: The Vietnam War, the AIDS*

Epidemic, and the Politics of Remembering (Berkeley: University of California Press, 1997). Cultural memory was a phrase originally coined by Jan and Aleida Assmann in 1995—Jan Assmann, "Collective Memory and Cultural Identity," *New German Critique* 65 (2005): 125–33; Christian Pentzold and Vivien Sommer, "Digital Networked Media and Social Memory: Theoretical Foundations and Implications," *Aurora* 10 (2011).

32. Lynne C. Manzo and Patrick Devine-Wright, *Place Attachment: Advances in Theory, Methods and Applications* (New York: Routledge, 2014), 17.

33. Ansel Adams, "Trees and Bushes in Foreground, Mountains in Background, 'In Glacier National Park,' Montana," National Archives RG: 79 Ansel Adams Photographs of National Parks and Monuments. https://catalog.archives.gov/id/519830.

34. Wendy Harding, *The Myth of Emptiness and the New American Literature of Place* (Iowa City: University of Iowa Press, 2014).

35. Crawshaw and Urry, "Tourism and the Photographic Eye," 183.

36. Sontag, *On Photography*, 13.

37. Crawshaw and Urry, "Tourism and the Photographic Eye," 179.

38. Crawshaw and Urry, 183.

39. Of course, this anonymity is always incomplete. The viewer may only see the back of a person, but it is almost always a white, thin, young person, an identity that is obviously difficult for many outdoorspeople to see themselves in. This both reinforces the colonial nature of the explorer while at the same time setting the young, white, fit person up as the aspirational identity for the outdoor community. Whiteness is so common and is such a standard that when the model is not white, it is immediately noticeable and often explicitly part of a diversity campaign. See the final chapter for a discussion of the lack of diversity in the outdoors.

40. Crawshaw and Urry, "Tourism and the Photographic Eye," 183.

41. Eddy Borges-Rey, "New Images on Instagram: The Paradox of Authenticity in Hyperreal Photo Reportage," *Digital Journalism* 3, no. 4 (2015): 586.

42. Goal Zero (@goalzero), "California Desert," Instagram, July 4, 2017, https://www.instagram.com/p/BWIYIRHjW76/.

43. Michele Zappavinga, "Social Media Photography: Construing Subjectivity in Instagram Images," *Visual Communication* 15, no. 3 (2016): 276.

44. Gunther Kress and Theo van Leeuwen, *Reading Images: The Grammar of Visual Design* (London: Routledge, 2006).

45. William Cronon, "The Trouble with Wilderness: or, Getting Back to the Wrong Nature," *Environmental History* 1, no. 1 (1996): 7.

46. Goal Zero (@goalzero), "Well, you can't win em all," Instagram, September 26, 2017, https://www.instagram.com/p/BZgpfDujHlT/; Huckberry (@huckberry), "There are things known," Instagram, August 4, 2017, https://www.instagram.com/p/BXYbFnGnEWB.

47. H.R.2491—Roadless Area Conservation Act of 2019, https://www
.congress.gov/bill/116th-congress/house-bill/2491/actions.

48. Clif Bar (@clifbar), "That Awe-Inspiring Moment," Instagram,
December 9, 2017, https://www.instagram.com/p/BcgE7UWAkjc/; Moun-
tain Hardwear (@mountainhardwear), "Huautla Cave System," Instagram,
June 1, 2017.

49. Bradley Mountain (@bradleymountain), "The Pine Collections,"
Instagram, August 13, 2017, https://www.instagram.com/p/BXwfuL_nu6d/.

5. The President Stole Your Land

1. Environmental nonprofits are a third player here, but each one has
individual goals, purposes, and philosophies that vary significantly, aligning along a spectrum from corporate models of environmentalism to more
noncapitalist Indigenous models.

2. As explored in detail in previous chapters.

3. Andrew Gulliford, "The Pothunting Problem," *Utah Adventure Journal,*
May 16, 2012, http://utahadvjournal.com/index.php/the-pothunting-problem
-thieves-of-time-in-the-american-southwest; see also Andrew Gulliford,
Sacred Objects and Sacred Places: Preserving Tribal Traditions (Denver: University of Colorado Press, 2000).

4. Bears Ears Intertribal Coalition, "Proposal Overview," Bears Ears
Coalition, 2018, http://bearsearscoalition.org/proposal-overview/. Officially
the Ute Indian Tribe of the Uintah and Ouray Reservation and the Ute
Mountain Ute Tribe, respectively. Note: The formation of an Indigenous-
managed national monument is itself a coalition of sorts between the five
tribes and the U.S. government, one that proved untenable in the wake of
the Trump/Zinke decision.

5. Zinke ended up resigning from his position as a result of corruption.

6. Julie Turkewitz, "Trump Slashed Size of Bears Ears and Grand Stair-
case Monuments," *New York Times,* December 4, 2017, https://www.nytimes
.com/2017/12/04/us/trump-bears-ears.html.

7. Eric Lipton and Lisa Friedman, "Oil Was Central in Decision to
Shrink Bears Ears Monument, Emails Show," *New York Times,* March 2, 2018,
https://www.nytimes.com/2018/03/02/climate/bears-ears-national
-monument.html; https://www.documentcloud.org/documents/4391967
-National-Monuments-a-Look-at-the-Debate-From.html#document/.

8. Lipton and Friedman, "Oil."

9. Lipton and Friedman.

10. Lipton and Friedman.

11. Martin Nie, "The Use of Co-Management and Protected Land-Use
Designations to Protect Tribal Cultural Resources and Reserved Treaty

Rights on Federal Lands"; Amy Joi O'Donoghue, "Zinke: Bears Ears Monument Boundaries Need to Change," *Deseret News,* June 12, 2017, https://www.deseretnews.com/article/865681811/Zinke-Bears-Ears-monument-boundaries-need-to-change.html.

12. Lipton and Friedman, "Oil."

13. The *Outside* Editors, "The Next Great Western Land War Has Begun," *Outside Magazine,* December 4, 2017, https://www.outsideonline.com/2264721/the-next-great-western-land-war; Abe Streep, "Patagonia's Big Business of #Resist," *Outside Magazine,* July 24, 2017, https://www.outsideonline.com/2201581/big-business-resist.

14. Terry L. Anderson, "Utah Faces Down the Rock-Climbing Industrial Complex," March 12, 2017, https://www.wsj.com/articles/utah-faces-down-the-rock-climbing-industrial-complex-1489187009.

15. Patagonia, "Protect Public Lands," Patagonia.com, accessed January 15, 2018, http://www.patagonia.com/protect-public-lands.html. As I describe, the claim that the move was illegal is disputed.

16. The Outdoor Industry Association, "The Outdoor Recreation Economy" (2017), https://outdoorindustry.org/wp-content/uploads/2017/04/OIA_RecEconomy_FINAL_Single.pdf; Jess Bernhard, "Outdoor Recreation Is 2.2 Percent of the U.S. Economy, New Report Finds," REI Blog, September 21, 2018, https://www.rei.com/blog/news/outdoor-recreation-is-2-2-percent-of-the-u-s-economy-new-report-finds; Bureau of Economic Analysis, "Outdoor Recreation," bea.gov (2017), https://www.bea.gov/data/special-topics/outdoor-recreation.

17. Abe Streep, "Patagonia's Big Business of #Resist," *Outside Magazine,* July 24, 2017, https://www.outsideonline.com/2201581/big-business-resist.

18. The North Face Inc. (@thenorthface), "Utah Diné Bikéyah," Instagram, December 4, 2017; this set has since been removed.

19. Chaco Footwear (@chacofootwear), "Standing Strong for Public Lands," Instagram, December 4, 2017; Chaco's Instagram feed now begins two days after this event.

20. At the time of this writing, the company has over 5.4 million followers.

21. Carolyn Webber and Kassondra Cloos, "Yvon Chouinard, Peter Metcalf Put Pressure on Utah for Fighting Public Lands," *SNEWS,* May 17, 2017, https://www.snewsnet.com/news/straight-outta-utah.

22. Patagonia (@patagonia), "Bears Ears Posts," Instagram.

23. Patagonia, "Two Old Friends Meeting Up," Instagram, March 8, 2017; Patagonia, "A Room with a True View," Instagram, June 10, 2017.

24. Patagonia (@patagonia), "Statement from Rose Marcario," Instagram, May 5, 2017.

25. Radwa Mabrook and Jane Singer, "Virtual Reality, 360° Video, and Journalism Studies: Conceptual Approaches to Immersive Technologies," *Journalism Studies* 20, no. 14 (2019), 2096–2112.

26. Patagonia, "Why Patagonia Is Fighting for Public Lands," YouTube, September 28, 2017, https://www.youtube.com/watch?v=3VmjDNL0-lE.

27. Patagonia Works, "Annual Benefit Corporation Report," Patagonia .com, April 30, 2017, https://www.patagonia.com/static/on/demandware .static/-/Library-Sites-PatagoniaShared/default/dw824facof/PDF-US/2017 -BCORP-pages_022218.pdf.

28. Utah Diné Bikéyah v. Trump, No. 1:17-cv-02605-TSC (D.D.C. December 6, 2017); Hopi Tribe v. Trump, No. 1:17-cv-02590 (D.D.C. December 4, 2017); Wilderness Soc'y v. Trump, No. 1:17-cv-02587 (D.D.C. December 4, 2017).

29. Utah Diné Bikéyah v. Trump; Hopi Tribe v. Trump; Wilderness Soc'y v. Trump.

30. Should President Biden issue an executive order restoring Bears Ears, it is possible the case will be considered moot and simply dropped without deciding upon the inherent vulnerabilities of using the Antiquities Act and executive action to preserve land.

31. Hopi Tribe v. Trump, "Bears Ears Complaint 2017-12-04 (00170516. DOCX; 13)," 4, https://www.courtlistener.com/recap/gov.uscourts.dcd .191691/gov.uscourts.dcd.191691.1.0.pdf.

32. David Gelles, "Patagonia v. Trump," *New York Times,* May 5, 2018, https://www.nytimes.com/2018/05/05/business/patagonia-trump-bears -ears.html; Patagonia, "How's That Lawsuit against the President Going?," *The Cleanest Line,* Patagonia.com, April 9, 2019, https://www .patagonia.com/blog/2019/04/hey-hows-that-lawsuit-against-the -president-going/.

33. Plaintiffs include Utah Diné Bikéyah, Friends of Cedar Mesa, Archaeology Southwest, Conservation Lands Foundation, Inc., Patagonia Works, The Access Fund, National Trust for Historic Preservation, and Society of Vertebrate Paleontology. Defendants include Donald J. Trump (President), Ryan Zinke (Secretary of the Interior), Sonny Perdue (Secretary of Agriculture), Brian Steed (Deputy Director of the Bureau of Land Management Exercising the Authority of the Director), and Tony Tooke (Chief of the United States Forest Service).

34. Utah Diné Bikéyah v. Trump.

35. Utah Diné Bikéyah v. Trump.

36. The Utah Diné Bikéyah suit that Patagonia is part of does cite cultural resources as one of the reasons for the suit, especially in damages to the plaintiffs Utah Diné Bikéyah and Friends of Cedar Mesa, but even these plaintiffs include recreational equally alongside Indigenous uses in ways the tribal coalition does not.

37. Importantly, President Biden's restoration of Bears Ears National Monument using the Antiquities Act doesn't change the systems that made the land vulnerable in the first place.

6. Indigenizing Instagram

1. Indigenous Women Hike, "Pursuit Series," Instagram, The Outbound Collective (original post deleted), December 18, 2018, https://www.instagram.com/p/BriiRbaFA4e/.

2. Jolie Varela (@indigenouswomenhike), "Native Culture Is Not for Sale," Instagram, December 18, 2018; Full caption: "@theoutbound Native Culture is not for sale. We are not your backdrop. We are not your trend. We are not your mascots. Our culture does not exist to sell tickets to your outdoor events. You mock us and you encourage our erasure. The United States government has barely granted us the 'freedom' to celebrate our identities and practice our ceremonies and traditions. You exploit us and encourage the idea that we no longer exist. And if we do exist as the Disney Pocahontas or Tonto. You are harmful to our Indigenous communities, to our future generations. We all celebrate and hold reverence for the land. No more tipis. Be original. Be respectful. Sincerely, A Native Woman who is tired of being used as a prop."

3. For example, the Native American Religious Freedom Act was only passed in 1978.

4. See Chapter 4 for more on how social media tends to favor corporate influence.

5. Although primarily an image-based platform, Instagram has proved an especially useful space for informal digital publishing. In general, the social media site does not allow links to outside websites—with the exception of a single link in one's profile and "swipe up" links in Instastories. This means that, unlike Facebook, most of the content shared in Instagram is written (or photographed) specifically for the site and unlike Twitter, the captions can be much longer (2,200 characters) and content heavy. Comments by the original poster are also generally prioritized by Instagram's algorithm, allowing for additional textual content. In fact, for many activists, the image is used to augment the caption rather than the other way around. The ability to share posts on Instastories has also facilitated much greater dissemination of these posts, drawing on extended networks instead of direct followers alone.

6. In this section, I follow digital theorists like José van Dijck and Lisa Nakamura, treating Instagram as both networked media as well as a living community and using a mixed-methods approach to engage with these accounts.

7. Lisa Nakamura, *Digitizing Race: Visual Cultures of the Internet* (Minneapolis: University of Minnesota Press, 2007), 5.

8. Nakamura, *Digitizing Race,* 178.

9. José van Dijck, *The Culture of Connectivity: A Critical History of Social*

Media (Oxford: Oxford University Press, 2013); Marisa Elena Duarte, *Network Sovereignty: Building the Internet across Indian Country* (Seattle: University of Washington Press, 2017).

10. Nick Couldry and Ulises A. Mejias, *The Costs of Connection: How Data Is Colonizing Human Life and Appropriating It for Capitalism* (Stanford: Stanford University Press, 2019).

11. Shoshana Zuboff, *The Age of Surveillance Capitalism: The Fight for a Human Future at the New Frontier of Power* (New York: PublicAffairs, 2019).

12. I think it is important to address critiques of this claim, especially Siva Vaidhyanathan's argument that the reestablishment of oppressive power structures in Egypt shows that Facebook was not a catalyst for actual revolutionary activity, but merely inflated the visibility of otherwise unconnected social media users. While I agree that social media is not a total replacement for on-the-ground organizing, I think the argument that Arab Spring would have happened regardless is counterfactual and difficult to prove. A failed revolution does not invalidate the factors leading to its attempt. Siva Vaidhyanathan, *Anti-Social Media: How Facebook Disconnects Us and Undermines Democracy* (Oxford: Oxford University Press, 2018), 133.

13. Yousri Marzouki and Olivier Oullier, "Revolutionizing Revolutions: Virtual Collective Consciousness and the Arab Spring," *Huffington Post,* July 17, 2012; Also see Carne Ross, *The Leaderless Revolution: How Ordinary People Will Take Power and Change Politics in the 21st Century* (New York: Blue Rider Press, 2011).

14. Adrienne Russell, "The Arab Spring: Extra-National Information Flows, Social Media and the 2011 Egyptian Uprising," *International Journal of Communcation* 5 (2011).

15. Nikita Carney, "All Lives Matter, but So Does Race: Black Lives Matter and the Evolving Role of Social Media," *Humanity & Society* 40, no. 2 (May 2016): 180–99; Abigail de Kosnik and Keith P. Feldman, "Introduction: The Hashtags We've Been Forced to Remember," in *#Identity: Hashtagging Race, Gender, Sexuality, and Nation,* ed. Abigail de Kosnik and Keith P. Feldman (Ann Arbor: University of Michigan Press, 2019), 1–19.

16. Leanne Betasamosake Simpson, *As We Have Always Done: Indigenous Freedom through Radical Resistance* (Minneapolis: University of Minnesota Press, 2017), 20.

17. Duarte, *Network Sovereignty.*

18. Joanne Waitoa, Regina Scheyvens, and Te Rina Warren, "E-whanaungatanga: The Role of Social Media in Maori Political Empowerment," *AlterNative* 11, no. 1 (2015).

19. Oliver Froehling, "The Cyberspace 'War of Ink-and-Internet' in Chiapas, Mexico," *Geographic Review,* 87, no. 2 (1997): 291–307; Duarte, *Network Sovereignty,* 3–5.

20. Nick Estes, *Our History Is the Future: Standing Rock versus the Dakota Access Pipeline, and the Long Tradition of Indigenous Resistance* (London: Verso, 2019), 252.

21. Estes, *Our History Is the Future.*

22. Merrit Kennedy, "More than a Million 'Check In' on Facebook to Support Standing Rock Sioux," *NPR,* November 1, 2016, https://www.npr.org/sections/thetwo-way/2016/11/01/500268879/more-than-a-million-check-in-on-facebook-to-support-the-standing-rock-sioux. Note: The claims that police were actually using Facebook to follow protestors remains unsubstantiated.

23. Marisa Duarte, "Connected Activism: Indigenous Uses of Social Media for Shaping Political Change," *Australasian Journal of Information Systems* 21 (2017).

24. Terry Wotherspoon and John Hansen, "The 'Idle No More' Movement: Paradoxes of First Nations Inclusion in the Canadian Context," *Social Inclusion* 1, no. 1 (2013): 21–36; Vincent Raynauld, Emmanuelle Richez, and Katie Boudreau Morris, "Canada Is #IdleNoMore: Exploring Dynamics of Indigenous Political and Civic Protest in the Twitterverse," *Information, Communication & Society* 21 (2018): 626–42.

25. See Glen Sean Coulthard, *Red Skin, White Masks: Rejecting the Colonial Politics of Recognition* (Minneapolis: University of Minnesota Press, 2014).

26. Laura Beaulne-Stuebing, "How Idle No More Transformed Canada," *CBC,* November 26, 2022, https://www.cbc.ca/radio/unreserved/idle-no-more-reconciliation-1.6663310.

27. Chelsea Vowel, Presentation at Indigenous/Settler Conference, April 6, 2019, Princeton, NJ.

28. Emily Riddle and Lindsay Nixon, "The Killing of Colten Boushie and Outcome of Gerald Stanley's Trial Represent a Bigger Problem," *Teen Vogue,* February 14, 2018, https://www.teenvogue.com/story/the-killing-of-colten-boushie-and-outcome-of-gerald-stanleys-trial-represents-a-larger-problem.

29. Patagonia, "Protect Public Lands," Patagonia Home Page, December 4, 2017, http://www.patagonia.com/protect-public-lands.html; Patagonia, "The President Stole Your Land."

30. David Clucas, "Patagonia 2011 Sales Surpass $500 Million," *SNEWS,* May 17, 2017.

31. REI, "The climate crisis," Instagram, September 16, 2019; The North Face, "Make America's Parks Open Again," Instagram, September 20, 2019; Columbia, "The Message Is Loudest," Instagram, January 11, 2019.

32. Jolie Varela, "Response to Patagonia," Instagram, December 5, 2017, https://www.instagram.com/p/BcVHO3YhcGu/.

33. Gregg Deal (@greggdeal), "Response to Patagonia," Instagram, December 5, 2017, https://www.instagram.com/p/BcVeFmHjAN4/.

34. Larissa Nez (@canoecanoa), "Response to Patagonia," Instagram, December 4, 2017, https://www.instagram.com/p/BcTGurXhDOx/.

35. Comments on @terraincognita, "Response to Patagonia," Instagram, December 4, 2017, https://www.instagram.com/p/BcTNmKmhOcy/.

36. Douglas B. Holt, *Cultural Strategy: Using Innovative Ideologies to Build Breakthrough Brands* (Oxford: Oxford University Press, 2010), 252.

37. Tara Johnson, "How Much Do Influencers Charge—Paying Influencers 2019 Guide," *cpcstrategy,* June 22, 2018, https://www.cpcstrategy.com/blog/2018/06/how-much-do-influencers-charge-paying-influencers-2018-guide/.

38. Native Women's Wilderness, "Lydia Jennings," Instagram, November 3, 2017, https://www.instagram.com/nativewomenswilderness/.

39. Although "late capitalism" in a Marxist sense originally meant a moment of pervasive and oppressive capitalism immediately preceding revolution, in social media and meme culture today, "late capitalism" is used almost in the manner of an emphasis hashtag to call out blatant absurdities, ironies, and contradictions in capitalist systems, mostly around marketing and labor practices. For example, while the commodification of a leisure activity like hiking, something that is by its very definition outside of labor, is just normal capitalism, a company making an advertisement selling the concept of hiking as a break from labor using an image created by an "ambassador" whose leisure has been commodified and is now labor is late capitalism because of its irony.

40. @thenortheface_climb, "Walls Are Meant for Climbing," Instagram, August 15, 2017.

41. @thenorthface, "Walls Are Meant for Climbing," Instagram, January 11, 2019.

42. See David Kozak, "Between a Rock and a Hard Place," *High Plains Society for Applied Anthropology* 26, no. 2 (2006).

43. Len Necefer (@lennecefer), "Tsé Nít'i' Éí Baa Nidajina'," Instagram, August 28, 2019.

44. Natives Outdoors, "Bears Ears," Instagram, October 18, 2017, https://www.instagram.com/p/BaZfıNJlmUh/.

45. Patagonia, "Dear Secretary Zinke," Instagram, May 5, 2017, https://www.instagram.com/p/BTt-g75F5b8/.

46. Patagonia does have media that engages deeply with Indigenous people around Bears Ears on other platforms like their website, but even these contribute to the portrayal of Bears Ears as a tourist space by pairing them with content about climbers and hikers, creating another false equivalency.

47. Jolie Verala (@indigenouswomenhike), comment on @indigenousgeotags, "What Should a Coalition Between Native People and Outdoor Corporations Look Like," Instagram, February 2, 2018, https://www.instagram.com/p/BetWyATllv_/.

48. Len Necefer (@nativesoutdoors), comment on @indigenousgeotags, "What Should a Coalition between Native People and Outdoor Corporations Look Like."

49. Len Necefer (@nativesoutdoors), comment on @indigenousgeotags.

50. Sophie Bowley-Aicken (@anarchopixie), comment on @indigenousgeotags, "What Should a Coalition between Native People and Outdoor Corporations Look Like"

51. Jennifer Earl and Katrina Kimport, *Digitally Enabled Social Change: Activism in the Internet Age* (Cambridge, MA: MIT Press, 2013); Marisa Duarte, "Connected Activism: Indigenous Uses of Social Media for Shaping Political Change," *Australasian Journal of Information Systems* 21 (2017).

52. Nüümü Poyo refers to the John Muir Trail in California.

53. For example, the company has funded and produced Indigenous-led media projects like Necefer's film *Gwichyaa Zhee* (2019) and has given money to Honor the Earth and the American Indian Law Alliance.

Conclusion

1. David Gelles, "Billionaire No More: Patagonia Founder Gives Away Company," *New York Times,* September 21, 2022, www.nytimes.com/2022/09/14/climate/patagonia-climate-philanthropy-chouinard.html.

2. Yvon Chouinard, "Earth Is Now Our Only Shareholder," Patagonia.com, September 14, 2021, www.patagonia.com/ownership/. Wealth created through extracting value from nature.

3. Carolyn Finney, *Black Faces, White Spaces: Reimagining the Relationship of African Americans to the Great Outdoors* (Durham, NC: University of North Carolina Press, 2014); Lauret Savoy, *Trace: Memory, History, Race, and the American Landscape* (Berkeley: Counterpoint Publishing, 2015); Sarah Jaquette Ray, *The Ecological Other: Environmental Exclusion in American Culture* (Tucson: University of Arizona Press, 2013).

4. On Instagram: @pattiegonia, @outdoorafro, @unlikelyhikers, @latinxhikers, @climbthegap, @browngirlsclimb, @brownfolksfishing.

5. Ray, *The Ecological Other,* 19.

6. Traci Brynne Voyles, *Wastelanding: Legacies of Uranium Mining in Navajo Country* (Minneapolis: University of Minnesota Press, 2015).

7. Mark Smith, *Against Ecological Sovereignty: Ethics, Biopolitics, and Saving the Natural World* (Minneapolis: University of Minnesota Press, 2011).

8. Erin O'Donnell, *Legal Rights for Rivers: Competition, Collaboration and Water Governance* (New York: Routledge, 2019).

9. Colorado River Ecosystem v. the State of Colorado, 28 U.S.C 1343 (2017); City of Toledo, "Lake Erie Bill of Rights" (2020), https://www.beyondpesticides.org/assets/media/documents/LakeErieBillofRights.pdf.

10. Erin Fitz-Henry, "Multi-Species Justice: A View from the Rights

of Nature Movement," *Environmental Politics* 2 (2021): 338–59; Zoe Todd, "An Indigenous Feminist's Take on the Ontological Turn: 'Ontology' Is Just Another Word for Colonialism," *Journal of Historical Sociology* 29, no. 1 (2016): 4–22.

11. Eve Tuck and K. Wayne Yang, "Decolonizing Is Not a Metaphor," *Decolonization: Indigeneity, Education, and Society* 1, no. 1 (2012): 1–40.

12. Mark Hefflinger, "In Historic First, Nebraska Farmer Returns Land to Ponca Tribe along 'Trail of Tears,'" *Bold Nebraska,* June 11, 2018, https://boldnebraska.org/in-historic-first-nebraska-farmer-returns-land-to-ponca-tribe-along-trail-of-tears/; Jim Robbins, "How Returning Lands to Native Tribes Is Helping to Protect Nature," *YaleEnvironment360,* June 3, 2021, https://e360.yale.edu/features/how-returning-lands-to-native-tribes-is-helping-protect-nature.

13. David Treuer, "Return the National Parks to the Tribes," *The Atlantic,* May 2021, 44–45. https://www.theatlantic.com/magazine/archive/2021/05/return-the-national-parks-to-the-tribes/618395/.

14. McGirt v. Oklahoma.

15. Originally posted as a comment by the author on @indigenousgeotags.

Index

Joseph Whitson is a marketing strategist and earned his PhD from the University of Minnesota. His writing has been published in *American Quarterly* and *The Public Historian*, and he is founder of *Indigenous Geotags*, an environmental and decolonial justice–focused blog.